FREE LOVE

The American Social Experience Series
GENERAL EDITOR: JAMES KIRBY MARTIN
EDITORS: PAULA S. FASS, STEVEN H. MINTZ,
CARL PRINCE, JAMES W. REED & PETER N. STEARNS

FREE LOVE
Marriage and Middle-Class Radicalism in America, 1825-1860

JOHN C. SPURLOCK

NEW YORK UNIVERSITY PRESS
NEW YORK AND LONDON
1988

LIBRARY OF CONGRESS
Library of Congress Cataloging-in-Publication Data
Spurlock, John C., 1954–
Free love / John C. Spurlock.
p.   cm.—(the American social experience series ; 13)
Bibliography: p.
Includes index.
ISBN 0-8147-7883-6 (alk. paper)
1. Free love—Unites States—History—19th century.   2. Middle
classes—United States—History—19th century.   3. Radicalism—
United States—History—19th century.   I. Title.   II. Series.
HQ967.US6S68   1988
306.7'35—dc 19   88-19916
CIP

Book design by Ken Venezio

To Becky

Contents

Illustrations

Acknowledgments

Summaries of helpfulness often have a breezy quality that belies the gratitude of the summarizer. In spite of this danger, I want to attempt to thank the many individuals who helped me during my research and writing. James Reed, John Gillis, Suzanne Lebsock, and Michael Moffat demonstrated not only intellectual insight but also patience and perseverance in carefully going over the drafts of this work with me. In particular, James Reed provided many useful suggestions and supported my efforts to bring the project to a timely conclusion.

Other colleagues at Rutgers, both faculty and graduate students, offered encouragement and advice, especially David Oshinsky, Tom Slaughter, and Gunther Piehler. Sections of this manuscript received careful evaluation at the Rutgers Graduate History Conference and in Carol Gilligan's seminar, "On the Psychology of Love." My thanks to participants in those discussions. Jacqueline Miller searched the entire manuscript to help me weed out errors of spelling and typing. Rutgers and the Department of History also provided me with fellowships during the final two years of research and writing.

Robert V. Hine, of the University of California, Riverside, proved to be, as always, both supportive and incisive in his talks with me on the project. George Sirgiovanni and Robert Johnston were good enough to carefully read and comment on large portions of the manuscript. Ann Braude provided a check on my speculations about spiritualism.

Librarians and archivists have extended their help during the entire process. The staff of the Rutgers University Libraries were very active on my behalf. In addition I have been aided by a number of individuals and institutions across the country. Keith Arbour and other staff at the American Antiquarian Society gave me access to the impressive collections held in Worcester, Massachusetts. I was able to visit the American Antiquarian Society several times thanks to the hospitality of Chuck and Polly Arneson. Kathryn L. Beam and Edward C. Weber of the Rare Books and Special Collections Division of the University of Michigan's Graduate Library worked with me both during my brief visit to Ann Arbour and by correspondence in the following months; Mr. Weber later provided valuable help in searching out pictures appropriate for the book. Donald Pitzer, Director of the Center for Communal Studies, University of Southern Indiana, the Center's archivist, Gina Walker, and Aline Cook, head librarian of the Workingmen's Institute Library, helped make my visit to Indiana extremely productive. Martha Stepsis of the Brentwood Public Library provided me with help both in correspondence and during my brief but profitable visit to Brentwood. Gould Coleman, Department of Manuscripts and Special Collections, Cornell University Library, and Andrew Dibble gave me access to that library's collection on spiritualism. Mark Weimer, librarian and archivist at Syracuse University, was most helpful in both the material he provided and the suggestions for locating other resources. John White, Southern Historical Collection, University of North Carolina, gave me the initial information I required about material there and then put me in touch with Walter Campbell, whose outstanding work in that collection allowed me to use materials when I could not go to Chapel Hill. Kelly Boyd did valuable work for me at the British Library. Jeff Wexler, State Historical Collection, Madison, Wisconsin, made copies of parts of the Stephen Pearl Andrews papers available for my use. Peggy Jewkes, Bloomsburg University Library, helped me track down those last few source materials as the project was drawing to a close. And Jim Sperry and JoAnn Mengel of Bloomsburg's history department provided both assistance and encouragement in the work of preparing the manuscript for publication.

Finally, I wish to thank my wife, Rebecca Spurlock, and to dedicate this work to her.

Introduction

By the middle of the 1850s a network stretched across the northern states composed of many hard-working men and women who would have been good neighbors in their communities except that they demanded the "disintegration" of American society, the repudiation of Christian orthodoxy, and the abolition of marriage. These were the free lovers. They published journals, wrote books, formed communities, and established a counterculture to the American middle class. Yet every element of their ideology had strong bonds to middle-class culture. Free lovers believed the most basic changes in American society would be to end the artificial relationships that tied the workingman to a commerce based on selfishness, the worshiper to bigotry and superstition, and the wife or husband to an unloving mate. At the same time, they condemned those whose behavior did not meet the exacting standards set by middle-class health reformers. On their farms and in their businesses they worked hard and extolled private ownership of land.

We must understand free love on its own terms. This study reconstructs the free love movement by identifying its leaders, its major ideas, and the institutional forms of the movement. Free love cannot be understood in isolation, however, but only in its relationship to the American middle class. For both those who called themselves radicals and those who did not, *free* and *love* were words with special meanings.

Free love grew out of concerns that were basic to the middle-class identity that was formed by men and women during the 1830s and 1840s. Many members of the middle class considered marriage the foundation of both personal happiness and social stability, because the love that bound two people was the one force that could overcome individual isolation and guarantee the coherence of society.

Among the members of this new middle class were some who refused to compromise their beliefs concerning sexual purity, marriage, and equality. They joined vigorously in the reforms of the period in an effort to redeem themselves and society. Many were strongly religious and continued their pursuit of spirituality with the aid of mesmerism and mediums. During the 1840s these men and women found themselves increasingly confused about marriage. If, as the middle-class marriage advisers had claimed since the 1830s, love made marriage genuine, then love held priority. And if love faded in marriage, then marriage might be as artificial as other false relationships. These ponderings partook of a wide range of ideas, from revivalist heterodoxy to spiritualist communications, from European socialism to an American brand of individualist anarchy. The free lovers help us understand the importance of religious conversion, personal purity, and marriage in the middle-class vision of American society by allowing us to look at some of the most uncompromising expressions of middle-class beliefs.

In addition to being a study of the middle class, this is also a study of radicalism. Free lovers helped to define a long tradition of radicalism that included antislavery activists, nonresistants, and feminists. An individual could be a radical, could adopt a consistent and socially unpopular version of any of these ideologies and not consider himself or herself a free lover. No one could be a free lover, however, without being a radical and therefore against the slavery of the black man and the married woman. Free love, to a large extent, defined what radicalism meant to the ante-bellum bourgeoisie. I have used the term *middle-class radicalism* to designate this extension of middle-class values into a criticism of American society. Following the Reconstruction, radicalism became largely a matter of working-class organization and left behind the cultural concerns that had been central to the free love ideology. These concerns, however, persisted throughout the century and have become more important in our postindustrial world when marriage and family, along with the middle class, seem to be in crisis.

The study begins with an examination of the emergence of the new middle class of the early nineteenth century and of the importance that marriage, sexual purity, and social genuineness played for the development of that bourgeois identity. Chapters 2 and 3 show the attempts by various socialist and religious systems to redefine marriage, to purify it, or to spiritualize it. We already find that the middle-class equation of marriage as the basis of society had entered the thinking of reformers and radicals. Free love, drawing upon earlier heterodoxies, appeared about 1850. Chapter 4 looks into the first free love community of Modern Times; chapter 5 deals with the network that spread over the northern states; and chapter 6 analyzes the pattern of individual development for those who became free lovers. The final chapter brings the story of free love to the end of the nineteenth century.

Although a small movement, free love expressed and evoked the passions of a broad range of middle-class thinkers. It stood as either a horrifying perversion or a gratifying possibility—but always as an extreme—to Americans throughout the nineteenth century. As such, it shows us the limits of middle-class thought and helps us understand how the nineteenth-century middle class understood both itself and radicalism.

CHAPTER I

Marriage and the Formation
of the Middle Class

Historians have traditionally considered the decades following the War of 1812 a time of prosperity and optimism in the United States. American culture until mid-century, according to historians like John Higham, was "characterized by boundlessness." The expanding economy freed young men from traditional occupations as the spread of the franchise and competing political parties involved them in the business of government. Men and women found salvation in revival meetings and studied the improvement of mankind at reform lectures. "In that time," Alice Felt Tyler wrote, ". . . the spirit of man seemed free and the individual could assert his independence of choice in matters of faith and theory." "To the new-born converts," according to Gilbert H. Barnes, "and their rejoicing brethren fresh from the ardor of the revival, social ills seemed easily curable and dreams of reform were future realities." The Republic's growing realization of individual freedom and political equality seemed to offer unlimited opportunity and inspired grand visions of the future.[1]

Recently, scholars have questioned this pervasive optimism. The individuals who took their chances in the commerce of the day, who faced the Creator without benefit of priestly intercession, and who sought personal perfection experienced anxiety as well as optimism, confusion as well as exhilaration. As social distinctions blurred and as individuals felt themselves more alone, both boundlessness and nervousness became basic to American experience. Americans in the early nineteenth century elaborated a social vision that emphasized their freedom from customary limits and concealed the contradictions in their lives. Far more dependent than their grandparents upon complex economic connections, they declared the primacy of the individual. Rejecting the traditional ranks of the colonial farming villages, they embraced equality as their social ideal even as they worked to define new gradations of status.[2]

In the decades preceding the Civil War, a new middle class emerged in the United States that glorified individuality and equality and assumed both the benefits and the contradictions of these ideals. Young men and women moved from rural areas to live in the prosperous towns and cities of the republic and make their livings in nonmanual occupations. However, this class was defined more by particular values than by residence or occupation, with individual liberty and social equality informing every aspect of middle-class life.[3] Small businessmen, clerks, teachers, and journeymen could meet in reform societies, militia troops, lodges, lyceums, and churches. Since neither inherited prestige nor income fixed the boundaries of this class, membership in the middle class became a matter of a young man's or woman's beliefs, goals, and behavior. Individuals were assimilated to the class as they adopted its distinctive assumptions and actions and joined its organizations. Especially in New England and the middle-Atlantic states, an individual's character came to be measured in terms of respectability and authenticity. Self-control was to allow young people to interact without artificiality.

The economic changes that fostered the new middle class also encouraged new family patterns. The Puritan ideal of marriage as the mainstay of a consensual society yielded to the new middle-class reality in which marriage served as an enclave where producers were prepared for the active life of commerce or nursed back to health from the wounds of competitive society. By 1800 household and shop production for local markets began to give way to large-scale production for distant markets. Consequently, the relationships that grew up between apprentice and master or among family members involved in piecework yielded to new forms of interaction and to a new ideal at odds with the Puritan vision. Clerks and apprentices lived apart from their employers and so found companions and recreation outside of the family. The married couple no longer formed a partnership; rather, each performed duties within his or her separate sphere.[4] As religion, reform, and behavior in society became means of self-creation for the middle class, each contributed to a particular ideal of marriage.

From 1800 to the Civil War, American Protestantism grew rapidly as it became increasingly evangelical. While not all Protestants accepted the emotionalism or the theology of revivalism, those churches that promoted revivals most aggressively grew spectacularly, accounting for much of the increase—from 7 to 23 percent of the population —in church affiliation. From the early years of the century, evangelical churches tended more and more to adopt practices and theology associated with Methodism. The Baptist associations cooperated to duplicate the successes of the circuit riders, and revivals rocked even stern Congregational and Presbyterian churches. The Presbyterian Charles Finney preached that salvation was in the hands of the sinner —a doctrine that horrified Princeton professors, but one soon adopted by most revivalists. Young men and women came to the anxious bench struggling to commit their lives to sanctification.[5]

Even alone before their God, however, sinners could serve social ends. "Revivals occasionally did save sinners deep in their sins," Gilbert H. Barnes has noted, "but their greatest execution was among earnest young people predisposed to morality and reform, who were sinners by courtesy only." As Barnes suggested, young men and women could lay aside other burdens than their sins and take on more than grace, when they were converted. By freeing themselves from traditional restraints, young men in early nineteenth-century America found new opportunities but lost the roles once provided by village churches, local customs, and shop rules. America was both exciting and frightening, offering new ways to wealth and new ways of losing it. Without fixed social roles, youthful opportunists often came to fear disorder in their own lives. Camp meetings and conversion allowed many young men and women to express their independence and also helped them establish a stable identity in a confusing world. The visible sign of conversion was a changed life, one that expressed the inner workings of grace. As the nineteenth century advanced, the ideal of conduct came to be termed character and expressed the belief that control of human impulses and destiny came from within. Character was a goal advanced by revival, but it was also cultivated within the family and in reform organizations.[6]

Evangelical Protestantism, for scholars like Mary Ryan, lay at the center of the new middle-class consciousness. The revival was part of a strategy, centered in the family, that allowed the middle class to form itself. In Utica, New York, the focus of Ryan's study, women saved in the revivals carried the message back home and "cajoled, manipulated, or simply led their children into the evangelical sects." As many as 54 percent of converts made their professions of faith with relatives. Evangelicalism permeated the home, shaping discipline, child-rearing, and schooling—all tending to extend the residence of children and allow their parents to guide them into adulthood and into the middle class. Although no longer a unit of economic production, the family took on enormous importance as the school of individual behavior where the wife was exhorted to reform the husband, the husband to cherish and support the wife, and both to convert their children. In this way Utica families maintained their status while they defined the behavior appropriate to that status.[7]

Reform ideology was also important to the emerging middle class. The master mechanics of Providence, Rhode Island, who supported the city's earliest temperance society in the late 1820s, viewed reform as a means of enhancing their respectability and labor discipline. After all, sober mechanics made better workmen. By 1830, with the organization of the Providence Association for the Promotion of Temperance, a shift had taken place. The new association was more democratic and egalitarian. Members expressed their zeal by seeking laws against the licensing of taverns, and they perceived those who opposed the total abstinence pledge as the dupes of fashion or appetite. Abolitionism also began during the 1830s in Providence, with a similar middle-class constituency. The movement stressed a more individualistic and egalitarian vision of society, in which a single personal vice became the basis for all the evil of the world. Whether it was drink or slavery, the results were idleness, vice, pauperism, insanity, cholera, and mob violence.[8]

Both reform and revivalism shaped and spread a new attitude toward sin. Protestant Christianity from Luther and Calvin to Jonathan Edwards had preached that sin was so ineluctably bound up with human life that individuals could not even seek righteousness. By the early nineteenth century, however, Unitarians, Arminian Methodists, and Finney-style revivalists were discarding original sin and proclaiming that the unaided human will could seek grace, reject sin, and accept salvation. Sin became not a condition but a problem; sin was the result of human actions and was therefore amenable to human reform. This doctrine tended toward perfectionism, the belief that human effort could eliminate all sin. It became necessary for those saved in revival to separate themselves from sin and to reject temptation, whether the temptation was drink or human bondage. As a problem of the will, sin also became far more individual, and for many sin became equated with personal desires and longings.[9] Overcoming sin meant self-control and the development of character.

Health reformers became the most important advocates of the new understanding of sin as individual lust, and of salvation as self-control. From the 1830s to the Civil War, physicians, writers, and lecturers, such as Sylvester Graham and William Alcott, spread the message that health demanded a life of order and restraint. Americans may have discarded total depravity, but depravity still existed and received detailed descriptions in the advice manuals, followed by exhortations to repent, to change habits, and live by system. While the constant and driving force of sin was human lust, which expressed itself in harmful habits, the occasion of sin was a social problem, one that seemed to be encouraging ever greater ravages upon human life. At stake was the health and happiness of the individual, the married couple, and the society.[10]

Just as damnation followed upon violating God's laws, disease resulted from violating the laws of nature. According to Sylvester Graham, the interdependence of all bodily organs meant that excitement to any one organ put a strain upon all others and tended toward general debility. Rich foods were very disruptive, but sexual excitements had the harshest effects. Regulation of the reproductive organs was particularly important because of the close relationship between these organs and mental processes. Many young men, Graham asserted, believed that unrestrained intercourse would be desirable, were it not for civil and moral restraints; they should know "that moral and civil laws, so far as they are right and proper, are only the verbal forms of laws which are constitutionally established in our nature." The violation of these physiological imperatives result in disease. "It seems unfortunate," John Ware wrote, "that the propensity of our natures which we find most difficult to control, and which, when uncontrolled, is sure to be the source of the greatest physical and moral evil, is that whose regulation is left most completely to chance." So unfortunate did this seem to Ware and others that they worked to take the chanciness out of control.[11]

For many ante-bellum advisers, masturbation was the most deadly and most insidious sexual disease. It destroyed attributes valued by a commercial class—health, vigor, desire to labor and study, mental acuity, and, worst of all, self-control. One case study summarized the fate of R.A., who at about the age of fifteen began to masturbate. "The result was epileptic fits, which increased with his increasing habit, till be became a *maniac*, and an IDIOT, and died in this deplorable state at less than thirty years of age." As he abandoned self-denial, R.A. soon lost control of his body then his mind. "Among the hapless inmates of the lunatic asylum," Sylvester Graham told the young men in his audiences, "none is more incorrigible nor more incurable than the wretched victim of this odious vice!" In a world obsessed with control—of self, of nature, of economic fortune—onanists lost everything. That the individual should find controlling his passions so difficult was due to an unhealthy environment. Once children become accustomed, warned Sylvester Graham, "to all the degenerating habits of luxury, indolence, voluptuousness and sensuality, we shall be more indebted to the want of *opportunity to sin*, than to any other cause, for the preservation of their bodily chastity." Water-cure physician Russell Trall agreed that danger lurked everywhere: " 'Train a child in the way it *should* go,' or be sure it will, amid the ten thousand surrounding temptations, find out a way in which it should *not* go."[12] Yet if individuals had the will to change, they could not only escape the degenerative influences of their environment, they could redeem it. Physicians and health reformers who translated sin into physiological terms also presented a plan of salvation proportioned to the individual.

As the revival preachers thundered again and again and as the reform societies taught in their lectures and tracts, the salvation of society depended upon individual actions.

Self-control as a means of salvation applied as much to relations between the sexes as to any aspect of life. Although bundling and other forms of premarital sexual exploration were common in the early years of the nineteenth century, the middle-class standard of premarital chastity seems to have become widespread as the century advanced. In the late eighteenth century, about one-third of all brides went to the altar pregnant. By the middle of the nineteenth century, premarital pregnancy had dropped to about 10 percent. Preachers of self-cultivation also demanded limits to sexual indulgence within marriage. Sylvester Graham believed that healthy couples could copulate safely once a month but never more than once a week.[13]

Sexual abstinence, at least in some respects, benefited both men and women. The development of character required that young men who wanted to conquer new economic horizons also conquer themselves. Churches and reform societies demanded appropriate behavior of young men, but so did their wives, mothers, sisters, and fiancées. For women, the new ideal drew from and promoted what historian Nancy Cott has termed "passionlessness." As women during the eighteenth century came to constitute the majority of congregants in evangelical churches, ministers eschewed the traditional idea that women were especially lustful and lacking in self-control and made them the spiritual and moral saviors of men. Culture and reform, as well as religion, became primarily female concerns, thus allowing women increased self-respect and education for pursuits other than attractiveness. "The tacit condition for this elevation," however, "was the suppression of female sexuality." The clergy generalized the idea of women's purity, "and they expected not merely the souls but the bodies of women to corroborate that claim." The new sexuality had important consequences for marriage. According to Cott, passionless women could demand the end of the double sexual standard by insisting upon the purity of both partners. Moreover, sexual restraint tended to raise the prestige of women and give them control over sexual relations and decisions relating to childbearing.[14]

As self-control became the basis of character, and therefore the measure of an individual's worth, it became necessary for middle-class Americans to establish criteria for recognizing good character. "Where no distinction is attached to rank or birth," Edward Strutt Abdy, an English traveler, noted in the early 1830s, "it is natural that 'outward and visible signs' should supply their places, and be proportionably valued." A class open at the lower end, shading into the working class for the ambitious to rise and the dilatory to fall, would leave insecure those who had only short or slight acquaintance with their new status. For the young clerk or ambitious journeyman, membership in the middle class, like grace, could never be certain. "In democracies," de Tocqueville commented, "all stations appear doubtful." The traditional cues coming from the family, the community, and the church were ignored by youth eager to strike out for the frontier or the main chance and were drowned out by the roar of revival. Revival religion, which insisted upon the unmediated experience of salvation, increased the suspicion of mere appearance.[15]

Edgar Allan Poe expressed the logical conclusion of false appearances in his story "The Man that Was Used Up." That "truly fine-looking fellow, Brevet Brigadier-General John A. B. C. Smith" turned out to be nothing more than false teeth, hair, and everything else. Even his voice was made by a machine. Professor Westervelt, in Nathaniel Hawthorne's *Blithedale Romance*, also seemed a handsome young man until the narrator noticed the gold band holding his false teeth in place.

This discovery affected me very oddly. I felt as if the whole man were a moral and physical humbug; his wonderful beauty of face, for aught I knew, might be removable like a mask; and, tall and comely as his figure looked, he was perhaps but a wizened little elf, gray and decrepit, with nothing genuine about him, save the wicked expression of his grin.[16]

The threat of falsehood required a powerful remedy, one that would shape social interaction. Writing in 1825, James Fenimore Cooper explained his solution to the problem of hypocrisy. He believed that so many people were constantly entering good society "that it is yet, fortunately, more likely to give distinction to be rationally polite, than genteelly vulgar." Even the best people in America "maintain their intercourse among each other, under far fewer artificial forms than . . . in any other country." Cooper admitted that not every American was "wise enough to discriminate between the substance and shadow of things," but once the mind had been thoroughly imbued with moral truths, the blandishments and exaggerations of conventional manners seemed noxious. To insure natural relations, Americans in the 1830s and 1840s took up the study of rational politeness. The message of advice manuals and popular periodicals, according to historian Karen Halttunen, was that the proper behavior for a republican middle class was complete sincerity and transparency. Beauty was not the product of cosmetics, taught the advice manuals, but the outward expression of a virtuous mind and heart.[17]

Far more dangerous than someone who appeared handsome but was not was someone who appeared virtuous but was not—someone searching not for a loving, but for a wealthy, partner. According to an English advice writer, Alexander Walker, courtship was a particularly difficult time to discover the true character of another, since "before marriage, the parties are always endeavoring to appear amiable to one another; and their real character and disposition are almost universally cloaked under a refined and, in woman, an instinctive dissimulation." Phrenologist Nelson Sizer believed that women played the coquette in self-defense, to deceive polished and polite young gentlemen as much as they were themselves being deceived.[18]

Marriages based on appearances could be disastrous. "Under this pleasing hallucination," wrote John Austin, "and in entire ignorance of each other's actual tastes, habits, and dispositions, the irrevocable vows are plighted, and the indissoluble knot is tied!" Thousands, it was believed, were annually united under these unfavorable circumstances. Marriage for companionship depended upon courtship free of material considerations. The fate of the virtuous young woman wooed and won by a rake, or of the Christian young man of fortune seduced by a gold digger, was horrible indeed. Marriage for life to a bad person corrupted the good individual when it did not destroy him or her.[19]

Marriage reformers stressed the importance of honesty during courtship. Nelson Sizer wrote that "CANDOR, should be the cardinal virtue of courtship." Failing such openness, those going courting must be wary of men and women who were used up or made up. "Scrutinize closely," Orson Fowler counseled young men, where is her color? *On* her cheek, not in it. Where her teeth? In her *tumbler*, not mouth. Where her fine rounded form? *On* her, not *of* her. Where her fine bust? Outside. Where her flesh? Nowhere—much. Alas, almost a bundle of dry-goods-artificialities.

Orson's brother Lorenzo advised that instead of superficial and easily imitated externals the courting young man should "prefer the amiable and affectionate disposition, a high standard of virtue and morality, correct principles, good intellectual powers, a well trained and balanced mind" and other qualities that would suit the woman to become "a companion and parent."[20]

The high value given to marriage, and consequently to courtship, by youthful members of the middle class is reflected in the courtship correspondence of Angelina Grimké and Theodore Weld. Theodore Weld was thirty-three when he first met Angelina Grimké. She was thirty-two. Weld had been converted by the preaching of Charles Finney and then assisted the revivalist during 1826 and 1827. After Weld embraced the immediate emancipationist view of antislavery, the same skills that helped save lost souls served him in his work as a spokesman for Garrisonian abolitionism. First at Lane Seminary, then for twenty months throughout Ohio during 1834 and 1835, Weld lectured on and debated the topic of slavery, establishing local antislavery societies and converting many to abolitionism. His voice, unfortunately, could not stand the strain and Weld had to turn to other types of antislavery work. In 1837 he helped train prospective antislavery speakers at a convention in New York City. It was there that Weld met Angelina Grimké, a daughter of South Carolinian slaveholders. A convert first to Presbyterianism and then, due to her sister Sarah's influence, to Quakerism, Angelina Grimké set aside social convention to urge her fellow church members to turn against slavery. She traveled north with Sarah in 1829 to live in Philadelphia. That year she wrote a letter to the *Liberator* that was later reprinted as a major statement of antislavery. In 1836 she and Sarah were invited to New York to speak to small groups about slavery. Their friend Elizur Wright helped organize the training convention in November of the following year.[21]

Neither Theodore nor Angelina gave the slightest hint that they felt anything more than respect and friendship toward one another during the month-long convention. Only after the sisters had gone to stay with friends in Providence, Rhode Island, did Weld, in a letter, finally reveal to Angelina Grimké that he had loved her since reading her letter to the *Liberator*. Amazed, but pleased, Grimké replied that she, too, had loved him ever since she read a letter of his in the *Liberator*. Neither Weld nor Grimké doubted that their earnest love would unite them in marriage. For Weld, this meant that courtship must proceed systematically. People who intend to marry must study each other closely. They must know one another's defects, habits, and weaknesses. After discussing all the aspects of marriage, they should establish "plans of life, modes of employment, the system by which to regulate their household." It was no wonder that Weld insisted upon such careful planning since he believed that if "among the Divine institutions ordained for human beings there be one whose issues involve responsibilities that are *infinite*, that is the institution of marriage." In Weld's scheme, society came into existence when the lone individual took and became a spouse. Marriage gave character to all other human relations; it was "the most *permanent* of all . . . and being itself the nucleus and original constituent of the social state. Every element of that state gravitates toward it with centripetal force and receives from it abiding impress."[22]

The importance that Weld and Grimké invested in marriage increased their concern over the danger of false appearances. Both feared that the other may have been deceived concerning some grievous faults. They wrote letters to reveal these shortcomings so they could enter marriage fully informed of one another. As much as he loved her, Weld wrote to Angelina Grimké, "I would break every link, cost me what of torture it might, rather than that you in the artless confiding of your nature should commit to me the custody of your happiness for life—blinded to the sad defects of my character." He obligingly listed the defects for her in a later letter: pride, selfishness, impatience at being contradicted, bad temper, severity, sarcasm, self-indulgence, and willfulness. While we can assume that Weld was being a little hard on himself, as lovers often are when they compare their poverty of attractions with the wealth they perceive in the loved one, he obviously understood the price he paid for character. The struggle to develop character had, for Theodore Weld, been a success, yet he perceived himself "as far as *emotions* are concerned, a quivering mass of intensities kept in subjection by the *rod of iron* in the strong hand of conscience and reason and never laid aside for a moment with safety."[23]

For young men, finding a proper partner took on the additional urgency of finding an ally to help wield the rod of iron over emotions and desire. "Every thing, domestic or social, depends on the female character," wrote a contributor to the *Liberator*. "As wives, they emphatically decide the character of their husbands, and their condition also." The love of a good woman accomplished seeming miracles, making men more industrious and less criminal, promoting health, peace, and sound sleep. "She diffuses around her a mild warmth, a pure light, that vivify and illuminate all that encircle her." "Woman, in the perfection of her nature, is as near an angel as is consistent with an abode on earth," rhapsodized the Methodist minister George Henry. The influence of women, proclaimed Alexander Walker, was potentially "equal to the moral regeneration of the world." A mistaken choice of mate, however, would not only rob a young man of expected reforms, but make his life much worse. George Henry warned that "virtue being lost, and shame lost, she is a fiend incarnate, the centre of a hell on earth." One writer speculated that half the misery of the country's families was due to the wife's bad temper or lack of frugality. If the wife did not make the home pleasant, the husband will tend to stay away, "And when the love of home is gone, the man is lost." Lost, that is, in vice.[24]

Finding the virtuous love made courtship a success; for marriage to succeed, however, more was necessary. The reason for many of the unhappy marriages of the day was the lack of self-knowledge and self-control. William Alcott, among the most prolific ante-bellum advice writers, was particularly concerned that discipline be practiced within marriage: "there is hardly any thing in the world which renders free agents so truly free, as living by system." He felt that the ten to fourteen hours spent each day attending to bodily needs and desires were too many. "It is not—it cannot be—the lot of humanity to be always a slave to the appetites and lusts—to spend and be spent for the mere house of the soul." Certain hours for sleep, eating, business, conversation, and study should be established. The Welds took this to heart and adopted a schedule included in one of Alcott's books. Other writers stressed eating habits, recommending temperance in (or abstinence from) the use of alcohol, tea, coffee, spices, and meat. Those virtues that would lead to success in most commercial occupations—order, discipline, attention to detail—would lead to success in other aspects of life. Just as young men were expected to establish habits of self-discipline, renouncing alcohol and self-stimulation, married men and women were expected to continue perfecting themselves. Alcott summed up the objects of marriage in the phrase "Christian education." "It is for Christians, especially in matrimonial life . . . to hasten the consummation of earthly human happiness."[25]

Alcott's phrase, "earthly human happiness," points to the importance of marriage for Americans in the early nineteenth century. To middle-class Americans the home appeared to be the one place of stability in an uncertain world; it was a retreat from strife, a school of perfection, and a means to happiness for the individual and for society. "Without it," John Ware wrote in 1850,

no individual can be considered as having answered the whole purpose of existence; of having arrived at the full development of which his character is capable. He is incomplete and imperfect. . . . Domestic life, and the domestic relations, are the essential element [sic] of human happiness and human progress so far as our moral and spiritual character are concerned.

"No part of any man's influence is wasted," wrote William Alcott. If a person could make some improvement it would benefit himself and also his offspring. Reasserting a version of his Puritan ancestors' faith, Alcott gave the work of salvation to the family—the husband would save the wife, the parents their children and neighbors. From a single pair now alive, he calculated, there may descend more people than have so far descended from Adam and Eve, and would not "the eternal well-being of these hundreds of millions . . . possibly depend on the effects of a single husband to emancipate the companion of his bosom?"[26] Marriage, at the center of all human interaction and vital to middle-class self-formation, became essential not only to the success of American society but to the salvation of the world.

Alongside this vision of marriage there arose the daily reality of sharply defined gender roles for men and women. Observers in America found that husband and wife "apparently move in different spheres, although they repose on the same bed." American men, according to one English traveler, ignored their wives because of the need to do business. "But the result is that the married women are left alone; their husbands are not their companions, and if they could be, still the majority of the husbands would not be suitable companions" because women had considerable cultural accomplishments while men did nothing but business and read nothing but newspapers. Frances Trollope wrote that married men managed to socialize almost entirely without women: "were it not for public worship, and private tea-drinking, all ladies in Cincinnati would be in danger of becoming perfect recluses."[27]

The separation of spheres and the inequality of husband and wife that characterized middle-class marriage seemingly contradicted the value placed upon marriage by those who claimed it was the foundation of society. Yet Americans perceived their world as both a great promise and a potential threat, and marriage served as one of the most important means of reconciling, or at least concealing, these conflicting visions. While the decline of customary forms of status allowed men to establish relationships with other men far more freely, they felt both optimism and uneasiness among their peers. Competition, as well as trade, was free; business partnerships could be formed without regard to status or custom, but partners contracted suspicion for one another with their other obligations. Tension probably figured prominently in relations among men because of the very equality that made these relationships so easy to establish. Marriage, then, became the antidote for bonds that may have seemed dangerous. Women, removed from male economic life, could nurture virtues that had no hint of competition and conflict.[28]

Writers of marriage manuals recognized the separation of sexual spheres, but they believed that a successful marriage would bridge the enormous chasm of gender. "The permanent union of one man with one woman," wrote John Ware, "establishes a relation of affections and interests which can in no other way be made to exist between two human beings." R. J. Culverwell agreed: "Man's earthly happiness . . . rests on no higher pinnacle than in the union of hearts as well as bodies." Though the spheres of the sexes continued to be separate, in marriage they intersected most fruitfully. A writer in the *Liberator* claimed that far from being a burden to a man, his wife "shares his burdens and she alleviates his sorrows." According to William Alcott, it was incumbent upon husbands to make continual efforts to perform kind services to the wife to maintain and improve the couple's love. Husbands should limit the amount of time they spent away from their wives, yielding "only to calls of a public nature; and let those be as seldom as possible."[29]

Essential to the transforming power of marriage was an ideal of love. Historian John Gillis has shown that an important shift in attitudes toward courtship took place during the late eighteenth and early nineteenth century in the British Isles. In earlier centuries, the relationship between prospective mates had been nurtured through the magic of ritual, communal pressure, and contact during betrothal. By the nineteenth century, love came to be viewed as a force beyond the control of those experiencing it, "inaccessible to both reason and ritual." It was this mysterious power that English and American lovers came to view as the basis for their relations. The self-control that made Weld and Grimké successful reformers, and that had allowed the two to hide their feelings for one another, did nothing to lessen the power of those feelings. Indeed, both Weld and Grimké believed that their passions had run completely amok: "I have prayed earnestly against them at times," admitted Angelina Grimké. She had implored her heavenly Father to reveal to her "why He had created these restless longings of my heart after communion and union, deep and pure and chaste and indestructible?" Weld believed that his other loves—for parents, siblings, friends—were under his will.

But my love for you Angelina does not seem to be anything that I *put forth*, but the *tendency*, the *gravitation* of all my inner being toward you to seek and mingle with its *own affinities*—as the deepest, *profoundest* want instinctively reached forth *of itself* for its own provided supply.[30]

By the late 1840s the work of marriage idealists had firmly established love as the ideal basis for marriage. James Fenimore Cooper reflected this new attitude toward courtship when he wrote that "married persons who love each other always live together agreeably." Other writers gave far more importance to love. "*Reciprocated love is marriage*," proclaimed phrenologist Orson Fowler. That this ideal spread beyond the advisers' tract is evident from one of Angelina Grimké's letters to Theodore Weld. "In the sight of God," she wrote, "we are married . . . ; from the moment you were assured that I loved you, we became one." The marriage that Weld and Grimké celebrated in May 1838 became possible for them because of their belief that each was joined to the other by the express intent of God. "Do you believe," Angelina wrote to Theodore, "that our Father ever begets such pure and holy feelings in one heart without touching the other?" She felt that "we are the two halves of one whole, a twain one, two bodies animated by one soul and that the Lord has given us to each other."[31]

One of the most widely known formulations of this ideal of married love comes from the work of Henry C. Wright. Wright had been a minister, education reformer, and advocate of home missions and Sunday schools before being drawn to abolitionism in the early 1830s. Converted to Garrisonian abolitionism in 1835, he became an agent of the American Peace Society in 1836 and the following year joined the agents of the American Anti-Slavery Society who were trained by Theodore Weld to spread abolitionism throughout the North. While Wright continued his work for abolition and nonresistance, he abandoned orthodox Christianity by the 1850s and became primarily a lecturer on health and the family. His biographer has shown that Wright's own development converged with the concerns of his audience. Lasting married love would provide, in Wright's thinking, permanence in the chaos of society and the basis for healthy development. Wright's listeners were also seeking to make the elements of their class identity into universal laws of behavior. Marriage, for the middle class, became the key to understanding society.[32]

For Wright, all social institutions existed to "perfect and ennoble individual man." Marriage was preeminent in this, being the only relation "in which the whole nature of man and woman can find a full development." The basis of true marriage was spiritual; if two people truly loved each other their union would be perpetual. Of course, disturbances can occur in the attraction, so the couple must strive to continue in each other's affection. True marriage, however, would never include deviation from complete affection for the partner. "The only marriage," wrote Wright, "that commends itself to the instinct, the reason and the heart, is exclusive; and therefore this alone will

elevate and purify man or woman." If affection for another enters the
heart, then the marriage is at an end. To assure that true marriages
took place, Wright urged proper care in the choice of mates. It was
obvious that this was rarely the case, since

society is full of inharmonious and most fatal alliances between men and
women, under the name of marriage,—alliances as unnatural and monstrous,
and as fruitful of evil, as a union between liberty and slavery, truth and
falsehood, purity and impurity,—alliances in which no compromises can ever
produce harmony or happiness.

While Wright would be accused of free love by middle-class critics and
congratulated upon his theories by free lovers, his real purpose was
the salvation, rather than the abolition, of the marriage ideal. Wright
wanted marriage to realize its potential for perfecting the individual. It
could do this, he believed, if it became subject to the spiritual power
of love.[33]

   The high standards of happiness and moral improvement inherent
in the ideal of bourgeois marriage, frequently in conflict with the sharp
separation of sexual spheres, inevitably created disappointment. Henry
Wright's own marriage was far from the blissful relationship he sketched.
He probably referred to it when he wrote, "I know full well what
depths of misery may lie behind a smile." Among the emerging middle
class were those who would find the gap between the ideal of warm
companionship and the routine of daily living intolerable. Marriages
that were productive of nothing but wretchedness must have seemed
much worse. A contributor to the *Liberator* echoed concerns that appeared frequently in ante-bellum popular literature, when he lamented
that many couples "instead of ministering to the happiness of each
other . . . possess no congeniality of feeling, and agree on only one
subject, that of increasing each other's wretchedness." Both Theodore
Weld and Angelina Grimké expressed horror at what they considered
substandard unions. Weld wrote that "among the dislocations of the
age marriage and the relations of husband and wife are perhaps as they
now are the most horrible perversions of all." Angelina Grimké admitted that she had

   . . . been tempted to think marriage was *sinful*, because of what appeared to
me almost invariably to prompt and lead to it. Instead of the higher, nobler

sentiments being first aroused, and leading on the lower passions *captive* to
their will, the *latter* seemed to be *lords* over the *former*.

She had feared being married to a man who believed that "women
were made to gratify their animal *appetites, expressly* to minister to *their*
pleasure." [34]

The vision of marriage for America's middle class in the decades
before the Civil War alternated between a blissful haven where the
work of redemption could proceed and a hellish prison where both
husband and wife found only misery. Tension between these perceptions fueled a growing interest in marriage and concern about its future
during the 1840s and 1850s. At least eleven books primarily concerned
with marriage were published in America in the 1840s, with five of
these appearing in 1848. During the 1850s, eleven more books on
marriage appeared. After a series of meetings in 1847 and 1848, a
group of prominent Bostonians commissioned John Ware to write a
work for the instruction of young men in sexual matters. William
Alcott published two volumes in the 1850s that reflected his sense of
urgency concerning the problems of marriage. His efforts were necessary, he felt, to counteract the plans of Satan, "by extending the
domain of conscience over that part of the Divine Temple which has
too often been supposed not to be under law, but to be the creature of
blind instinct, in which we are only on a par with the beasts that
perish." Marriage, Alcott warned, was "the golden chain that binds
society together. Remove it, and you set the world ajar, if you do not
drive it back to its original chaos." [35] Having accepted an ideology that
made society a result of individual interactions, Alcott and others
recognized that a threat to the most intimate of interactions endangered
all of society. And if love was essential to marriage then the nature of
love determined the fate of society.

Among the middle-class individuals who came of age following the
Era of Good Feelings, marriage served as the major bulwark against
social and personal chaos. It was both a basis for and an extension of
evangelical religion, individual reform, and the search for authentic
relationships. As the primary social contract, marriage served to mask
the contradiction between the middle-class reliance upon individuality
and its increasing dependence upon invisible forces in the market,
government, and society. Yet it often seemed that marriage actually

contributed to disorganization, both of an individual's life and also of social life in general. As men and women searched for some explanation for this incongruity between expectations and results, they often found the most convincing answers in the radical critiques of bourgeois society. From the 1820s onward, criticisms of marriage emerged along with attacks upon the other flaws in American society. By the 1850s, a long tradition of both secular and religious marriage reforms was already known to many Americas. In the last decade before the Civil War, the criticisms assumed a new stridency, culminating in the free love movement that demanded the abolition of marriage. Paradoxically, so pervasive was the ideal of middle-class marriage that those who sought to reform the institution—and even those who called for its abolition—assumed many of the beliefs of the romantic and evangelical ideologues.

CHAPTER 2

Marriage and Utopia,
1825 to 1850

In May 1845 Robert Owen visited Brook Farm. Twenty years had passed since New Harmony had tested his reforms in the New World. Now seventy-four, Owen distanced himself from the failure of New Harmony, saying it had been "conducted by people who understood not his principles." Although still a major reform movement in England, in America Owenism no longer exerted much influence. Brook Farm, at that moment, seemed destined to be the model for future communitarian movements. Originally a transcendentalist community, Brook Farm was reconstituting itself as a Fourierist phalanx. "He expressed himself much pleased with our experiment," wrote Marianne Dwight of Robert Owen, "and wondered at our success."[1] Owen's brief visit symbolized the convergence of three communitarian reform movements: Owenism, transcendentalism, Fourierism. Even though each had unique origins and diverse goals, all three offered challenges to middle-class social values and especially marriage.

While evangelical religion, economic opportunity, and the idealized family gave direction to the aspirations of many young men and women during the decades following the War of 1812, two groups remained unassimilated to the emerging middle-class society. Many journeymen and rural immigrants to the city found that the promises of the Era of

Good Feelings and Jacksonian America were made to others. Unlucky at speculations or slowly undermined by unseen economic forces, those who had once held middling status and the hope of a master's shop found themselves becoming part of a working class that lacked control over working conditions. Others, who retained their status or even prospered, found intolerable the gap between the ideal of economic and social equality and the reality of growing wealth and poverty and rejected in part, or entirely, the bourgeois system. Both groups discovered a need to rewrite the social contract according to their understanding of society and their aspirations for justice.

In Europe, two of the earliest thinkers to inspire their countrymen with visions of a better future were Robert Owen and Charles Fourier. Born in 1771 and 1772 respectively, both men condemned the system of inequality and oppression that characterized the new bourgeois society, and both proposed sweeping changes in economic production, religion, and family. Their reconstructions of society were based upon cooperative villages or associations that would realize the goals of justice, equality, and harmony within their precincts and so serve as models for other units. Owen recognized America as the ideal location for the beginning of his cooperative scheme, and many Americans responded enthusiastically to his proposals. Fourier had never considered America a likely place for his phalanxes; but some Americans, converted to his teachings, adapted Fourierist thought for domestic use.

American socialist thought was often derivative of European models. However, transcendental social thought during the 1830s resulted from conflicts with local religious and social hierarchies. Drawing upon European and American ideas, transcendentalists engaged in their own social activism and attempted two experimental communities. By the end of the 1840s, the small social movement inspired and led by transcendentalists was absorbed into the larger Fourier and antislavery movements.

Owenism, transcendentalism, and Fourierism challenged the bourgeois ideal of marriage on three levels. First, the systematic thought of all three movements questioned basic assumptions of middle-class society, including its forms of family life. Second, even though the official arrangements of the communities left marriage untouched, the nature of community life often had the effect of bringing marriage into question. Members of a community that had abandoned the social norms of the world faced the need to either retreat into familiar forms or create new patterns. Generally, this resulted in some doubt or testing of the limits of acceptable behavior. Finally, within all experimental communities, no matter their provenance, discussion of every aspect of life pervaded the leisure hours. Whether an individual communitarian accepted wholly or partially the visionary ideas, the beliefs that inspired Owenism, Fourierism, and transcendentalism would become a creative element within the widespread discourse on marriage and sexuality taking place during the early nineteenth century.

The reforming goals of many communities resulted in special constraints and problems. On the one hand, valued reforms might be detrimental to the harmony of the community. Even before the founding of New Harmony, some Shakers gave Owen fair warning of this. They asked what religion his community would consist of, "Quakers? or Jews? or what? and shook their heads when they found it was for all sects." On the other hand, the reform movements often raised questions that communities were unable to address. Owen and his followers, for instance, intended to improve marriage but never found adequate means to attain this goal. The importance of sexual relations in community life was suggested by a Shaker whom Owen met. The Shaker invited Robert Owen and his son to join the Society of Believers. "We said we would make some communities still better than theirs and that they would come to us. He asked if we forbid marriage. We said no. He replied then you can't agree; there will be continual quarrels."[2]

Yet in spite of the limitations of communitarian reform and the frequently timid attitude that communitarians took toward marriage, any system that challenged the values of the new middle class also, to some extent, challenged bourgeois marriage. The communitarian experience of thousands of Americans by the late 1840s left them unwilling to accept the system of economic laissez-faire or of marital free trade.

Owenism

Robert Owen and his disciples in America offered one of the earliest nonreligious attacks on the ideal of middle-class marriage. Rather than understanding marriage as the consequence of an unwavering and purely private experience of love, Owen viewed marriage as a social product serving the ends of a class-bound society. Love, outside the control of the will, could fluctuate wildly. Marriage, Owen believed, must receive entirely new social circumstances. Owen's doctrines, with their strong blend of free thought, were branded as irreligious and pernicious at a time when church membership and influence were growing, especially among the middle class. At the same time, Owen's forthright treatment of marriage as an individual contract reinforced the growing belief that marriages should be ended at the discretion of those within them.

During their visit in November 1824, both Robert Owen and his son William were impressed with the Shaker settlement north of Albany, New York, at Wiskeyana. "All the society . . . appeared happy and contented," recorded William. The ninety-nine men and women lived with property in common, working according to their own choice of trade and occupation. Although men and women worked jobs traditional for their sex, they changed jobs frequently. They ate well, too, if the meal taken by the Owens was any indication. It included three kinds of meat, potatoes, turnips, mashed squash, pies, cheese, butter, and two kinds of bread.[3]

Robert Owen had come to America to negotiate with George Rapp for the purchase of the lands and buildings of Rapp's religious community in southwestern Indiana. The evident success of the Shaker community and of the Rappites must have reinforced Robert Owen's conviction that cooperative settlements would be the foundation of a new moral world. Historian Arthur Bestor has shown that Americans perceived religious communities as models of separate societies in miniature, functioning without the growing division between rich and poor evident in the young republic. Reformers established dozens of communities in the years following Owen's visit, seeking to duplicate the prosperity of the religious communities, to change the nature of labor, and to create an environment for improvement and tolerance. It was Robert Owen who converted a primarily religious effort into a reformist vehicle. "Owen was the first Socialist that stirred the enthusiasm of the whole American people," wrote John Humphrey Noyes, himself a community builder and historian of communitarianism, "and he was the first, so far as we know, who tried the experiment of a nonreligious Community."[4]

Robert Owen's faith in cooperative communities grew out of his experience in managing cotton mills during the 1790s and from his work at New Lanark in Scotland. From 1800 Owen had been a partner in the mill and manager of the concern that included the village of New Lanark. His success in increasing the efficiency of the factory and improving the living and working conditions of the workers drew visitors to New Lanark from all over the world. Owen was his own best publicist, celebrating his achievements in lectures and essays and publicly proposing new schemes for manufacturing, education, and poor relief. He evoked sympathy from those concerned with the changes brought about by Britain's industrial advance. "Since the general introduction of inanimate mechanism into British manufactories," wrote Owen in *A New View of Society*, "man, with few exceptions, has been treated as a secondary and inferior machine; and far more attention has been given to perfect the raw materials of wood and metals than those of body and mind."[5]

Owen assumed that an individual's character was produced by the environment. "Withdraw those circumstances which tend to create crime in the human character, and crime will not be created. Replace them with such as are calculated to form habits of order, regularity, temperance, industry, and these qualities will be formed." Owen placed his faith in the rational individual following his enlightened self-interest. Once relieved of superstition and trained in true principles, people would eschew intemperance and licentiousness, "for such conduct in itself is neither the immediate nor the future interest of man; and he is ever governed by one or other of these considerations, according to the habits which have been given to him from infancy."[6]

Frustrated by his efforts to have Parliament enact remedial legislation affecting factories and poor relief, Owen developed his own ideas of reform during 1817 to 1820, moving from cooperative villages for poor relief to communities designed to cure capitalism. Even with his great wealth Owen could hardly hope to begin his experiment in England on the grand scale he envisioned. He estimated that a cooperative village for one thousand would cost almost half a million dollars. The prospects for a cooperative village brightened in 1824 when Owen met Richard Flower, an English settler in Indiana who had been commissioned by George Rapp to sell the property of the Harmony Society. For $100,000 Owen could purchase the extensive acreage and buildings he considered necessary to establish his society. By the fall Robert Owen and his son William set sail for America to inspect the property, conclude the deal, and spread the Owenite gospel in America.[7]

Although Owen's ideas had reached America in the Scottish and English reviews, his visit in 1824–25 created far more interest and enthusiasm for reform. Owen stirred those in America whose faith still rested in human reason and offered hope to those who feared that America's commercial and industrial expansion might create a stratified society in which the poor sought their living in degradation and crime. Owen's success as a cotton lord gave him access to the highest levels of American society, where he could preach equality through paternalism. The day after leaving the Shakers in November he spent with General Van Rensselaer, whose dinner guests included a senator from New York and DeWitt Clinton. In Washington, D.C., Owen visited with President Monroe, Secretary of State John Quincy Adams, and Secretary of War Calhoun. During the rest of his stay, Owen continued to explain his plans, inspiring volunteers for the New Harmony community, for the Owen clubs, and for communities independent of New Harmony.[8]

Back in Washington, D.C., in February 1825, Owen was given his bulliest pulpit in the New World. Speaking before the members of Congress with President Monroe, president-elect Adams, and the members of the cabinet in attendance, Owen offered his message to the last American government strongly tinctured by Enlightenment ideals. The object of society, he lectured, was to "secure happiness for the greatest number of human beings." This would be accomplished by giving everyone education from birth, providing means for all to obtain the necessities for "human nature," and uniting all individuals in a social system that would give them "the greatest benefit from society." The basic flaws in society were errors of training, the "imaginary notions of religion and prejudice that led groups to condemn and torment other groups and resulted in the formation of institutions in opposition to the nature of man. He especially condemned commerce. "The whole trading system is one of deception; one by which each engaged in it is necessarily trained to endeavor to obtain advantages over others, and in which the interest of all is opposed to each." "The consequence of this inferior trading system is to give a very injurious surplus of wealth to a few, and to inflict poverty and subjection on the many." The new system would produce wealth so efficiently that everyone would have adequate goods from the common store.[9]

During his further travels in 1825 Owen left the management of the community under the direction of a committee dominated by his son William. He returned to New Harmony in January 1826, bringing his oldest son Robert Dale and a "boatload of knowledge"—educators and scientists who had been fascinated by Owen's vision. The Preliminary Society already numbered about one thousand volunteers who had come from throughout the United States and northern Europe to begin building the new society.[10] Even in January it should have been apparent that the experiment was in serious trouble. The colony had attracted all kinds of people, from poor farmers to professionals. Since there were few spinners or dyers to manufacture yarn, or millers to make lumber or flour, equipment left in good condition by the Rappites stood idle. Craftsmen who came to the colony found ready work, though compensation was often a problem, and those who provided productive labor strained their equalitarian beliefs to put up with those who did none. John Humphrey Noyes compared the open admission policy of New Harmony with advertising for a wife, "and we never heard of any body's getting a good wife by advertising." Robert Owen, out of his own wealth, provided for the needs of the community during these months, but even his largesse proved inadequate.[11] So did his leadership. In April 1826 Owen promulgated the community's first constitution. By the time the seventh constitution was published in September 1827, New Harmony had run its course. Lack of income, poor manufacturing, poor husbandry, little housing, and constant controversy over major decisions finally wore down the community's spirit and hopes for improvement.

John Humphrey Noyes compared New Harmony to "a great ship, wallowing helpless in the trough of a tempestuous sea, with nine hundred *passengers*, and no captain or organized crew!" Noyes was sensitive to a community's ability to balance its books and to house and feed its members. At the same time, he recognized that other and more important processes than bookkeeping were the soul of community life. The fellow-feeling engendered by community life, the approach to more just social systems and less onerous labor routines, and the enrichment of individual lives made utopian colonies important to thousands of Americans during the early nineteenth century. Noyes assured his readers that "the *idea* of Owen and his thousand was not a delusion, but an inspiration, that only needed wiser hearts, to become a happy reality."[12]

Josiah Warren, who had sold his prosperous lamp-making business in 1825 in order to move his family from Cincinnati to New Harmony, reflected that at New Harmony "everything went delightfully on, except pecuniary affairs!" Warren led the community orchestra that gave concerts each Thursday evening and played for the frequent dances. These musical performances were fondly remembered fifty years later by Robert Dale Owen who also enjoyed the discussion groups and balls held in the community. "There is a great charm in the good-fellowship and in the absence of conventionalism which characterize such associations," Dale Owen decided. Even Paul Brown gave a backhanded testimonial to community life. Brown, a young school teacher who had arrived in April 1825, quickly went into opposition, damning Robert Owen for living in luxury at the tavern while shortages plagued the community and for demanding payment for his land while denouncing the commercial system. He felt that Owen's insistence upon balanced ledgers and proper payment for labor killed any community spirit. "The people of this town continued strangers to each other in spite of all their meetings, their balls, their concerts, and their so frequent occasions of congregating in the Hall, and all their pretence of co-operation." In spite of its invidious intent, Brown's list makes life at New Harmony sound full and rich rather than bankrupt.[13]

William Pelham, who would become an editor of the *New Harmony Gazette*, also commented on the social life of the community in letters to his son. "The utmost order, regularity and good humor exist here," he said of the dances. On Sunday he went faithfully to the church to listen to the Scottish rationalist Robert Jennings lecture or to hear William Owen read from his father's works. In the evenings Pelham joined others at the tavern where only conversation of "a serious philosophical cast" was served. Although he was put to work at an occupation he had little knowledge of—bookkeeping at the general store—he wrote to his son that "I *at once* found myself *at home*, though among strangers—such is the frankness of manners prevailing here." [14]

New Harmony's discussion, publication, and "absence of conventionalism" made the community important in the debate over courtship, marriage, and sexual relations. New Harmony and Owenism reinforced in America a tradition of British feminism associated with Mary Wollstonecraft and William Godwin. Wollstonecraft had eloquently appealed in 1792 for women's right to education for something other than servitude or beauty: ". . . in order to preserve their innocence, as ignorance is courteously termed, truth is hidden from them, and they are made to assume an artificial character before their faculties have acquired any strength." This inferior education meant that "when they marry they act as such children may be expected to act. . . . Surely these weak beings are only fit for a seraglio!" Mary Wollstonecraft called for women to improve their health through exercise and their minds through study. Marriage, she felt, should not be based on love but on friendship, a more moderate and reasonable passion. Better educated women would improve marriage, since rational women "would be contented to love but once in their lives; and after marriage calmly let passion subside into friendship." Without developed reasoning and equality, however, women could never enter marriage as anything but slaves. [15]

William Godwin, influenced by the woman he would later marry, incorporated Wollstonecraft's ideas into his 1798 analysis of government. Building upon the democratic ideas of the eighteenth century, Godwin showed that government had far fewer legitimate functions than it in practice usurped. While the rights of each individual were limited by the equal rights of other individuals, within marriage this principle had no currency. Marriage was a system of fraud that young people encouraged by ignoring the shortcomings of their beloved. The

result was the permanent union of incompatible persons. Compound-
ing this problem was the cohabitation of the married couple:

. . . it is absurd to expect the inclinations and wishes of two human beings to
coincide, through any long period of time. To oblige them to act and live
together is to subject them to some inevitable portion of thwarting, bickering
and unhappiness.

Godwin considered that the present system could be abolished with
no attendant evils. Each person should choose his or her partner
voluntarily and continue with that partner as long as it was mutually
agreeable. Like Wollstonecraft, Godwin believed that friendship would
be the true bond in these relationships.[16]

Editions of *The Rights of Women* appeared in the United States within
two years of its English publication. The ideas of both Wollstonecraft
and Godwin found an American advocate in the novelist Charles
Brockden Brown. Brown's 1798 book *Alcuin* was largely a long discussion between a bachelor and a married woman on the institution of
marriage. Alcuin's hostess, Mrs. Carter, criticized marriage, saying
that in it the woman "loses all right to separate property. The will of
her husband is the criterion of all her duties. All merit is comprised in
unlimited obedience." "Marriage is a sacred institution," states Mrs.
Carter later, "but it would argue the most pitiful stupidity to imagine
that all those circumstances which accident and custom have annexed
to it are likewise sacred." Among the changes that Mrs. Carter believed
necessary were the freedom of women to choose whom they will marry
and freedom of divorce. When Alcuin objects that free divorce would
lead to licentiousness, his hostess counters that it "would eminently
conduce to the happiness of mankind." In Mrs. Carter's view, women
should retain their property within marriage and maintain homes
separate from their husbands. She summarized her view of marriage
as "an *[sic]* union founded on free and mutual consent. It cannot exist
without friendship. It cannot exist without personal fidelity. As soon
as the union ceases to be spontaneous it ceases to be just."[17]

Although his ideas on the subject developed slowly, domestic reform
became crucial to Robert Owen's thinking. In 1825 he had condemned
the divisive effects of commerce before the Congress and had implied
in the same speech that religion was a major source of the evils in

society. In Philadelphia, during his second trip to America, he told an audience that it was "his opinion most distinctly that the Scriptures were no more inspired than any other book." Although he made no condemnation of the family, Owen saw that it was a source of exclusiveness. One of his speeches in New Harmony, published in the *Gazette*, held up the world's institutions, past and present, as "proof of the ever-changing insanity with which the human mind has been enveloped." While he saw that the present institutions of society had to be endured temporarily, he looked forward to a time when families would live in cooperation, protecting, educating, and caring for children communally. The intellectual ferment at New Harmony helped Owen define his own ideas more clearly, drawing upon the insights of past thinkers and of those contemporaries who gathered each week for discussions. An article in the *New Harmony Gazette*, for instance, found exclusiveness at the root of evil, and this included exclusive affections.[18]

Owen summarized his agenda for reform in the "Declaration of Mental Independence" delivered on a rainy July 4, 1826, to the inhabitants of New Harmony. To gain mental independence, Owen thundered, it was necessary to destroy "the threefold causes which deprive man of mental liberty, which compel him to commit crimes, and to suffer all the miseries which crime can inflict." These monster evils were private property, irrational religion, and marriage based upon private property. The only question was which was worst? "They are so intimately interlinked and woven together by time that they cannot be separated without being destroyed." The solid foundation of this hierarchy was private property, which combined the evils of poverty and wealth. Religion was the handmaiden of this system, destroying the judgment and making men slaves.

Marriage allowed the wealthy to separate their children from others and so retain for them the advantages of their position. At the same time the daughters of the poor, bartering their affections for wealth and power, could be added to the property of the rich. Since an individual's circumstances determined his actions, Owen asserted, affection could not be controlled by the individual. And if it was impossible for someone to promise to love another in perpetuity, then there should exist some means to end the relationship when affection ceased.

More importantly, equality must be established or the bartering of affection would continue. When equality became general, individuals could make rational decisions about their choice of partners and so insure that unions would be more likely to last. With the destruction of the three evils, man would cease to be dependent upon a powerful few and give up his superstitious fears, and he would "no longer unite himself to the other sex from any mercenary or superstitious motives, nor promise and pretend to do that which it depends not on himself to perform." [19]

Owen's views of religion had already earned him the intense, persistent, and ultimately successful opposition of church leaders. His Declaration of Mental Independence enlarged the polemic possibilities available to his enemies and probably increased opposition. "If we are allowed to judge," howled the *Indiana Journal*,

of the moral character of New Harmony society, by the licentious principles of their founder and leader, it would be no breach of charity, to class them all with whores and whoremongers, nor to say that the whole group will constitute one great brothel.

William Maclure, who headed the community school and helped Owen pay for the mortgage on the Harmony property, approved of Owen's statements in a private letter to his assistant, Madame Fratageot. "His 4th of July oration is all true and told in a masterly manner," Maclure wrote on August 2, 1826. His letter to a resident of Philadelphia, written September 20 and published in a Philadelphia magazine, took a different approach. "I did all I could to bridle the impetuosity of the enthusiastic reformer," Maclure assured his reader. The opinions expressed in the speech were those of Mr. Owen alone, "who is, perhaps, the only one within five hundred miles of him, who thinks them fit or necessary in the present state of society." [20]

Maclure's letter was meant to calm critics of Owen's ideas on marriage, but it was misleading on two important points. Maclure knew very well that many at New Harmony shared Owen's beliefs about marriage, including Madame Fratageot, who wrote Maclure that the speech "will no doubt open the eyes of a great many and be useful to the progress of truth." It was also incorrect to imply that Owen believed the new order of marriage could be instituted in society as it was. On July 30 a meeting was held in the Harmony Hall devoted almost entirely to the question of marriage. Owen told the audience that it would be almost impossible "under the present anti-social system" to establish "natural marriages" because of the continuing strength of religions of mystery and the inadequate education that individuals received. "Nor could any individual contract a natural marriage, when the universal custom was to give perpetuity to unnatural ones." Asked what he meant by natural marriages, Owen replied that the ideal was for the union to be formed within social institutions that provided equal education for all and allowed both parties to gain a thorough knowledge of themselves and of their prospective partner, so that a decision to marry could be made "where the judgment has been the guide and director." This, he believed, would make marriage far more permanent.[21]

Even if outsiders believed the worst, New Harmony never attempted domestic reorganization. In Cincinnati, William Maclure heard the stories of Mr. Owen's amorous overtures to women who had been in New Harmony. "This, beat up with the discourse on the antient mode of marriage, forms the nostrum that gives currency to all the stories about indiscriminate intercourse and all things being in common." Maclure wrote to Mrs. Joseph Sistaire, whose three daughters were living in New Harmony, assuring her "of the morality of the inhabitants of Harmony being more correct than in any part of the Earth I ever was in, touching . . . the sexual intercourse." Historian Arthur Bestor found no authenticated instance of license in the community, a remarkable record, if true, for a village of a thousand inhabitants during two years of constant change.[22]

While the community never abolished any of the irrational institutions of society, its principles constantly called the practices of society into question. Soon after his arrival William Pelham "discovered that forms and ceremonies have no place here." This was evident a few weeks later when he attended the funeral of a female member who was buried in the corner of an apple orchard "without any of the parade and *cant* that I have formerly seen and heard on such occasions." The disdain of ceremony was accompanied by a lively social life. One visitor, Duke Bernhard, was certain that the dances were divided along class lines, but William Maclure believed that the people of the community acted with "sobriety, order . . . and friendly conduct etc."[23]

When Robert Dale Owen wrote in the *New Harmony Gazette* that there was no harm in considering various alternative arrangements in domestic life he was only encouraging discussions already being made. Robert Dale Owen later remembered the

> . . . free and simple relation there existing between youth and maiden. . . . We called each other by our Christian names only, spoke and acted as brothers and sisters might; often strolled out by moonlight in groups, sometimes in single pairs; yet, withal, no scandal or other harm came of it (except perhaps improvident love-matches).

Community life brought together young men and women frequently and familiarly. Even Paul Brown indicates the pervasive interest in courtship and marriage. "The sexes fought like cats about individual marriages," he claimed. "There was not true politeness between the single persons of the two sexes; but a dark, cold, sullen, suspicious temper, and a most intolerable miserly allusion to individual property as the standard of worth." "At their balls and social meetings, instead of learning affability, they learned little or nothing but pride." His comments make it clear that marriage was a popular topic among the young people.[24]

One story indicates both the direction and the type of reform endorsed by the New Harmony communitarians. On April 2, 1826, Philip M. Price married Matilda Greentree and Robert Robson married Eliza E. Parrin in New Harmony, with the Rev. John Burkitt presiding. The ceremony departed rather sharply from custom, however, with this pledge being recited before the religious vows were taken: "I, A.B. do agree to take this woman (man) to be my wife (husband) and I declare that I submit to any other ceremony upon this occasion, only in conformity with the laws of the state." The formula embodied the belief that marriage was a voluntary, civil affair, without extraneous ceremonies or expectations. The *New Harmony Gazette* editorialized that those who believed that an individual's character was formed for him could not in good conscience solemnly promise to love another "during their *whole* lives, while at the same time they are conscious that their affections do not for one hour depend upon them-

selves." Changes such as the simplifying of the ceremony or the loosening of divorce laws were more commonly topics for the *Gazette* than
were profound changes in the social system. In this respect the community marched in step with American practices. Auguste Carlier
reported in the 1860s that marriage required little legal and no religious
sanction in America (something that was discovered in New Harmony
soon after the double wedding was performed) and that divorce, as
compared with Europe, was relatively easy to obtain.[25]

Although Owen had intended New Harmony to be the test for
Owenism in America, the failure of the colony was not the sole reason
that the Owen movement fragmented into short-lived communities,
clubs that celebrated their leader's birthday, and local efforts. The
year before Owen's return to New Harmony in 1825 was the beginning of Charles Grandison Finney's revival work in New York as an
agent of the Utica Female Missionary Society. As more Americans
came to the anxious bench, fewer could be convinced of reforms so
tightly bound up with freethinking as Owen's. The Awakening contributed to a larger trend in American life that focused attention upon
the individual and away from his or her social environment. Reform
societies, often extensions of evangelical renewal, urged young men
and women to renounce alcohol, meat, or other harmful practices.
Physiological reformers like Graham and Alcott preached that the
millennial hopes for the nation could be realized through proper physical and spiritual health. At a time when Americans by the thousands
were coming to believe that regenerate individuals could save society,
Owen's attack upon social institutions seemed irrelevant.[26]

By the time Owen departed for Europe in June 1827 any possibility
of a structured movement in America had been lost. However, long
after the demise of New Harmony, echoes of the Owenite melody
persisted. The leader of New Harmony's band, Josiah Warren, composed his own plans for creating harmony in human relations. Warren
would implement Owen's idea of a labor exchange and even reorganize
a school along principles derived partially from Owen. Warren's settlement of Equity, in Ohio in 1831, was one of the last Owenite communities formed in the country. By then Warren's career had taken a turn
that we will follow later.[27]

Even without its leader, Owenism persisted in America. Franklin community in Rockland County, New York, was formed by those who had been attracted to the vision of "a state of society in which pride of rank, and the insolence of wealth, shall be unknown—and where each shall see in every face a *brother* and a *friend*." By April 1825 several families had taken possession of the land, even though Jacob Peterson, the leading financier of the community, was still negotiating for the purchase. By the time the deal had been concluded in June, Robert Jennings had arrived from New Harmony to help organize the community. Jennings was made president of Franklin's board of directors, and George Houston was appointed secretary. Freethinkers Jennings and Houston made freedom of opinion in religious matters more or less mandatory at Franklin. The community school offered no religious education, and on Sundays the residents were called to the main building to give reports of their week's work and to listen to rationalist lectures by George Houston. Before he left, resident James M'Knight claimed to have heard complaints that the young men had kissed the women, even married women, with whom they danced, " 'And *something else* very often takes place.' 'And what of that?' " Robert Jennings replied, " 'you must become naturalized to our *social system!*' " Jennings also decided that married couples were unfit for the community and intended to accept only young people as colonists in the future. Franklin had very little future. The departure of outraged residents ended the project after only five months.[28]

During the mid- to late 1820s, other small Owenite communities in Valley Forge, Pennsylvania, and at two places in Ohio widened the audience for Owen's ideas. As late as 1844, a Massachusetts community of 150 people was founded upon Owenite principles. Organized by John Collins, general agent of the Massachusetts Anti-slavery Society, Skaneateles community rejected government based on force, held all goods in common, assumed responsibility for educating the community children, refused to follow any religious creed, and endorsed divorce. The community lasted about three years.[29]

Individuals, sometimes in alliance with small groups and sometimes alone, also carried on Owen's attack against priestly institutions—including marriage. The Franklin community's secretary, George Houston, had emigrated to New York City from England where a freethinking publication had earned him two years in Newgate. In

New York he was supported by a group of "Painites" who eagerly subscribed to his paper, the *Correspondent*, from 1827 to 1828. The paper scoffed at reports of New Harmony's end as it published articles supporting freethinking, Thomas Paine, and Robert Owen. The priesthood feared Owen, claimed one writer, because

> . . . if Mr. Owen's system prevails . . . *religion* will cease to be a *trade*, whereby they can live a life of idleness and hypocrisy—man will no longer suffer his *reason* to be trampled under foot, to support them in a *profession* which, in all ages, has occasioned more dissention and bloodshed than any other cause.

New York freethinkers also supported the Institution of Practical Education, a project of Franklin's past president, Robert Jennings. The tradition of free thought continued as a challenge to evangelicals throughout the early nineteenth century, giving workingmen an alternative rationale for sobriety and solidarity.[30]

Paul Brown, though an opponent of Owen, carried on many of Owen's ideas in his paper, the *Radical*, in the early 1830s. An advocate of working-class power, Brown called for the equalization of all property and education and the end of representative government controlled by the prosperous. Like Owen, he scoffed at the idea of promising fidelity in marriage for life. "Now if any person were to make so rash a bargain about any other sort of transaction, our laws would rate him *non compos mentis*, and from thence make the obligation void." Paul Brown rejected the normal marriage oath of love, honor, and obey until death. "Marriage is a private agreement between two individuals of different sexes. Wherefore should we require it to be solemnized with a public confirmation by oaths, more than any other private agreement?" As long as affection lasts, the two should live together, and part when affection ends. An honest man, Brown pointed out, would support his children without an oath if he could, and no oath would compel him to if he could not.[31]

The most widespread influence of Owenism emanated from the careers of Frances Wright and Robert Dale Owen. Frances Wright, born in Scotland in 1795, was already a well-known author in the early 1820s when she became acquainted with the work of Robert Owen. She was so impressed with New Harmony during a visit in 1826 that she tried to model her Nashoba colony for training slaves for freedom after the Indiana community. While selection of the colonists was more careful than at New Harmony, management at Nashoba was quite poor. Wright was generally absent, leaving the plantation in the charge of James Richardson, who took to heart the radical notions on marriage current among the reformers when he began living with a beautiful mulatto girl. We can assume he was sincere in his views, since he did not act in secret but had an account of the liaison published in a national antislavery journal.

Wright ignored the scandal following Richardson's indiscretion and proceeded with an idea she had conceived during her stay at New Harmony. Nashoba would be converted into a colony for whites as well as blacks. The races would live together and work for human progress. As a partial answer to the problem of racial tensions, Wright suggested intermarriage as a way of merging the races. This idea alone would probably have been enough to doom the community, but Frances Wright was not one to be radical by halves. Having imbibed the strong drink of mental independence at New Harmony, she also announced that whatever marriage meant outside of Nashoba had no currency inside. Relations between the sexes would be based strictly upon the equality of the parties:

No woman can forfeit her individual rights or independent existence, and no man assert over her any rights or power whatsoever, beyond what he may exercise over her free and voluntary affections; nor, on the other hand, may any woman assert claims to the society or peculiar protection of any individual of the other sex, beyond what mutual inclination dictates and sanctions.

New Harmony attracted a thousand settlers; Nashoba never really began. In 1830 Wright took the slaves to Haiti to give them their freedom.

In 1828 Wright purchased half interest in the *New Harmony Gazette*, then being edited by Robert Dale Owen. She rechristened it the *Free Enquirer* and moved it to New York City. At its greatest the paper had one thousand subscribers, with articles on reform topics, freethought, and divorce. Frances Wright purchased Ebeneazer church as a Hall of Science where she and others gave lectures to promote reform. Wright and Owen helped organize an early labor movement in New York, though their faction lost control of the Working Men's Party by 1831. In 1831 Frances Wright married Phiquepal D'Arusmont, a rather unsavory character who had been one of Maclure's teachers at New Harmony and whose students had set the type for the *New Harmony Gazette* and *Free Enquirer*. The newlyweds departed for Europe in 1831. After that date the *Free Enquirer* became decidedly less devoted to the cause of marriage reform. The Hall of Science was sold to a Methodist church, and by 1835 the *Free Enquirer* had ceased publication.[32]

Although closely identified with Robert Owen through the late 1820s, Robert Dale Owen (who was born in 1801) moved away from communitarian reform after his father's return to Europe. From envisioning a society completely remade, so that communal child-rearing could take the risk out of marriage, Robert Dale Owen turned to support for divorce as the most important reform of marriage. He agreed with his father that love could not be guaranteed but believed that the availability of divorce would make marriage more nearly a union of two freely consenting individuals and guarantee the affections of those involved. In 1828 he felt it was up to the community to see that the children were properly cared for and educated; he would stress community education much more in later years. Under Robert Dale Owen's editorship, the *New Harmony Gazette* serialized "Milton's Discipline of Divorce." He opened the columns of the *Free Enquirer* to correspondence on the marriage questions. As part of his effort to make marriage less burdensome for the poor, in 1830 Robert Dale Owen wrote *Moral Physiology*, which would soon become one of the most widely circulated birth-control tracts of the nineteenth century.

After 1831 Robert Dale was no longer a major player in labor politics. He turned over editorship of the *Free Enquirer* to Amos Gilbert and returned to New Harmony to help manage the western property left to him and his brothers and sisters by their father. This ended neither his idealism nor his commitment to reform. In the simple ceremony at the marriage of Robert Dale to Mary Jane Robinson in 1832, the statement of each included no vows of eternal affection. Later, as a state legislator in Indiana, Owen worked for both the protection of women's property within marriage and for more realistic divorce laws. This led to an 1860 exchange between Owen and Horace Greeley in the columns of the *Tribune*, in which Greeley accused Owen of making Indiana a paradise for free lovers.[33]

Like Alcuin's hostess, Robert Owen's American followers retained marriage within their reorganized society and within their less sweeping reforms. Not all of the accidental attributes of marriage, however, were sacred. Owen's followers believed that the institution should be deprived of irrational authority by separating it from religious symbolism and ceremony. Better marriages would be built upon equality between the sexes and fraternity between the spouses. And mistakes in choice of partners or changes in passions could be corrected through divorce. The English feminist tradition as preached by the Owenites would have made marriage into a wholly civil agreement between citizens.

Appreciating the Owenite contribution to marriage reform through the middle of the nineteenth century carries us only part of the way toward understanding its importance. Owenism, like liberalism and the other intellectual systems of the period, sought to reconcile the needs of the individual with those of society. On many points Owen's thinking completely agreed with that of Graham, Alcott, and other marriage experts who sought to make marriage the basis for social harmony. With common roots in the Enlightenment, the socialist and middle-class views of society sometimes resulted in identical conclusions. Owen believed that the passions were largely beyond human control and needed to be subject to systems that were based on human reason. Since vows could never guarantee fidelity, it was necessary that marriages be entered into with open eyes. Owen would have excoriated John Austin, who wrote that marriage was a divine institution, but would have agreed with Austin that much of the unhappiness in marriage was due to lack of proper precaution in choosing a mate.[34] Neither Owen nor the conservative advisers doubted the ability of a bad marriage to create intense and prolonged misery for those involved. And, although there were many who rejected divorce as a remedy for a bad marriage, Owen's position was held by many of those who wrote on the subject during the decades after New Harmony. Owenism would thus serve as a foil and as a prop to the new ideal of marriage, as well as inspiring later radicals who called for the institution's abolition.

Transcendentalism

The appeal of Owenism in America was limited by the growth of revival religion and individualism. In the very years that Owen received a warm welcome, middle-class Americans were forming a consensus that held up individual regeneration as the basis of religion and social improvement. While Owen's belief in renewed social institutions was losing currency, other groups committed to individuality were questioning the value of certain social institutions. Transcendentalism offered a new perspective on both American society and middle-class marriage. The New England sages came to see the individual as the fount of eternal truths and society as a conspiracy to silence these truths. Both the condition of women and the institution of marriage received critical attention, though in both cases transcendentalists believed that solitary individuals could redeem a flawed environment. At Fruitlands and Brook Farm, disciples of the "New View" attempted to release the individual's creative potential.

The "New View" appeared in the Boston area in 1836. During that year Ralph Waldo Emerson published *Nature* and Bronson Alcott, George Ripley, and Orestes Brownson published books challenging Puritan and Unitarian orthodoxy. That same year a series of meetings began, the first at the home of George Ripley. Henry David Thoreau, Margaret Fuller, Frederic Hedge, Alcott, Brownson, Emerson and others met to discuss theology, law, truth, personality, and individuality. Other members had imbibed the latest literary works of Carlyle, Coleridge, and Wordsworth. "From that time," Emerson wrote later, "meetings were held with conversation—with very little form—from house to house. Yet the intelligent character and varied ability of the company gave it some notoriety, and perhaps awakened some curiosity as to its aims and results." Outsiders believed the group was developing its own dogma and called the members transcendentalists.[35]

At odds with the intellectual establishment from the first, proponents of the New View were denied the columns of the Unitarian *Christian Examiner* after 1839 when James Walker stepped down as editor. Members of the club decided to publish their own journal called the *Dial*, which was first edited by Margaret Fuller and later by Emerson. Through the *Dial* and other literary works, "transcendental-

ists" would influence literature, religion, and social thought throughout the United States. One of the movement's earliest historians,
O. B. Frothingham, traced the intellectual roots of transcendentalism
to Germany, calling it the "transfigured protestantism of the land of
Luther." For Frothingham, the essence of the New View was the
"fundamental conceptions, the universal and necessary judgments,
which transcend the sphere of experience, and at the same time impose
the conditions that make experience tributary to knowledge." It was a
philosophy that sought the primary, unconditioned laws of life within
the individual and assumed that each person was capable of this fundamental knowledge.[36]

Transcendentalists wanted to anchor the dignity of man in his inner
being at a time when the business of the world tended to reduce him
to an economic function. Emerson's belief in individualism rested on
his faith in the essential divinity of man—thereby making individual
freedom a guide for American ideals and social identity. "I think that
the intellect and moral sentiments are unanimous," wrote Emerson in
1849, and that "the wiser a man is, the more stupendous he finds the
natural and moral economy, and lifts himself to a more absolute reliance." As early as 1830 Amos Bronson Alcott proposed infant instruction as a means of awakening "the nobler affections and pure sympathies of infancy." In 1836 Alcott wrote his "Doctrine and Discipline of
Human Culture," which viewed man as fallen from divinity but capable of redeeming his fallen state, individually and collectively. "Man's
mission," he urged, "is to subdue Nature; to hold dominion over his
own Body; and use both these, and the ministries of Life, for the
growth, renewal, and perfection of his Being."[37]

Although the truths preached by Emerson, Alcott, Ripley, and
others seemed so profound and ethereal that they defied human manipulation, the transcendentalists recognized that life was largely determined by outward circumstances. Man might partake of the eternal,
but he was conditioned by a society with evident, if remediable, flaws.
Alcott lamented that "the Divine Idea of Man seems to have died out
of our consciousness. Encumbered by the gluts of appetites, sunk in
the corporeal sense, men know not the divine life that stirs within
them, yet hidden and enchained." Human weakness is created, insisted Alcott, by human agency. Like his cousin William, Bronson

Alcott condemned self-indulgence and other abuses of nature. "We train Children amidst all these evils. We surround them by temptations, which stagger their feeble virtue, and they fall too easily into the snare which we have spread." John S. Dwight lamented the growing complexity of material existence.

> We do not properly live, in these days; but everywhere with patent inventions and complex arrangements are getting ready to live. . . . life is smothered in appliances. We cannot get to ourselves, there are so many external comforts to wade through.[38]

Transcendentalist social thought emerged from the social tensions in Boston during the early nineteenth century. By 1830 Boston had both benefited and suffered greatly from the growth of commerce, industry, and immigration. From 1820 to 1830, the city grew by about one-third, to sixty thousand, with many of the new residents crowded into the poorer district. During the 1820s journeymen, tradesmen, and the sons of farmers who had moved to the city were finding employment as clerks, tavernkeepers, and grocers or were becoming owners of small businesses or factories. From these occupations arose a new middle class, distinct from the old middle and upper classes and the emerging working class. Social harmony, as preached from Unitarian pulpits, disappeared in the struggles of the marketplace. The Second Great Awakening, reaching Boston by 1822, inspired Unitarians to crusade for greater religious conviction. It was from this evangelical Unitarianism that the transcendentalists derived their visions of personal and social malaise and redemption. Many who first embraced the New View—Emerson, Ripley, Dwight, Hedge, Theodore Parker, James Freeman Clarke—were either Unitarian ministers or ex-ministers. Paul Boller has described transcendentalism as an effort "by bright young Unitarians to find meaning, pattern, and purpose in a universe no longer managed by a genteel Unitarian God."[39]

The New View inspired faith "in boundless possibility, and in unimaginable good." Emerson believed that individuals and especially young people, were they to follow their natural inclinations, would resist conformity. "To every young man and woman," Emerson lectured in 1838, "the world puts the same question, Wilt thou become one of us? And to this question the soul in each of them says heartily,

No." Such inspiration as transcendentalism offered could lead to separation or symbolic action, as with Thoreau's retreat to Walden, or to
confrontation and agitation, as was evident from Thoreau's jail sentence in Concord. Both transcendentalist responses tended to operate
outside of and with deep suspicion of institutions—an attitude that
shaped the translation of social criticism into action.[40] Characteristic of
the transcendentalist attack upon social problems was the movement's
advocacy of women's rights.

An 1841 article in the *Dial* by Sophia Ripley makes clear the difficulty of applying the insights of human divinity to the constraints of
domestic life. Beginning with a direct challenge to the notion of woman's sphere, Sophia Ripley claimed that the character and intellect of
each woman created her own sphere. Woman, however, was educated
to be an appendage, first of her parents and then of her husband.
Selected as a wife, she invests all of her affection in her husband, but,
eventually, "she finds him not what she expected; she is disappointed
and becomes captious, complaining of woman's lot, or discouraged and
crushed by it." Assuming that her husband is always right, she adopts
his prejudices. The home is supposed to be woman's special domain,
but while the wife is only a nurse to the children, the father is an
oracle. Although Sophia Ripley's analysis pointed toward the need for
changes in marriage and family life, her recommendations bore entirely upon the individual wife and mother. Women should see reality
more clearly and have leisure to contemplate and study. She did not
indicate how this leisure would be created or how reality could be seen
more clearly. She advised women, "Let no drudgery degrade her high
vocation of creator of a happy home." Housekeeping, she concluded,
should be related to cosmic realities.[41]

Sophia Ripley's article is curious because it describes the problems
facing middle-class women so accurately, yet calls for reforms that
combine impracticality and conventionalism. The transcendental preoccupation with the immanence of deity within the autonomous individual is probably the root of this contradiction. Women lacked real
power and economic independence, so the ideals of individuality as
preached by Emerson and practiced by Thoreau had little correspondence in women's experience. The reconciliation of the condition of
bourgeois women with transcendental individualism was approached

(while at the same time exaggerated) in the thought of the New View's most remarkable feminist, Margaret Fuller.

Born in 1810 in Cambridgeport, Margaret Fuller grew up in the Massachusetts countryside. Brilliant even when young, she drove herself to learn ancient and modern languages. An early interest in European transcendentalism helped attract her to the Boston movement. She wrote short pieces for James Clarke's *Western Messenger*, became acquainted with Ralph Waldo Emerson, and taught at Bronson Alcott's Temple School from 1837 to 1838. In 1839 Fuller began five years of annual conversations with groups of Boston women. An article by Fuller in the July 1843 issue of the *Dial* set forth her basic arguments on women's rights. In 1845 she expanded the article into *Woman in the Nineteenth Century*, a book, wrote Edgar Allan Poe, that "few women in the country could have written, and no woman in the country would have published, with the exception of Miss Fuller." Poe's unkind remark reflects the extraordinary way in which the book made women agents of transcendence.[42]

Margaret Fuller wrote of the fulfillment of the destiny of man and added, "By Man I mean both man and woman." In order for mankind to realize its divinity, woman would have to realize hers. "We would have every path laid open to Woman as freely as to Man. Were this done, and a slight temporary fermentation allowed to subside, we should see crystallizations more pure and of more various beauty." Fuller insisted, however, that the real issue was not employment but spiritual and intellectual development. Fuller's preoccupation with spiritual attainments tended to deflect her discussion from more mundane matters. "The especial genius of Woman I believe to be electrical in movement, intuitive in function, spiritual in tendency." She rejected, on behalf of all women, money, notoriety, and authority, in favor of the freedom to learn the secrets of the universe. Having defended the essential equality and incomparable value of each soul, however, Margaret Fuller could go on to claim for women the full dignity of their immortal essence. Once this became the norm in society there would cease to be varieties of marriage bonds according to relative social existence.

She would not, in some countries, be given away by her father. . . . Nor, in societies where her choice is left free, would she be perverted, by the current of opinion that seizes her, into the belief that she must marry, if it be only to find a protector, and a home of her own.

It may have been that Margaret Fuller considered marriage too hard a bargain, a virtual guarantee that a woman's instincts would be lost. Those who live too much in relations, she wrote, lost an understanding of their own resources. Women who believed that they must remake their entire lives around their husbands were victims of the "vulgar error that love, *a* love, to Woman is her whole existence; she also is born for Truth and Love in their universal energy." She praised women such as George Sand, Madame Roland, and Mary Wollstonecraft, who had struggled against social conventions, pointing to Eloisa's choice to remain Abelard's mistress because she "saw in practice around her the contract of marriage made a seal of degradation."[43]

Fuller's suspicion of marriage resulted from her recognition of the contradiction between the bourgeois woman's sphere and the individual's search for transcendence. Her conclusions are important for showing that transcendentalism brought into question important middle-class institutions. Emerson expressed some of the tension in transcendental thought concerning marriage when he reflected in 1841 that the "most rabid radical is a good Whig in relation to the theory of Marriage." Marriage during the 1830s was being given ideal attributes and virtues quite beyond the capacity of any human relation. Emerson recommended skepticism: "Is not marriage an open question, when it is alleged, from the beginning of the world, that such as are in the institution wish to get out, and such as are out wish to get in?" Skepticism tends to questioning, and so restless a group as the young transcendentalists could hardly be expected to allow even marriage to remain sacrosanct. Not surprisingly, it was the praise of spiritual freedom that first led to the poetic phrase *Free Love*, the title of a poem by Henry David Thoreau.

> Be not the fowler's net
> Which stays my flight,
> And craftily is set
> T' allure the sight,
>
> But be the favoring gale
> That bears me on,

And still doth fill my sail
When thou art gone.[44]

The attempts to put the transcendental philosophy into practice at
Fruitlands and Brook Farm carried the renegade Unitarians more directly into conflict with the emerging pattern of middle-class marriage.
Fruitlands was largely a joint venture of two men, Amos Bronson
Alcott and Charles Lane. Alcott was born in 1799 and grew up on his
family's farm in Wolcott, Connecticut. A bright student, he competed
for academic honors with his second cousin, William Andrus Alcott.
The cousins remained close throughout their lives. During the early
1820s William accompanied Bronson on one of his trips to Virginia to
sell housewares and other items to the planters. They taught at schools
in neighboring districts from 1823 until 1826, when William began his
medical studies. By then Bronson was well along in developing the
philosophy of education that he applied in 1828 as schoolmaster of an
infant school in Boston. He courted Abby May for two years, marrying her in time to take her to Germantown, Pennsylvania, where he
was a schoolmaster for almost four years. Returning to Boston in 1834,
Bronson Alcott began his Temple School for young boys with the
support of many prominent Bostonians. Conversations held with the
boys on a wide variety of topics were integral to the curriculum. His
assistants, first Elizabeth Peabody and then Margaret Fuller, recorded
the conversations held with the boys on the gospels.

Contact with prominent Unitarian evangelicals in the Boston area
brought Alcott into the sphere of the transcendentalists. Inspired by
the ideas of Ripley, Emerson, and others, Alcott contributed his *Conversations with Children on the Gospels* to the transcendental publications
of 1836. Unfortunately, the unorthodox view of Christ presented in
Conversations shocked the parents of his students, and by the beginning
of the fall term of 1837, Alcott had only six students left. Forced to
close the school in June 1838, he taught briefly at a school for the poor
in Boston, but this also failed when Alcott admitted a black girl and
the white parents withdrew their children. For the next few years, the
Alcotts lived on what Bronson earned from chopping wood and cutting
hay and what Abby and the girls earned with their sewing.[45]

Alcott's setback as an educator was irrelevant to the influence of his
educational philosophy. His writings so impressed a group of educa-

tors in England that they began a school called Alcott House. In 1842 Emerson raised enough money for Alcott to visit England where he met many of the island's prominent thinkers, attended anticorn-law rallies, and argued with Carlyle. Alcott spent most of his visit with members of the Alcott House faculty, especially Charles Lane and Henry G. Wright. Lane had studied the work of the French Socialist, Fourier, and in 1841 had written an introduction to a translation of a work by French Fourierist Gatti de Gamond. Although Lane agreed with Alcott that people made their own institutions and then became enslaved to them, Lane also believed that people needed to act to alter or construct institutions that would provide an appropriate environment for development.[46]

Lane, Alcott, and Wright conceived of a method of reform that would use Graham's ideas of diet to inspire universal love among a small group of people. Lane and Wright offered to underwrite the cost. They returned to America in October 1842 with Lane's son and immediately put their plans into operation at Alcott's home in Concord. Henry Wright tired of their ascetic existence by January 1843 when he abandoned the experiment and his investment. Lane and Alcott persisted, however, and by the following spring they purchased a farm in Harvard Township for eighteen hundred dollars. Although they traveled widely to recruit members and to spread their beliefs, the Fruitlands colony attracted only seventeen members, including Alcott's family. Seeking to free themselves of as many encumbrances of the surrounding world as possible, they rejected all trade, hired labor, and animal labor. The colonists abstained from tea, coffee, meat, and milk both because these were rejected in Grahamite diets and because the money required to purchase these luxuries would connect them to the outside world. Limited farming experience, a poor harvest in the fall, and the cold of winter thoroughly demoralized the utopians. Lane argued with Abby Alcott over her devotion to the nuclear family. In January 1844 the experiment ended, with the Alcotts moving back to Concord and the Lanes leaving for a brief sojourn with the Shakers before returning to England.[47]

Fruitlands expressed the self-reliance so important to the New View. So short-lived a colony could not establish an alternative to middle-class marriage, but it could help define the contrasting visions of married life of Alcott and Lane. For Alcott, Fruitlands was based firmly upon the model of the family as the point of reconciliation between the needs of the individual and the demands of the world. The colony was to extend the benefits of the nuclear family to a larger sphere and so provide a means of realizing the most sublime needs of the individual and of the society.[48]

Charles Lane had no such sanguine view of the family. Like Alcott, Lane believed in the necessity of reconciling the spiritual with the material world. However, Lane viewed the family as a divisive element. "The universal bond is so weak," he wrote in William Channing's *Present*,

or the individual bond is so strong, that one married pair is deemed a sufficient swarm of human bees to hive off and form a new colony. How, then, can it be hoped that there is universal affection sufficient to unite many such families in one body for the common good?

Lane offered a hard choice for those who supported communitarianism: "If, as we have been popularly led to believe, the individual or separate family is in the true order of Providence, then the associative life is a false effort."[49]

The opposition of the world of society and the world of association held little attraction for most transcendentalists. Historian Richard Francis has written that the more typical attitude was displayed at Brook Farm in an effort to combine the old and the new orders. Brook Farm began when George Ripley and his wife Sophia took possession of a farm in West Roxbury, Massachusetts, in April 1841 as the core of a new community. A graduate of Harvard Divinity School, Ripley believed that the purpose of Christianity was to redeem both the individual and society from evil. Ripley's community would combine manual and intellectual labor, thereby ending the separation of workers from the product of their labor, consumers from the source of their goods and services, and class from class. The end to be gained was a community of educated and cultivated persons who worked the soil and provided for their other needs. Among the original colonists were many middle-class intellectuals, including not only the Ripleys but Charles Dana and Nathaniel Hawthorne. As the years passed, the middle-class constituency of the farm declined and more working-class applicants passed through the two-month waiting period for admission.[50]

Variety was both a goal and a reality at Brook Farm. By 1842 the colony had outgrown the large farmhouse, called the Hive, and new buildings were constructed for the residents. The Eyrie was built in 1842, followed by the Cottage, the Pilgrim House, and a workshop. Occupations included farming, schoolteaching, carpentry, shoemaking, and printing. In addition to their traditional household chores, the women made fancy lampshades for sale in the city. The community's school had a good reputation, attracting thirty boys and girls by the end of the second year and providing needed income. In contrast to Fruitland's asceticism, Brook Farm's inhabitants tried to accommodate all tastes. Smoking was discouraged, but some continued to smoke. Convinced Grahamites had their own table in the common dining room. Those who wished to take their meals alone in their rooms were free to do so. Variety also characterized the amusements of the community, including frequent dances, amateur theatricals, outings, churchgoing, occasional parties, and, on almost all occasions, conversation. These formed part of the community's effort to give everyone opportunities for spiritual and intellectual development.[51]

John Humphrey Noyes, who made careful investigations into such matters, wrote that he found "nothing that indicates any attempt on the part of Brook Farm to meddle with the marriage relation." He suspected something had been overlooked. As Noyes knew, it was the nature of community life to bring together men and women outside of social forms and so make them face problems of sexual relations. Nathaniel Hawthorne's *Blithedale Romance*, a tale that incorporated many of Hawthorne's experiences at Brook Farm, suggests the heightened awareness of sexuality and affection characteristic of community life. One of the major female characters is Zenobia, whose sexual desirability is repeatedly described. Hawthorne recorded that the footing on which men and women met at Blithedale "seemed to authorize any individual, of either sex, to fall in love with any other, regardless of what would elsewhere be judged suitable and prudent." In general, he assured his readers, the results were harmless.[52]

While Hawthorne may have taken some poetic license, the testimony of residents shows that Brook Farm encouraged men and women to test convention, even if only in matters of romance. There were few married couples on the farm as late as 1844, and many of the community's amusements would have been most suitable for young people, including dancing, boating, and picnicking. According to historian Lindsay Swift, the women, many of them well educated, were quite capable of "fellowshipping with men in a serious endeavour lying well outside of domestic relations." Of the fourteen marriages Swift traced to friendships begun at Brook Farm, remarkably few were mismatched. "Intellectual equality and unusual opportunity for discovering real character would go far to explain the gratifying result." That the young people discussed their concerns about courtship shows through Sophia Ripley's exhausted patience with "the extravagant moods of the young girls" and the use of the word "affinity." " 'Morbid familism'," Swift recorded, "was a frequent reproach brought against exoteric civilization."[53]

The only marriage to take place at Brook Farm was between Marianne Dwight and John Orvis. Orvis had been a student at Oberlin and joined the antislavery cause after coming to Boston. He joined Brook Farm about 1843 or 1844 and was one of the lecturers sent out by the colony to spread Fourierism when that became the community's gospel. Marianne Dwight arrived with her father, mother, sister Frances, and brother John in the spring of 1844. She ate at the Graham table and soon came to see the necessity for women to make their own money in order to attain actual independence. Writing to a friend, Marianne Dwight expressed the vision of the transcendental community for the kind of spiritual development preached by Margaret Fuller: "Much shall I rejoice when I see the day . . . that will not find me surrounded by any enslaving circumstances." She hoped that association would raise women to spiritual equality with men, freeing their intellectual development.[54]

Before Marianne Dwight's marriage in 1845 she took part in the many activities of the colony's young people. Her letters were full of talk about work and leisure, but news of the latter was more prominent. She remembered an evening walk in the woods with a small group. She and two others, Frederick and Dora, "threw ourselves upon our backs . . . and talked till about nine o'clock when the dampness warned us home." Her flirtations were innocent but frequent enough that she was teased by her friend about them. "You ask how many flirtations I carry on. Why, you saucy thing. . . . But I never '*evade.*' *One* with almost any body—no, one with Christopher List,— two with J. Orvis, and Miss Russell says, 'and *seven with Fred.*' " Apparently the young women gained a certain notoriety. Marianne's brother John overheard a conversation between two young men, new-comers to the community. "The girls here are *pretty slick*," said one. "Yes!" replied his companion, "a very good place for a fellow to come who wants to look up a girl."[55]

Marianne Dwight's letters testify to her enjoyment of the "absence of conventionalism" that Robert Dale Owen remembered of New Harmony. She wrote to her brother Frank, "I could not feel contented again with the life of isolated houses, and the conventions of civiliza-tion." Conventional society was probably farther removed from Brook Farm in work and the status of women than in the latitude given young people for courtship. Travelers to America found that American youth, especially young women, had great freedom during court-ship.[56] Brook Farm, however, unlike "exoteric civilization" and unlike New Harmony, promised to extend the family to include the commu-nity, so that a single pair would not "hive off" but remain integrated in the larger community. Thus the concerns of housing, childcare, and employment would diminish for the couple as they were subsumed in the general maintenance of the community. In this way the separate spheres of the man and woman would be more likely to break down. Marriage would still exist, but it would no longer be the marriage that isolated individuals and families.

Brook Farm's success seemed to offer a permanent alternative to middle-class society, but the end would come soon enough. During 1844 and 1845, discussions of industrial organization in the community led to interest in and then the adoption of the French socialism of Charles Fourier, which seemed the wave of the future. Brook Farm began publishing the Fourierist organ, the *Harbinger*, in 1845. The colonists took on a large debt to build a phalanstery, a project ending in disaster in 1846 when the uninsured building burned down. Finan-cial problems crowded upon the colony then. Brook Farm survived for another year before the land was put up for sale.[57]

With the end of Brook Farm came the decline of transcendentalism as a social movement. George Ripley moved to New York City, where he worked for Horace Greeley and slowly paid the debt left over from the colony. Alcott had become a farmer, but during the 1850s he began a series of travels throughout New England and the West holding conversations on human culture. In 1859 he was asked to be superintendent of schools for the Concord school district, a position he held with distinction until 1865. Margaret Fuller went to New York City to work for the *Tribune* after editing the *Dial*. In 1846 she went to Europe where she soon became involved in the movement for Italian liberation. She met and married an Italian nobleman whose son she bore. The family sailed for America in 1850 but was lost at sea during a storm. Those transcendentalists who remained in the Boston area became part of a new social elite, and their reform efforts were caught up in larger movements, especially the antislavery agitation. In 1854 Bronson Alcott joined a vigilance committee in a failed attempt to free a black man arrested under the fugitive slave law. Even before the Fugitive Slave Act of 1850, transcendentalism was being replaced as an intellectual alternative. The search for divinity after 1848 turned to attempts at communicating with the dead, and Fourierism already had become the most important model for communitarian reform.[58]

Even in decline, transcendentalism left an impressive intellectual critique of middle-class society. The essential divinity of each soul made all people equal and so undermined the separate spheres in which men and women apparently moved. The New View also offered new perceptions of the family, both as a means of realizing individual genius and as a trap for human aspirations. At the same time, transcendentalism formulated the evangelical and capitalist conception of individuality in universal terms. The man on the make or the sinner alone in the throes of regeneration became the irreducible human soul on a journey toward its own transcendence. Transcendentalism expressed the reliance upon individual action and the rejection of institutional reform that characterized much of middle-class thought during the 1840s and 1850s. As such, transcendentalism formed part of the repudiation of Owenite socialism and helped prepare for later reform movements that would seek to reduce government, commerce, and marriage to freely contracted relationships among individual sovereigns.

Fourierism

The French socialism of Charles Fourier reached America in a revised version, specially edited for American tastes. Where Owen had disparaged organized religion and the growth of private wealth, American Fourierists claimed that their reforms would promote true Christianity and would aid the rich and poor alike. Where Owen condemned the institutional framework that destroyed marriage, Fourierists wanted to realize the highest ideal of middle-class marriage. Even so, Fourierism, like Owenism, was ultimately declared anathema by editors, ministers, and other middle-class intellectuals. Fourier's beliefs, rather than their American version, became issues in the late 1840s. By then, the high hopes for communitarian reform had been lost with most of the Fourierist associations. What remained, however, was a widespread agreement among former associationists on the ills of society and marriage and both a vocabulary and a network that facilitated the spread of discussion of social ills.

Although the ideas of Charles Fourier received some attention in the United States as early as 1838, Fourierism became familiar to Americans only after 1840 through the work of Albert Brisbane. Brisbane was born in Batavia, New York, in 1809, the son of a wealthy retail merchant. At age 17 he went to New York City to begin two years of study with the French expatriate Jean Manesca, who taught him French and Enlightenment philosophy. In 1828 Brisbane left for Europe, where he attended the lectures of Victor Cousin at the Sorbonne and the lectures of Hegel at the University of Berlin. From 1830 until 1832 he traveled widely in Europe, Greece, and Asia Minor, reflecting upon the conditions he encountered and meeting many of the great men of the day. When Brisbane returned to Paris he became a student of Charles Fourier. In 1834 he returned to upstate New York a convinced Fourierist and attempted to make a fortune that would enable him to begin a phalanx with his own resources. The panic of 1837 ended these hopes.

In 1840 Brisbane took over the propaganda arm of the small Fourierist society then in the United States. That same year he published *The Social Destiny of Man*, the first major work on Fourierism in English. By 1842 Brisbane had abandoned his first attempt at a Fourierist journal in favor of a scheme suggested by the journal's publisher, Horace Greeley. Brisbane purchased a front-page column in Greeley's new paper, the New York *Tribune*, that carried the Fourierist message to the paper's subscribers from March 1842 until 1843. By 1843 the *Tribune* articles had recruited a substantial following for the new Fourierist journal, the *Phalanx*.[59]

In New York, Fourierism became a major movement. People throughout the state adopted the ideas of Fourier in response to the publications and lecturers in the region. Fourierist missionaries, such as Theron Leland, toured New York from 1844, holding meetings and helping to organize local Fourier societies. Six phalanxes began that year in the Rochester area, and Theron Leland estimated that there were twenty thousand converts west of Rochester waiting to join an association. Leland's figure may have been optimistic, but it is certain that there were thousands who embraced Fourierism as a social philosophy and plan of community building. Phalanxes were established across the nation, from Red Bank, New Jersey, through upstate New York to Brook Farm, and across the West through Pennsylvania, Ohio, and as far as Wisconsin.[60]

While the conversion of Brook Farm in 1844 was only one of many triumphs for American Fourierism that year, it signaled a division within transcendentalist thought. Transcendentalists had stressed the perfection of man and had generally conceded the importance of environment. Individual development, however, remained largely idiosyncratic in the minds of most transcendentalists. Reform, in Emerson's mind, would proceed through "the simplest ministries of family, neighborhood, fraternity." Emerson outlined the divergence between transcendentalist and socialist thought in an article for the *Dial* in 1842. Having heard the Fourier system explained by Albert Brisbane, Emerson recalled that "it appeared to us the sublime of mechanical contrivance; for the system was the perfection of arrangement and contrivance." Its stress upon environmental changes struck Emerson as the core of the program. "Society, concert, cooperation, is the secret of the coming Paradise." An impressive system, but one that Emerson refused to accept. "Our feeling was that Fourier had skipped no fact but one, namely Life. He treats man as a plastic thing." What Fourier ignored were those qualities of humanity that constitute individuality.[61]

That George Ripley and others at Brook Farm should have adopted the associative route to reform probably resulted from their experience of community and common needs. By the 1840s many Americans were seeking collective measures to solve social problems. The aggressive propaganda of Brisbane and other leading Fourierists coalesced with economic and social changes in America and offered new ways of explaining and controlling America's destiny. New Harmony had been founded in 1825, the year that the Erie Canal was completed. The economic optimism of those years had been tempered, if not shattered, by depression in the late 1820s and the panic of 1837, which turned into a depression in the years following. The promise of prosperity had been fulfilled for many; but for workingmen, the mills in New England and the factories in New York had dimmed the prospects for shops of their own and had destroyed their hopes of becoming master craftsmen. Many workers accepted Fourierism during the 1840s as a means of retaining their independence as artisans by creating a social republic that would free them from dependence upon their employers. Middle-class Fourierists, on the other hand, viewed the movement as a means of eliminating tensions between classes. While about half of those in the Fourier organization in Rochester and two-thirds of the leadership were from the middle class, those who joined the Fourierist communities were more likely to be men who practiced mechanical crafts. Their interest was in the possibility of gaining control over their own financial arrangements.[62]

In addition to economic factors, there were religious developments that created an environment favorable to Fourierism. Revivalism in America blazed with particular fury through upstate New York along the route of the Erie Canal. As early as the 1830s, many people, emotionally overwrought after repeated struggles with salvation, had abandoned evangelistic Protestantism for Universalism. Universalists had always been at the forefront of reform, though they lacked the passion evinced by the evangelicals. With their evangelical recruits, however, many Universalist groups began pressing for total reforms by the 1840s. For instance, John Allen, one of Brook Farm's itinerant lecturers on Fourierism, had been a Universalist minister as well as an abolitionist.[63]

Another path for those who abandoned orthodoxy was perfect sanctification. Even within orthodox religion many Americans assumed that moral perfection, generalized to all of American society, was attainable. This belief was a powerful tendency outside of its religious context, expressed in transcendentalism and providing the New View with much of its popular appeal. As the depression of the late 1830s and 1840s turned speculation to social forms of perfection, Fourierism seemed to offer the correct analysis of economic ills, the reconciliation of individual and communal values, and the exact science to realize the millennium. Fourier, who had considered man to be essentially good, sought to create a social environment that would release this goodness and obviate both class divisions and the industrial city. Many of these attributes Fourierism shared with Owenism, but Owenism had been closely identified with free thought and had called for the end of private wealth. The American disciples of Fourier, on the other hand, made no attack on Christianity and presented their system as a means of reconciling rich and poor.[64]

Fourier taught that while the human passions were divine instruments for ordering humanity, they created suffering when denied proper expression. The evolution from savagery to civilization had proceeded with the creation of institutions that thwarted passions and so perverted human life. Like savages, children instinctively repudiated civilization and had to be forced into its routine. Once oppression ceased, claimed Fourier, "the next day you will see the whole people in revolt, abandoning work and returning to the savage state." Albert Brisbane faithfully presented this part of the master's analysis to the American public. "The Creator," wrote Brisbane, "distributes Attractions to all his creatures in *exact proportion* to their Destiny; . . . he connects their happiness with the functions they are to exercise, and secures the performance of them without resort to constraint." He cited the vicious habits of many in society, "the Duplicity, Discord, Vice and Crime . . . which has led Moralists, Philosophers and the World in general to suppose that Human Nature was inherently depraved." These evils did not make our social order necessary, he assured his readers, but were products of it. We are not attracted to poverty or monotony, wrote Brisbane, so we obviously are not des-

tined for it. "But it is in the revolt of the passions against our odious
societies, that we find a condemnation of those societies, and a proof
that they are NOT the social destiny of man."[65]

American Fourierists were less faithful about their presentation of
other aspects of Fourier's thought. Fourier believed that man could yet
evolve beyond the chains of civilization to higher and freer levels of
being, progressively replacing the institutions of oppression with freely
functioning passions. The summit of human evolution would be experienced in the phalanstery, or association, where the variety and frequent change of occupations would make work one among many
pleasures available and where each individual would follow his or her
affinities in work, leisure, diet, and love. Brisbane also looked forward
to the phalanstery, but Fourier's American disciples promoted Fourierism as a cooperative solution for unemployment and poverty and as a
promise of abundant wealth. Americans could accept association as a
model of industrial relief because of the evident success enjoyed by the
frugal Shakers and Rappites. Brisbane's brand of Fourierism, according to historian Arthur Bestor, was "the culminating expression of all
those social ideals that had built the American republic." With few
translations of Fourier's original work available in America, the version
presented in the columns of the *Tribune* and in the Fourierist pamphlets and periodicals stood for all of Fourierism.[66]

Parke Godwin wrote in 1844 that the great accomplishment of
civilization was that it eschewed war and embraced commerce and
industry. This development, however, generated a multitude of isolated interests, all in conflict, and so set each individual against all
others. Among the miseries of civilized life was the aversion to work,
creating the need for oppression. In his introduction to *The Social
Destiny of Man* (1840), Albert Brisbane stressed that the goal of Fourierism was a reorganization of industry. Oppression to enforce labor
violated fundamental laws of human behavior:

> . . . any passion which is suddenly arrested, thwarted or disappointed in its
> course, takes a subversive development or false direction, and turns to enmity,
> jealousy, revenge, antipathy, regret, and sometimes to despair and insanity.

The means of freeing the passions, and particularly of establishing
industrial liberty, was to form associations. These would offer the

Albert Brisbane (1809–1890).
Brisbane was instrumental in promoting the ideas of Fourier in America. During the 1840s Brisbane and other leaders of the American Fourierist movement carefully avoided attacking marriage, claiming that any changes in the relations between men and women would only appear in the distant future.

individual many forms of labor and frequent changes of routine and would guarantee food, clothing, lodging, and other material benefits. Working in groups, individuals would emulate the good workmanship of others, thereby improving industry. Association would create greater interest in work and would stimulate greater efforts and better working habits. Increased production, first in agriculture then in other forms of industry, would lead to peace and the end of armaments and armies. Once it became general among nations association would also solve the problems of the industrial cities by dividing production among independent phalanxes, each with a population of about two thousand in settings combining natural beauty and material needs for comfort.[67]

Brisbane distanced himself from the Owenites, whose "ideas of Community of Property, Abolition of Worship, etc., have excited the deepest antipathy and the strongest prejudices against the magnificent problem of Association." Brisbane's articles in the *Tribune* repeatedly insisted on the essential agreement of Fourierism and Christianity. Association was meant to realize the divine plan for humanity without threatening any religion. It would also completely reorganize society without disturbing property. Indeed, the rich had as much to gain as the poor, since "they are harassed by physical debility and disease, and are devoured often by mental sloth, ennui, apathy, melancholy and hypochondria." Association offered them moral riches, the pleasures of social relations, cultivation of the arts and sciences, and work to suit their passional attractions. The phalanxes would be organized as joint-stock ventures, with interest paid to stockholders who could cash in their certificates when they wished. While Brisbane agreed with Owen that private property was the basis of society, he concluded that it must therefore remain inviolate lest its destruction lead to injustice, anarchy, and bloodshed.[68]

Reflecting the success of the movement were the reports of meetings and organizational matters published in the columns of the *Phalanx*. By the Civil War, ten thousand people had been involved in American Fourierism. The transition from an intellectual movement to a communitarian movement had taken place by October 1843, when the Rochester Fourier society made preparations to purchase land and buildings belonging to the Shakers at Sodus Bay on Lake Ontario. The experience at Sodus Bay indicates that Fourierism was a different matter for those who merely discussed it and those who attempted to establish associations. Fourier's doctrines played a limited role in the organization of the Sodus Bay community in May 1844, and the building of the proposed phalanstery was less important than running the sawmill that provided needed cash. Income distribution and labor groups were greatly simplified. These emphases reflected the concerns of the working-class members who had seen Brisbane's plan for association as a means of taking control of the industries in which they labored. Sodus Bay lasted only until 1846, a victim of the slight productivity of the community's industries, an overreliance on agriculture, divisions among the participants, drought, overcrowding, and typhoid fever.[69] In fact, so many problems assaulted the community that its end was certainly inevitable.

The transition from intellectual critique to industrial reform was essential, since association had been the core of Brisbane's program. At the same time, the importance of the associational phase meant that the movement would stand or fall with its phalanxes. Of the twenty-nine associations established in America, twenty-two began in the three years from 1843 to 1845. Of these, all but two had ceased operation by 1847. The longest-lived phalanx was the North American, in Red Bank, New Jersey. Started in 1843, it survived until 1855, one year after a fire convinced its stockholders to liquidate their holdings. The Wisconsin Phalanx, founded in 1844, overcame religious divisions and prospered financially, but the rise in property values was too great a temptation for many of the members. The association disbanded after selling the property in 1850. Only three phalanxes were founded after 1846, one of them a settlement of French Fourierists near Dallas, Texas, that existed from 1855 to 1859.[70]

The movement had stalled long before La Reunion expired. By the middle of the nineteenth century, both the new industrialism and the new middle class had become dominating influences in America. The economic recovery that began by 1843 continued through 1854, making the Northeast a manufacturing region. During these same years, the men and women who had discovered new opportunities as clerks and managers and new duties as wives were gaining both social and economic self-confidence. According to historian Karen Halttunen, the sentimental critique of fashion that had characterized the 1830s and

1840s gave way to an acceptance among the middle class of "self-display, social formalism, and ceremonial ritual" and to the struggle for status. As the middle class became something distinct and self-aware, so did the working class. The continuing growth of manufacturing and of the factory system during the 1840s robbed workers of both independence and hope. Rather than the social republic uniting all classes, opposing visions of politics and society came to typify working-class and middle-class attitudes during the 1850s, making the promises of associationism irrelevant.[71]

Middle-class critics of Fourierism could point to the movement's departures from the newly ascendant moral conventions. As early as 1844 Donald M'Laren quoted scripture to underscore the basic conflict between Fourierism and middle-class society: " 'Every man is tempted, when he is drawn away of his own lusts and enticed.' " M'Laren continued, "When any man is thus drawn away and enticed, he exemplifies fully what Fourierism means by 'attraction.' " As Fourier's writings became more widely known, critics easily found points that offended the public. Fourier, as opposed to his American disciples, challenged each of the major institutions of bourgeois civilization— church, home, and counting house. The purpose of the phalanx was not to relieve unemployment but to free the passions, not to reform trade but to abolish it.[72] Outside criticism and disarray within the movement led many Fourierists to a careful scrutiny of Fourier's writings and to a reevaluation of some of the essential goals of reform.

In shaping Fourierism for its American audience, Brisbane, Godwin, and other publicists had carefully avoided for as long as possible any discussion of Fourier's writings about sexual relations. This is easy to understand, since Fourier's comments could hardly be construed as supporting marriage. "One must be born in Civilization," he wrote, "to tolerate the sight of those indecent customs known as marriages, where one sees the simultaneous coincidence of magistrate and priest with the fools and drunks of the neighborhood." According to Fourier, marriage, like the state, the factory, and the schoolhouse, was a form of oppression that distracted passions from their healthy expressions. It might be possible to force some to stay with a single spouse, but "perpetual fidelity in love is contrary to human nature; . . . the mass of men and women will never be reduced to monogamy." The social system that fostered dishonest trade and poverty also found it "necessary to stupefy women from their childhood, so as to make them fit the philosophical dogmas, the servitude of marriage and the debasement of falling into the power of a husband." For the impoverished woman, civilization offered only one means of subsistence, the bedpost.[73]

To say that the American Fourierists softened the master's teachings on sex and marriage is a considerable understatement. John Humphrey Noyes recorded that "it was always the policy of the *Harbinger*, the *Tribune*, and all organs of Fourierism, to indignantly protest their innocence of any *present* disloyalty to marriage." Projecting Fourier's marital prescriptions into the future became a tactic only when Fourier's ideas started to become generally known in America. According to historian Carl Guarneri, the Fourierists originally disclaimed any desire to promote changes in the marital system.[74] In fact, many of the early writings of American Fourierism falsified the intent of the system to make it acceptable to American readers. By the middle of the 1840s, however, questions concerning marriage were forcing themselves forward in the debate among Fourierists and in the polemics against the movement. In 1848, when the views of Fourier concerning love and marriage became generally known, the movement faced a crisis. Most Fourierists repudiated the master's vision. Surprisingly, others embraced it and would carry on even as the Fourier movement disintegrated.

Implicit in the language used by Brisbane, Godwin, and other writers for the *Phalanx* and *Harbinger* was a criticism of the social order concerning love, marriage, and the family. "Ambition and Love," wrote Brisbane, "are true and noble Passions and produce good when legitimately developed or called out; but still these same Passions may, if thwarted and outraged, turn to Envy, Jealousy, Hatred and Revenge." As Brisbane showed, the separated interests of civilization reduced society to warring among isolated households. Seeking a haven from the competition and animosity of civilization within the home gave rise to "that family-selfishness, which, concentrating all affections and hopes within its own little circle, leaves the heart indifferent to the woes and sufferings of mankind." According to J. A. Saxton, the isolated household became a school of selfishness, passing it from generation to generation. The result was to reduce women to servitude within their homes. "No class could bring so many well founded complaints against the social mechanism as women, for they are truly its slaves."[75]

According to American Fourierists, the cure was association, which would extend the household, foster cooperation, reduce the burden of housework, and give woman her natural and political rights. Although the household of the phalanx would include not six or eight persons, but two thousand, associationists denied that this threatened the family. "Some persons suppose that in Association the family and marriage ties will be dissolved," wrote Brisbane. "This is the grossest of errors." It was the isolated household and the deformed characters produced by civilization that deranged marriage; only association could redeem it. Brisbane predicted that the present state of marriage would continue unchanged for three generations after harmony had been established. By then women would have overcome their dependence and so be able to reshape the relationship, "uniting female liberty and independence with moral harmony and Christian purity." Women would force men to be honorable, chaste, and moral.[76] In other words, the phalanx would so improve marriage that its establishment would be the realization of the middle-class ideal.

Translations from French Fourierist Gatti de Gamond in both the *Tribune* and the *Phalanx* pictured marriage in association as a better form of the same institution that civilization nurtured. According to Mme. de Gamond, traditional marriage within civilization was the goal of a woman's education. Dependent upon father and then husband, a woman even lacked the choice of whom she would marry. For the poor woman, poverty and misery would drive her into "the abyss of degradation." The wealthy woman, isolated, bored, disgusted with her marriage, suffered as well. Chastity existed, if at all, only as a result of fear, oppression, and punishment. "And man rules in the social desert, where all the generous sentiments remain barren, where all true affections are subverted." Just as Gatti de Gamond's polemic is reminiscent of Sophia Ripley's, so is the solution she projects. Women will be well educated and given some industrial occupation in association, thereby ending their dependence upon men. Even working at home, the wife or daughter will be part of a series, "engaged in art or

industry, religion or instruction." Vice, a product of woman's degradation, would no longer exist.[77]

By 1844 Parke Godwin delicately suggested that some of the problems of society might be associated with marriage and could be amelio-
rated by various changes. Like Robert Dale Owen sixteen years before, Godwin wrote that while some persons were formed for constancy
in love, others were not. Marriage, therefore, should be a voluntary
contract that could be dissolved. This failed to satisfy the suspicion of
critics or the interest of the sympathetic. By 1845 opponents of the
movement were accusing it of undermining the family. Charles Dana,
a Brook Farm resident, wrote that "we make no attack upon the family
in itself." Family relations "originate in the most delicate and elevated
sentiments of the human heart; they are the crown and flower of life."
Rather, it was the isolated household that burdened families with
"tedium, petty vexations, anxieties, discord, unhappiness."[78]

Basing his attack upon the writings of Albert Brisbane, Donald
M'Laren claimed in 1844 that

marriage, as an institution, cannot subsist in the combined order. How can it
be maintained, when there is to be the greatest intimacy and freedom of
intercourse between the sexes, and that intercourse regulated, not by conscience, or moral duty, or reason, but by the passions alone?

The marriage issue became a major point of attack from critics of
Fourierism. The New York *Observer* accused the Fourierists of planning to abolish marriage and legalize unlimited licentiousness. The
Harbinger reiterated the position of Brisbane, Godwin, and others that
no change in marriage was to take place immediately; when reforms
were instituted, they would be made by "the noble Women of that
purer and more enlightened era." One week later the *Harbinger* again
answered a critic of Fourier. There existed wide divergence of views
on the marriage question among associationists, wrote the apologist;
and while Fourier had taught that attraction was the most important
guide to life, no associationist believed that men and women could
trust their passional attractions in the present state of civilization.[79]

It may have been that George Ripley, editor of the *Harbinger*, and
other leaders of the movement decided to handle the issue by maintain-
ing that changes in marriage would be far in the future. A major

recapitulation of the Fourier system appeared in the *Harbinger* during November and December 1846 and in January 1847. The author was Marx Edgeworth Lazarus, a southerner who had studied medicine in Philadelphia and was living at Brook Farm. "It would be idle," Lazarus wrote, "for us to speculate on the forms and institutions which will grow out of the Harmonic order and constitute its expression in the relations of the sexes." Lazarus deplored

> . . . the evils now resulting from constraint in the relations of love, and its false dependence on pecuniary interest, the withering of true affections, the false and unhappy marriages, the adultery, the libertinism and the prostitution with which our civilized cities are rotten.

Perhaps for the first time among American Fourierists, Lazarus admitted that married life in the phalanx of the future would be much different. Improvement would follow with the end of dependence for women and better opportunity for men and women to become acquainted. It was not just the perfection of bourgeois marriage that Lazarus predicted for harmonial society, but "perfect liberty to this and every other attraction must be not only compatible with a divine order, but absolutely essential to it."[80]

Until the mid-1840s American Fourierists embraced no marriage reforms not already put forward by Robert Owen twenty years before, some of which were endorsed by middle-class marriage experts. Lazarus went beyond these reforms, suggesting that the topic of marriage was becoming an issue. His article also alerts us to the growing importance of Fourier's writings, as opposed to those of his followers. This was not because of the power of Fourier's prose or the brilliance of his analysis, but because Fourier's conclusions were more comprehensive than those of his followers. By 1847 there were many who questioned the elements of society and marriage in particular. Among these were Fourierists, or persons interested in the movement, who sought a system to define their complaints against society. Even though the leaders of the association movement insisted that debates on the future relations of the sexes distracted from the reorganization of industry, Fourier's writing answered the need of many to probe, and even repudiate, social institutions. By 1847 business was pretty bad for the phalanxes, a trend that would soon undermine the mainstream of the movement. The failure of practical utopias, however, seemed to increase interest in theoretical matters. When a translation of Victor Hennequin's *Love in the Phalanstery* appeared in 1848, American readers could finally begin to judge for themselves the relation of Fourierism and marriage.

Hennequin, like his American confreres, rejected any call for a change in marriage until far into the future, a disclaimer reinforced by the translator in a lengthy preface and by George Ripley in his review. Fourierism aims only at the reorganization of industry, wrote Ripley, and "the objections which have been brought against it on account of Fourier's anticipations in regard to the future relations of the sexes, are irrelevant and unfounded." Even if Fourier's ideas were presently irrelevant, Hennequin's language in attacking the marriages of civilization must have left a deep impression upon the minds of those who already disagreed with Fourierism or with marriage.

To be sure, adultery, abortion, infanticide, the conjugal employment of arsenic, go on increasing—the wages of laboring women, every day more niggardly and contemptible, forces them to sell themselves to protectors—the register of prostitution unceasingly enlarges itself—but these women are not reckoned, of course. Their mission is to suffer and die, in order to preserve the security of marriage.

We think, or rather we know, that the present relations of the sexes are a hotbed of lying, deception, avaricious maneuvering, and infamous traffic: we know that they engender adultery, prostitution, disease, abortion, infanticide, fictitious paternity.

Prostitution is one of the columns of your social edifice, and you sacrifice to it without compunction hecatombs of young girls.[81]

Hennequin's description of the *vestales, damoiselle,* and *angelicate,* with their sexual duties ranging from chastity to fidelity to variety, must have shocked conservative readers. But it was his polemical language far more than Hennequin's frequent disclaimers, or even his description of the love life in association, that focused the marriage debate. Writers would soon be dealing with the central issue of whether marriage was good or bad. The official movement clung to a fencepost, but once marriage was damned, even the assurance that it would be changed only in the distant future made no difference. Those who had embraced the more radical conclusions of Fourier would soon advance one of their own: If marriage were bad, why should its destruction be delayed?

Hennequin's translator became an important participant in the debate. Henry James spent several months in late 1848 and in early 1849 defending the Fourierist view of marriage and advancing his own ideas on the topic. Although a youthful game caused an accident that led to the amputation of his leg, Henry James was still a drinker and a reprobate when he went off to Union College in 1829. He was cured of alcohol in 1830 but not by evangelical conversion, for by then his speculations had led him away from orthodox Christianity. The death of his father in 1832 left Henry James independently wealthy, enabling him to follow his peculiar intellectual interests. He studied at Princeton Theological Seminary from 1835 to 1837, where he met the brother of the woman he would marry in 1840. James was a friend of Emerson, and during his visit to England in 1843 to 1844 he met Carlyle, Tennyson, and John Stuart Mill. It was in England that James began the study of Swedenborg that would lead him to a kind of conversion and enable him to form a theological system blending his Puritan heritage with Swedenborg's mysticism.[82]

James's respect for the family was evident in his defense of *Love in the Phalanstery* against the criticisms of the New York *Observer*. "Our present society," he wrote in the *Harbinger*, "is founded on the family institution or marriage, and whatever tends to weaken this institution proportionately endangers the stability of society." Civilized morality, however, supported the family for the sake of raising children rather than seeking to make marriage the true expression of love between a man and a woman.[83] James was answered in the columns of the *Harbinger* by "AEF," a Fourierist who believed that Fourier's notions about sex were "folly, and to all my moral perceptions they are defilment. The fact that married women live in 'series' with others than their husbands, does not alter the nature of the connection; it is adultery." James protested that adultery was a creation of the law. If society became responsible for the maintenance and education of the young, then "marriage would appear in its true light, as an exclusively spiritual, private, and therefore free, relation of the parties, and no violation of it consequently would be possible." AEF responded a few weeks later that marriage was not a social convenience but inherent in nature. Society was based upon a divine principle, claimed AEF, "which is, that vice and wickedness, in those forms which infest society, *tend* toward suffering in some shape or other."[84]

Not one to let his opponent have the last word, Henry James took up several columns on the next page answering AEF's letter and continued his response in the subsequent issues of the *Harbinger*. James claimed that the marriage relation of civilization was based upon the exclusive property of a man in a woman. This could not be a product of nature, he asserted, so it must be imposed by society. Marriage was an external compact, creating licentiousness because it forced adherence to sexual exclusiveness. Since James wanted to avoid advocating the abolition of marriage or the repudiation of fidelity, he claimed that the contradiction between the self-ownership of each individual and the union required of marriage would be resolved when the partners attained a purely spiritual union transcending their separateness. "Marriage is thus the strict apotheosis of Love."[85]

James would have preferred to keep his vision of marriage on the plane of Swedenborgian spirituality, where all problems could be poetically resolved. Love and marriage had material and physical aspects, however, that James's discussion could not ignore. In "Postscript to Y.S.'s Reply to A.E.F.," James claimed that true marriage was the perfect union of man and woman, distinct from the marriages forced upon men and women by society. He wanted to undergird marriage by making it a spiritual ideal, but when he wrote that "the institution of external or bodily marriage, slays the very life of love, and turns marriage itself into a caricature" he placed himself at odds with the only kind of marriage that most people had any knowledge of. He believed spiritual union would result from liberty in love, but he also endorsed liberty in love. G.F.T. pointed this out in the following issue. While marriages might not always be perfect in spiritual, mental, and physical adaptation of the couple, society, in its enforcement of chastity and exclusiveness, was approximating the "true law."[86] Both men agreed that marriage should be a spiritual union. Their differences were in their reliance upon society or upon freedom to foster such spiritual unions.

The argument never ended, both because the interested parties were unmoved and because the *Harbinger* stopped publication in 1849. By then the nationwide enthusiasm for communitarian utopia had greatly decreased. The legacy of these movements, however, would help determine the debate over love and marriage in the years to come. Thousands of Americans had read the socialist and transcendentalist publications, lived in communities, and questioned the middle-class consensus. They had absorbed at least the rhetoric of a new system that would provide them with the concepts they needed to forge their own alternatives to middle-class ideals. The end of the official voice of the Fourier movement meant that many voices would now interpret the true meaning of marriage in a flawed society.

CHAPTER 3

Spiritual Wives and Elective Affinity: Perfectionist and Harmonialist Transformations of Marriage

In the same decades that Owenism and Fourierism provided secular alternatives to marriage, revivalism and special revelation fostered some of the harshest attacks on marriage. For many Americans conversion transformed marriage into a religious vocation—that is, a means of salvation for the married couple and a source of regeneration for the world. For a minority, however, the intense personal experience of redemption made the compromises of middle-class life seem intolerable. They came to view marriage, like intemperance and slavery, as an unnecessary evil. The possibility of reaching beyond sordid reality to spiritual truth also inspired many Americans, even those who had abandoned or rejected revivalism. When calmer approaches to special revelation became widely known in America by the late 1840s, they frequently encouraged the dissolution of unhappy marriages.

The results of revivalism varied greatly during the first half of the nineteenth century. While the earliest revivals led to renewed efforts to convert the backcountry, by the early 1830s those who had experienced repeated awakening were seeking to express their religion within the world and spread salvation in such forms as sabbatarianism and temperance. Reform societies with growing evangelical memberships often abandoned their moderate programs for more extreme positions, as in the total abstinence pledge demanded by the ultra wing of temperance reformers in 1836.[1] Out of the hybrid of secular and religious reforms grew a critique of American society that can be called middle-class radicalism. In general, those who advanced this critique were typically of the new middle class in their economic aspirations and status, yet they claimed the term radical for themselves, believing that their program of reforms would change every aspect of American life. Combining elements of socialism with decades of revival experience, the radicals condemned false relationships. While they attacked both slavery and bourgeois marriage and hoped for a system of equitable reward of labor, radicals never broadened the scope of their attack to include all forms of property. With the failure of Fourierism to establish society upon the basis of its industrial associations, radical reform became strongly individualistic. Middle-class radicals were also perfectionist—that is, intolerant of the division between their ideals of society, government, and marriage and the reality that they saw around them. In order to understand the attitudes and ideas adopted by the middle-class radicals, we must examine the understanding of marriage that emerged from revival and special revelation.

Revival and Perfection

Among the middle class, even among the pious, many believed that unhindered revivalism could be fatal. Some cases reported in a medical journal in 1835 show the connection that doctors assumed existed between morbid religiosity and social deviance. One young woman "imagined her stomach was gone and there was a vacuity in that part of her abdomen. She imputed the removal of her stomach to the vengeance of God on account of her sins. She said she constantly felt the burnings of hell." A forty-five-year-old woman believed she had been spiritualized, so resumed her maiden name and refused to consider herself married. "She said she had constant intercourse with her heavenly Father—her body was incorruptible, and she never should die—always should exist in her present body." Aside from this monomania, she was perfectly sound in body and mind.[2] In both cases women sought resolutions to religious fears through physical changes that were, at least implicitly, sexual.

Both the sympathetic and the skeptical assumed that revivals encouraged sexual, as well as spiritual, sensitivity. An English observer of American religion, William Hepworth Dixon, wrote that men and women in the camp meetings were keenly alive "to something more than gospel freedom." "Much whispering in corners, lonely walks at sundown, and silent recognitions, were in vogue." A Methodist camp meeting in Louisiana in 1831 offended the son of a New England Baptist minister.

I witnessed among the camp enticements of a kind not altogether religious which startled my puritan sense of propriety. . . . The flank of a beautiful leg or ankle . . . frolicsome girls or matrons under the light of torches and bonfires glowing through the woods, added sometimes to the zeal of greedy young gentlemen whose grade of piety was not high.

Presbyterian historian Benjamin Warfield explained in 1931 that frequent and intense revival experiences produced a "nervous exaltation" that "seems not merely to have broken down the restraints to the unchecked discharge of other than religious emotions, but . . . even to have incited it."[3]

More frightening to the middle class than individual aberrations or the flirtations of the camp meeting was the suspicion that mass enthusiasm could inspire wholesale rejection of morality. While men of God like Charles Finney brought multitudes to salvation, the same charisma commanded by a mountebank could undermine society. In 1835 William Leete Stone gave credence to this fear in his book on religious charlatanism. Stone was a conservative editor in New York, an abolitionist, and an active public servant and reformer in education.[4] His account of religious hucksterism and insanity encouraged the established churches in their attempts to control the effects of religious zeal.

The story of Jacob Cochrane goes back to the first wave of the Second Great Awakening, just following the War of 1812. An unemployed ex-army officer, Cochrane posed as a clergyman throughout rural Maine in 1817 and 1818. Stone ascribed Cochrane's success to animal magnetism and accused the preacher of using his charisma to insure himself an easy life and to gain power over his female followers. "The consequence," wrote Stone ". . . was the most open and loathesome sensuality. . . . he seduced great numbers of females, married and unmarried, under the pretext of raising up a holy race of men." A slightly more sympathetic account by a former follower recalled that Cochrane's preaching was a manifestation of grace and the means for the revival of many until he started teaching that those married to Jesus Christ were married to one another. His disciples taught this doctrine at least until Cochrane's death in 1834.[5]

In contrast to the brevity of the Cochrane story, Stone's study of Robert Matthews was rich in detail and clearly documented the progress from self-appointed preaching to megalomania. Matthews was a carpenter and millwright from Washington County, New York, who had gained a good living and respectability by his hard work. He joined Presbyterian or Dutch Reformed churches as he moved from place to place. In the late 1820s Matthews was living in Albany, where he was excited by the preaching of Edward Kirk and then of Charles Finney. By 1829 he was preaching to his fellow workers and predicting the destruction of Albany. In 1830, Matthews entered a church service to preach without invitation. Trouble with the authorities soon convinced Matthews to take his message to the country. He traveled as far west as Arkansas then returned through Georgia and up the coast.

In New York City, Matthews, now calling himself Matthias, met members of a Bible-study group who were seeking the inspiration of the Holy Spirit. Matthias converted several members of this group, including two wealthy merchants. One of these invited Matthias to live with him and provided the prophet with fine clothing and a carriage so he could ride down Broadway to the Battery and promenade with the city's finest. Although his preaching led to arrest and confinement in Bellvue, Matthias soon returned to his small group and moved them all to the Singsing estate of Mr. and Mrs. Folger. By this time Matthias identified himself so closely with Jehovah that he often spoke of God's message using the first person. He preached against the gentile system, whose marriages he regarded as illegitimate. "God, he said, had nothing to do with the marriage of the wicked." Consequently, the marriages of the gentiles "were generally productive of unhappiness, and to most of the female parties, it was a state of wretchedness." Matthias's mounting demands finally alienated his wealthy converts. The Folgers ordered him to leave and later had him arrested and tried for crimes he was suspected of committing when living with them. None of the charges were proven in court, however, and Matthias acted reasonably during his trial.[6]

To middle-class Americans already concerned with the excesses of revivalism, the stories of Cochrane and Matthias proved that religious enthusiasm could lead the unwary into fatal delusions. The accounts also indicated what two of the worst delusions were. Both Cochrane and Matthias offered closer identification of the believer with God and both attacked marriage. While these cases involved only two men with limited influence, the belief in individual holiness and the rejection of marriage appeared again and again among converts to revival religion.

Perfectionism was among the important religious consequences of the pervasive revivalism of the early nineteenth century. The desire to destroy evil could lead to reforms, such as abolitionism, or to the conviction that conversion would continually subject the faithful to the will of God. Perfectionism, one of the primary religious expressions of the American faith in individuality, frequently called socially approved morality into question. Once assured of the gift of grace, the individual became responsible to God alone for his or her conduct. Those who were no longer conformed to the world were expected to transform the values by which they acted.

For many perfectionists, the gift of grace required a new understanding of the relationship between men and women. Lucina Umphreville, an early perfectionist preacher, claimed in 1832 that in the day of grace all love between men and women would be chaste. She called for men and women to eschew carnality and frivolity and to unite on a higher spiritual plane. "A mob of lasses," one writer recorded, "began to dream dreams, to interpret visions, directed against love and marriage, as love and marriage were understood by an unregenerate world." Some young women gave up their admirers, and married women questioned their duties to their husbands. Erasmus Stone's revelations also attacked temporal marriage. Believing that most men and women were wrongly matched, Stone claimed that the only real marriages were based on spiritual affinity and that these took precedence over any previous, mistaken unions. Stone soon entered into such a spiritual match with Eliza Porter. Another preacher, Hiram Sheldon, joined spiritually with Sophia Cook.

Benjamin Warfield believed that at first the spiritual husbands and wives were simply companions, sharing in the work of ministry. As they traveled through New England and upstate New York and lived together, however, the physical nature of their relationship became more important. Simon Lovett, for instance, upheld the doctrine of spiritual husbands and wives by allowing Mary Lincoln and Maria Brown into his bedroom. Unfortunately, other residents of their village discovered them "in the act." In 1836 Jarvis Rider, Lucina Umphreville, Charles Lovett, and Mrs. Chapman decided that the relationship of the two couples could now include physical intimacy. Although the four appeared embarrassed when Mr. Chapman returned home, Chapman was struck blind when he tried to attack Charles Lovett. This sign from God assured these four perfectionists that they were free from sin and could follow their beliefs without guilt. Soon the spiritual unions of Stone and Porter and of Sheldon and Cook included physical intimacy. "What was in the first instance only an incredible folly and dangerous fanaticism," Warfield lamented, "soon became an intolerable scandal and dissolute practice."[7]

The perfectionist teaching of "spiritual wives" emerged during the same years as the middle-class ideal of marriage. Both ideals gave a central and spiritual importance to relations between men and women. Sylvester Graham's doctrine, however, made sexual restraint the foundation of lifelong monogamy, while Lucina Umphreville and Jarvis Rider attacked marriage as a product of an unregenerate world. The perfectionists' audience was probably as important as theology in determining their attitude toward marriage and sexual intimacy. Sylvester Graham published his "Lecture to Young Men" in 1834 in Providence, Rhode Island. His audience included immigrants from the farms and villages of New England, seeking to order their lives while they pursued riches.[8] The ideas of Graham, Alcott, and the Fowlers —like Bibles, tracts, and canals—would eventually penetrate into rural areas, but in the 1830s New England's villages retained other traditions of courtship and marriage.

In the late eighteenth and early nineteenth century, courting couples engaged in a wide range of physical contact and perhaps even more in fantasies of such contact. In rural areas the practice of bundling—couples spending the night together, normally with caresses but without intercourse—persisted at least to the 1820s. A teacher in Cape Cod in 1827, during an evening call, was surprised to be matter-of-factly invited to spend the night with the family's nubile daughter. A young woman wrote to the *Yankee* in 1828 that during her visit to a Maine village she had been shocked when a young man asked her to sleep with him. "I have since made inquiries about *bundling*, and find that it is *really* the custom here, and that they think no more harm of it, than we do our way of a young couple sitting up together."[9]

The freedom enjoyed by couples before marriage ended abruptly at the altar. Especially for women, marriage meant separation from intimate friends and relations. Adolescent women would have been most apprehensive of their impending change of status and thus were most receptive to the gospel of Lucina Umphreville. To men and women alike, unhappy marriages provided further proof that marriage as it existed was wrong. The perfectionist rejection of marriage was a defense of the traditional freedom of rural courtship. By the time the idealized marriage doctrines of the seaboard cities encroached upon the villages of New England and upstate New York, a theological critique of marriage had been fully elaborated.

John Humphrey Noyes carried the analysis and rejection of marriage farther than any of his contemporary perfectionists. Born in 1811 in Brattleboro, Vermont, Noyes had been a graduate of Dartmouth for one year when he was converted by a revival in 1831. He consequently studied at Yale Theological Seminary and later became an advocate of perfectionism, using scripture to support his claim that the millennium was not at hand but in progress. Those who sinned were of the Devil; those who surrendered themselves to God would be perfected and saved, not only from sin but from disease and death.[10]

Noyes's involvement in the perfectionist movement in upstate New York and New England and his own sense of having overcome sin led him to question the institutions of the world, especially private property and marriage. During the period of spiritual crisis in 1837, Noyes concluded that marriage was too wrapped up with selfishness to be part of the Kingdom of God. "When the will of God is done on earth

John Humphrey Noyes (1811–1886).
Noyes firmly rejected the selfishness and isolation that he believed was inherent in marriage. In his community of Christian perfectionists, each man was husband to all the women and each woman a wife to all the men.

as it is in heaven, there will be no marriage," he wrote in a letter to Theophilius Gates's periodical, the *Battle-Axe and Weapons of War*. "In a holy community there is no more reason why sexual intercourse should be restrained by law, than why eating and drinking should be; and there is as little occasion for shame in the one case as in the other." For many years Noyes maintained that this referred to the future, when the Kingdom of God would be established on earth. He had no doubt that revival would lead to new sexual standards and eventually to the reorganization of society. "The next thing a man wants," he wrote years later, "after he has found the salvation of his soul, is to find his Eve and his Paradise."[11]

Rather than reject revivalism because it challenged social values, Noyes concluded that the logic of revival required "a divine organization of society, which all who love Revivals and the good of mankind should fearlessly seek to discover and inaugurate." By 1838 Noyes had gathered around him a small group in Putney, Vermont, including his wife, brother and sisters, and a few other families. In 1841 the study group constituted itself a community, and by 1843 thirty-five people were supporting themselves in common. During these years Noyes continued his search of scripture and of his own soul, even as he led others to find the will of God. Holding property in common freed the Putney community from one of the snares of the world. By 1846 it had cast off another. Noyes and his wife Harriet, along with George and Mary Cragin, discovered that each was willing to abandon the bonds of exclusive marriage, and soon a small group at Putney agreed to a "community of hearts." Noyes later summarized the developments of the years from 1840 to 1847 as the working out of the principles of the association in theory and practice, "and step by step, the school advanced from community of faith, to community of property, community of households, community of affections." The introduction of male continence (*coitus reservatus*) made birth control general, thus eliminating the fear of unwanted pregnancy and allowing the group to establish new sexual standards.[12]

The residents of Putney who did not share Noyes's theology also rejected his new dispensation in sexual matters. Charged with adultery in October 1847, Noyes fled the state and soon most members of the community followed him to Oneida in upstate New York. Offshoots of the Oneida community would be planted in other areas, including in Brooklyn where their *Circular* was published, but most of the members lived in the Oneida community. The first major publication of the community attacked both property and marriage. All "systems of property-getting in vogue in the world," stated the *First Annual Report*,

are forms of what is vulgarly called the 'grab game,' i.e. the game in which the prizes are not distributed by any rules of wisdom and justice, but are seized by the strongest and craftiest; and the laws of the world simply give rules, more or less civilized, for the conduct of this game.[13]

A long section of the *First Annual Report* was devoted to the "Bible Argument," showing that the end of sexual exclusiveness in love was "required between all believers by the express injunction of Christ and the apostles. . . . 'The new commandment is love one another,' and not by pairs, as in the world, but *en masse*." Love, the argument pointed out, was simply attraction to congenial persons and the tendency for those attracted to become one. The natural result of this was sexual intercourse. Because it interfered with the normal course of attraction, "the law of marriage 'worketh wrath, . . .' " leading to secret adultery, keeping unmatched couples together, and providing too little satisfaction to the sexual appetite.

Prostitution, masturbation, and obscenity in general, are injurious explosions, incident to unnatural separations of the male and female elements. Reform, in order to be effectual, must base itself on the principle of restoring and preserving equilibrium by free intercourse.

In the *Oneida Circular* in 1851, Noyes wrote that the association did not separate husbands and wives, "but we teach them the law of love: 'Thou shalt love . . . thy *neighbor* as thyself; and when they have got that lesson by heart, they *separate themselves* far enough to let in their neighbor."[14]

Noyes recognized that publishing the "Bible Argument" would bring down a storm of abuse on him, but he aligned his theories with other challenges to marriage. These principles, he wrote, ". . . are not more revolutionary and offensive to popular sentiment, than the speculations of Fourier on the same subject," and they simply paralleled ideas that "Robert Dale Owen and Frances Wright propounded some years ago, in the public halls of New York, with great eclat." The Bible Communism of Oneida, however, was not like earlier socialisms. The Oneidans believed that men and women must be regenerated in order to attain higher institutions.[15] The discussion of marriage reached even the unregenerate, however, so that after 1848 those who found marriage an inadequate expression of love or a cause of strife could look to Oneida as a model of sexual relations and a source of challenge to the bourgeois ideal. For several years after the *First Annual Report*, Oneidan publications used the term *free love* to describe their system of complex marriage. The term was adopted by others who did not share Noyes's hope for Christian perfection, but who shared his rejection of the social system founded upon isolated households and of marriages that produced exclusiveness and separation.

Harmonialism and Spiritualism

During the 1830s and 1840s, personal, direct, and special insight vied with individual perfection as the most important American heterodoxy. The revelations of the 1840s ascribed the problems of American society to sickness rather than sin. Like the perfectionists, the prophets of special revelation wanted this world to be transformed by the heavenly, but they spoke of harmony rather than sinlessness as the key to remaking the world. In conflict with middle-class values, the new prophets almost inevitably thundered against middle-class marriage.

Intense and individual experience had always been a hallmark of revival religion, and the process had frequently been accompanied by changed understanding of religious truth and social duties. The claims of personal piety and revelations probably became far more pronounced during the 1840s with the predictions of William Miller that the earth would soon end, leading believers by the thousands out of churches and onto the mountainsides to await the Second Coming. The intensity of Millerism is reflected in the lament of a former adventist:

My advent experience has been the richest and brightest of all my Christian experience. If this had proven a failure, what was the rest of my Christian experience worth? . . . Is there no God, no heaven, no golden home city, no paradise? . . . Is there no reality to our fondest hope and expectation of these things?

The failure of the Millerite charisma may have sent many back to the established churches and led some to reject religion; others, however, continued to seek a form of spirituality that was intensely personal. Theodore and Angelina Weld, for instance, had been interested in Miller's predictions. By 1845 they replaced public worship with family Bible study.[16] The Welds, like many earnest Christians during the 1840s, reshaped their religious understanding in opposition to ritual order and in conformity to personal insight.

In response to the growing antiritualism of the 1830s and 1840s, Protestant church leaders sought more control over the revivalists. Denominational leaders like William Stone attacked the special revelations and inspirations of the Awakening in an attempt to warn converts from the camp meetings back into the churches and back under the tutelage of properly ordained male clergy. For many women this meant the loss of leadership roles and a return to the ritualized worship that revival had either superseded or subverted. Their protest was to abandon the established churches. Whether these women escaped to join the Hicksite Quakers, the Universalists, or the perfectionists, they agreed in their rejection of church organization and stringent norms for behavior and in their preference for intuitive forms of knowledge or experience.[17] Among those seeking a new spiritual wisdom during the 1840s were men and women interested in supernatural or paranormal phenomena. At least in the Northeast and Midwest, groups of investigators had gathered to seek wisdom that transcended known categories. Harmonialism will serve as a general name for the network of groups and individuals that formed around this search for supernatural enlightenment—*harmonial* because of their stress upon harmony among people and between the spiritual and the carnal. In these harmonial groups, an understanding of marriage and society developed that was heavily indebted to middle-class concepts but that also called for far-reaching changes in middle-class society.

"In the America that we consider so sober," wrote German traveler Moritz Busch in the early 1850s, "prevails three times as much belief in the shadow side of nature as we imagine." He listed the spirit-rappers and soothsayers advertised every day in New York City newspapers and the mesmerists, phrenologists, physiognomists, astrologers, and geomancers that practiced their trade throughout the land. During the 1830s and 1840s many people became fascinated with the phenomena of animal magnetism, or mesmerism. William Stone, who condemned extraecclesial religion, reported that mesmeric experiments were conducted among clergymen, businessmen, and state senators. "In nearly every city, town, or hamlet," recalled one early spiritualist, "the itinerant mesmerizer made his rounds, operating upon chance subjects as opportunity offered." By 1843 perhaps as many as thirty mesmerists were lecturing in New England. In Boston, two hundred magnetizers practiced their craft. Near Boston, at Brook Farm, mesmerism and other unusual phenomenon provided recreation for community members. In addition to Fourier's writings, *Die Seherin von Prevorst*—reports of a German seeress—fascinated some of the colonists. Marianne Dwight, the enthusiastic associationist, was told to recommend the book to her friend Ann Parsons, a woman with the ability of reading characters of people by passing her hand over something they had written. Miss Dwight's future husband, John Orvis, also possessed this ability, and her friend Fred Cabot healed minor ailments by putting people into a trance.[18]

When mesmerism came to the United States in 1836 it was a method of curing sickness—a scientific triumph over magic. Mesmerism's capacity to heal appealed to a society in which medicine offered few genuine remedies and such contagious diseases as cholera spread rapidly. Healing appeared again and again as the initial vocation of magnetizers and clairvoyants. During the early nineteenth century, healers often turned their attention to wider social ills, as had William Alcott. It was an easy transition for mesmerists from curing patients to giving advice in other fields. Mesmerism seems to have been assimilated in America to the more prevalent form of entering a trance and became, like revivalism, a means of transcending mundane existence and of attaining an abnormal state of consciousness and thereby gaining new insights.[19] Healers became seers. Because of their growing suspicion of emotional excess, many members of the middle class rejected revivals, but they were attracted to mesmerism. Instead of the press of the camp meeting with its confusion and wild religiosity, mesmerism was administered, like medicine, calmly and scientifically to the individual.

Even as mesmerism became a religious experience, it retained the medical model.

Magnetic enthusiasts rarely confined themselves to one line of investigation. Americans interested in the supernatural could find heavenly truths described in baroque detail in the writings of Emanuel Swedenborg, whom Ralph Waldo Emerson called the "last Father of the Church." Following his first interviews with the spirits in 1745 in Sweden, Swedenborg wrote about trips to heaven and hell and discussions with beings from distant times and superior states. By the early nineteenth century, the Church of the New Jerusalem based its theology on Swedenborg's revelations. Theodore Parker wrote of the attraction of the Swedenborgian church, commenting that "the Swedenborgians have a calm and religious beauty in their lives which is much to be admired." Those who examined Swedenborg's writings found communication with spirits and mystical experiences taken entirely for granted. He pictured the spirit world as a perfected version of life on earth.[20]

Henry James, the Fourierite apologist and father of the novelist, exemplified the pilgrimage from religious doubt to Swedenborgian certainty. During his unruly youth, James never felt oppressed by a sense of sin as a condition of life but only by acts that assaulted the "vital self-respect" of others. He believed that his religious conscience developed along natural rather than theological lines. Orthodox Christianity, with its doctrine of original sin, "revolted instead of conciliating my allegiance," James recalled, "inasmuch as it put me at internecine odds with my own nature, or obliged me to maintain an ascetic instead of a spontaneous relation to it." In spite of his contempt for Protestant orthodoxy, James came face to face with the problem of evil during a stay in England when he was already a married adult. Sitting in his study one evening, he was suddenly overwhelmed with "abject terror" seemingly emanating from "some damned shape squatting invisible to me within the precincts of the room, and raging out from his fetid personality influences fatal to life." This terror persisted, and James controlled his horror only with acts of will. He finally managed to understand the phemonenon when he began studying the writings of Emanuel Swedenborg, who called such experiences "vastation." In these writings James found Swedenborg's "fundamental postulate, which was that a new birth for man, both in the individual and universal realm, is the secret of Divine creation and preponderance." For James, the dark night of the soul came as a ghostly apparition, and salvation —the second birth—came from the visions of the Swedish mystic.[21]

Swedenborg's impressive philosophy appeared to gain support from the advanced thought of the day. "Genuine science," wrote one Swedenborgian editor, "is never in collision with genuine theology." George Bush, professor of Hebrew at New York University, turned from speculating about biblical prophecy in the early 1840s to examining the relationship between mesmerism and Swedenborgianism. Essential to Swedenborg's system, Bush wrote, was the insight that the human being was a spirit clothed in a body, "so constituted as to be even now a denizen of the spiritual world and constantly associated with kindred spirits." Bush believed that the facts of mesmerism supported the revelations of Swedenborg. Where Swedenborg had taught that all minds were constantly in contact with various "societies," mesmerism showed that the mind of the magnetizer could be directly in contact with the mind of his subject. During the trance, the magnetic sphere of magnetizer and subject became intermingled. Objects could be made to appear to the mesmerized subject or disappear from his vision; Swedenborg had said that in the spiritual realms spirits acted on one another by infusing each other with their fantasies. Bush concluded that, taken together, mesmerism and Swedenborgianism had opened "a new chapter in the philosophy of mind and in man's relation to a higher sphere. It would seem that the veil was about being removed which has hitherto shrouded in darkness the deep arcana of the spirit-world."[22]

By the late 1840s many believed that the veil had been stripped away by a popular Swedenborgian prophet, Andrew Jackson Davis. His supporters portrayed him as an "uneducated, unsophisticated child of Nature, entirely free from the creeds, theories, and philosophies of the world." Born to a poor farm family in 1826, Davis was raised in upstate New York and eventually became an apprentice tailor. His experience of Methodist revivals left Davis unconverted but with an enhanced fear of death that persisted until his mother died in 1841. At that time a vision of her convinced Davis that spirits of the dead could contact the living. During 1843 and 1844 he began to participate in experiments with mesmerism, finding that while in trance he could accurately tell sick people how to regain health. Davis soon met George Bush and then the spirit of Emanuel Swedenborg who instructed him in the secrets of the universe. During 1845, in a series of deep trances, Davis dictated his revelations to a group of trusted coadjutors, including the former Universalist ministers Thomas Lake Harris and S. B. Brittan.[23] Davis's practice had shifted from personal to social diagnosis.

Davis's messages from the spirit world, published in 1847 in *The Principles of Nature*, began by deploring the conditions of society that led to isolation and thus to the warring of various systems of thought. "Institutions which have been founded upon the artificial demands of a dominant ignorance," he warned, "cast at this time a mantle over the world which prevents unrestrained and free inquiry." Unable to perceive the designs of the motive power of the universe, mankind remains divided and in conflict. "Here, then, are the creations of man: a God after his own image, a devil after his own likeness, a theology after his own interest, and a system of practice after his own prejudices." It was not individual vices that were at fault, Davis taught, but the social system that caused character to unfold favorably or unfavorably. "Mankind as one human body must have a constitutional cleansing and renovating." His plans for this new social order sounded curiously similar to those of Fourier: "Men should be rewarded in proportion to the *amount of labor* they accomplish, and then they would feel an interest in *industry*, and not merely in its *reward*." In association, the needs and desires of each should be met; otherwise, harmony could not be accomplished.[24]

Andrew Jackson Davis became both the prophet and the philosopher of harmonialism. Harmonialism appealed to middle-class Jacksonians for much the same reasons that transcendentalism did. Faced with the confusion of a new social order, men and women universalized assumptions that were then emerging as the bases of middle-class culture. The human spirit, taught Davis, was the "ultimate—*man* . . . individualized forever" out of the infinite ocean of spirit.[25] Harmony, between heaven and earth as well as among men, became the basic prescription for social ills. Like transcendentalism, harmonialism found a home wherever the culture of New England had taken root. In Ohio it achieved one of its most ambitious forms.

Around May of 1846 John O. Wattles, attorney J. P. Cornell, editor Lorenzo A. Hine, and other respected citizens of Cincinnati met at the Kemble Street Church to discuss "Religious and Social Questions." They agreed "to conduct business on the highest principles of Christian equity, and thus show men how to live the true life and serve God in the midst of the universal Mammon worship." In addition they planned to form a Christian community and published a magazine, the *Herald of Truth*, in which Wattles announced the purpose of the Cincinnati Brotherhood:

The friends of God and Humanity in this vicinity, are labouring to make a commencement of a Social Reform, one that shall not need to be reformed, by effecting a Unity with each other mentally, and with the great influence of the Universal Mind.

Combining study of Swedenborg and mesmerism with their interest in social reform, the circle hoped to isolate the "First Principles" that would guarantee personal and social harmony.

Aided by J. T. Mahan, formerly an employee on an Ohio River steamboat who had demonstrated clairvoyant abilities to detect disease, members of the Cincinnati Brotherhood tried to clear their mental vision. Already in 1847 they professed "to have discovered the laws of spiritual communication, and to be governed in all their movements by information received from the world of Light." Even if human existence was a preparation for life beyond the grave, their reformist convictions dictated that they strive for more than heavenly bliss. "The objects of this association are practical," wrote Cornell, who helped finance Fourierist associations, "and look to the regeneration of society upon principles of natural affinity." Wattles, who had helped found the short-lived Prairie Home Community (a phalanx) in 1843, proclaimed that in the beginning of every new era there were "new arrangements of human duties, destined for the greater development of mental powers; and a more perfect Order, for the ready attainment of higher harmonies."

In 1847 the Cincinnati Brotherhood launched a cooperative associa-

tion using some of the property and buildings of the recently failed
Clermont Phalanx. One of the managers, a Mr. Porter, suggested they
use Mahan's power to guide them in investment. This mysterious
associate had claimed to be a merchant worth $20,000 but turned out
later to be a fraud. Cornell and the others agreed to pay Mahan $4,000
for home furnishings and other expensive inducements. When the
chicanery was discovered, the Brotherhood's directors called Porter
and Mahan to account. In the meantime, however, a flood destroyed
one of the main buildings at their community, and seventeen lives
were lost. Although the Cincinnati Brotherhood tried to continue its
work, the cooperative failed.[26] Even so, the Cincinnati group indicates
the close relation between spiritual crisis and renewal on the one hand
and the reform of society on the other.

The centrality of marriage to middle-class society meant that social
and spiritual progress required a new understanding of marriage. On
the subject of love the harmonialists benefited from the work of Emanuel Swedenborg, whose *Conjugial Love* had become an important source
of inquiry for those who, like Henry James and Andrew Jackson
Davis, questioned the relations of the sexes. Swedenborg's attitude
was that the "love of the sex," the desire for bodily pleasure and
conjunction, was common to all people and would survive death.
"Conjugial" love, however, required internal unions between two individuals. When this was achieved both unity and pleasure would
continue to increase and endure through eternity. Such spiritual unions
almost never happen until after death when the two spirits progressively put off their external natures and so are able to recognize the
one spirit with whom they can share "conjugial" love. When bodies
were joined without union of souls—even in marriage—Swedenborg
called the union adultery or fornication. When body and soul were
united in love, in or out of marriage, that love was truly "conjugial."
The difficulty of finding the true love made it necessary, while in the
flesh, to love others. Swedenborg believed that even fornication was
useful; it satisfied the sexual appetites of the young and preserved the
sparks of "conjugial" love.[27]

Harmonialists were indebted to Swedenborg, but their writings
about marriage also owed a heavy debt to the idealization of marriage
and love that had been developed in the early nineteenth century. The

Univercoelum, edited by S. B. Brittan, promoted Davis's revelations and featured the writings of several contributors. Believing that society was in chaos, the Brittan group in 1848 called for reform based upon the principle of gravitation: "by which we mean simply the tendency of particles and substances, organic and inorganic, *to associate according to the principle of elective affinity.*" In this way the interests of mankind, presently in conflict, would attain harmony. That this principle applied equally to marriage is obvious from an anonymous poem that appeared a month later.

> Love is attraction. So the magnet doth
> Attract the particles of finest steel,
> And so in all affinities of matter,
> In chemical, electrical, and in all
> The nice adhesion of the delicate parts . . .
> . . . One vast law
> Unites their destinies, prescribes their course.
>
> And so with human hearts, when souls akin
> By more than earthly marriage. . . .[28]

Like the middle-class marriage advisers, Davis's followers believed that only love could create a true marriage. The spiritualization of marriage, however, meant that a mistaken choice affected not only an individual's life but his or her afterlife.

Andrew Jackson Davis drew his messages about marriage from his own experience as well as the sources used by his associates on the *Univercoelum*. In 1847 or 1848 Davis received a vision revealing that one of his female followers and financial supporters was not only his spiritual sister but his future wife. Mrs. Dodge was apparently already separated from her husband and was powerfully attracted to the Seer from Poughkeepsie. With the help of the divorce courts, she threw off her "hateful bondage." While awaiting the final dissolution of the first marriage, Davis and Mrs. Dodge gave some of Davis's friends the impression that they were having sexual relations. By the time of the marriage in 1848, Davis had convinced Brittan that nothing scandalous had taken place. It seems that Mrs. Dodge, who died in 1853, had not been destined to become Davis's eternal partner. In 1854 Davis received a letter from Mary F. Love about her unhappy marriage. Sam-

uel and Mary Love met Davis during one of his speaking tours of
upstate New York and discussed their problems with him. Samuel
Love had located someone whom he considered his true partner for
life. This was unpleasant news for Mary Love, but she believed that
her husband might be right. Davis offered his help and brought through
a revelation that, indeed, Samuel Love should follow his affinity and
that Mary Love was destined to be the wife of A. J. Davis. She
obtained an Indiana divorce and married Davis in 1855.[29]

In 1855 the fourth volume of Davis's the *Great Harmonia* appeared
containing his insights about hygiene, physiology, and marriage. Re-
peating the nostrums of the physiologists and sex reformers, he declared, "Consumption or scrofula, dyspepsia, insanity, imbecility and
idiocy rage in all portions of our beautiful globe—the effects of exces-
sive and irregular sensual indulgence!" In general, Davis's remarks
were in line with the writings of marriage idealists. He maintained
that men and women were equal, but each had his or her own sphere.
Marriage was to be entered cautiously due to the prevalence of artificiality in the social world. A man might end up marrying "a laboratory
of prepared chalks; a quintal of whalebone; . . . and a system of *weak
nerves.*" A woman might acquire, in addition to her husband, "a mass
of unpaid tailors' bills; a broken constitution; with a brain, which
considers Business a ridiculous as well as a vulgar way of spending
life."

Davis recast the Swedenborgian concept of "conjugial" love. Monogamy on earth might one day be possible, he believed, but it would
require that each person find the one love. In the meantime, what he
called minor marriages were useful in developing the power and unity
that would aid in the individual's elevation and perfection and in
perpetuating and harmonizing the race. The goal of these minor marriages, however, was the "one true marriage, namely: *the marriage of the
right man with the right woman, forever!*" Davis rejected free love (which
he sometimes called free passionism) but believed that divorce was
useful while humanity remained on the natural plane. Divorce should
be made easier to obtain, and the children of a divorced couple, if not
provided for by the parents, should be adopted by the state.[30]

By the time Davis's book on marriage was published, the spiritualist
movement had displaced harmonialism as the source of supernatural

Andrew Jackson Davis (1826–1910).
Davis claimed that two people who were spiritually united would be married forever. Spiritual unions and earthly marriages, however, might be in conflict. After his first wife died in 1853, Davis married Mary Love who was to be his eternal mate. This turned out to be a mistaken spiritual intuition, for in 1885 Davis divorced Mary Davis to marry again.

FRONTISPIECE, ANDREW JACKSON DAVIS, The Magic Staff [1857].

wisdom. Special revelation came within the reach of virtually everyone in 1848 when the Fox sisters found that they could communicate with the ghost inhabiting their house in Hydesville, New York. Inspired by the example of the Fox sisters, hundreds of Americans soon discovered some ability for communicating with the spirits of the dead. By 1859 New York State supported seventy-one of these mediums, Massachusetts fifty-five, and Ohio twenty-seven. Lecturers were much more numerous, spreading interest and conviction and paving the way for the work of the mediums. John Edmonds, a justice of the New York Supreme Court before he became an ardent spiritualist, estimated in the early 1850s that the movement numbered four million people. This was only a guess since spiritualists never organized very well. Their lack of organization, according to Unitarian minister Theodore Parker, partly explained their popularity. Additionally, they provided evidence for their claims (the raps, table turnings, and, later, materializations) and were open to all religious truths and to possible future discoveries of truth. In spiritualism inspiration was available to all, a condition that suited the assumptions of individualism and equality that pervaded the young republic.[31]

Spiritualists accepted Davis as a kind of superior medium and eagerly attended his lectures, even though his revelations lacked the dramatic effects of table-tipping and materializations. It was more than just the quantity or even the type of phenomena that set spiritualism apart. The most important distinction is that harmonialism had been a thoroughly male business, a network of "brotherhoods." Its most prominent medium was Davis, and its leaders were virtually all men —Bush, James, Brittan, Cornell, Wattles. This contrasted markedly with spiritualism, in which women served as mediums and organizers. An instance of the transition to spiritualism appears in Boston, where the medium who introduced the city to rappings, automatic writing, and other spirit communications was Margaret Cooper, the daughter of mesmeric authority LaRoy Sunderland. Spiritualism not only allowed women the religious prominence they had experienced in revivalism, it also corresponded closely with the view of womanhood prevalent in Jacksonian America. Supposedly more delicate and nervous than men, women obviously had more sensitivity to spiritual exhalations. Confined within her role as queen of the household, the woman who accepted spiritualism could move church into the home. "Spirit circles gathered around dining room tables," comments historian Ann Braude, "an appropriate place for women to preside."[32]

Other differences separated harmonialism from spiritualism. Mesmeric experimenters and Swedenborgian philosophers tended to be financially well off and were either middle class or upper-middle class. Also, the spirit voices that appealed to the harmonialists spoke in foreign accents and recondite English. Both mesmerism and Swedenborgianism were European imports, and the social vision that emerged from Davis's encounter in the spirit world was modeled after Fourier. The complex language of Henry James in his *Harbinger* columns and the careful comparison of mesmerism to Swedenborg's thought by Bush show that harmonialists tended to be elitist in their revelation of truth. One account of the prespiritualist enthusiasm for mesmerism reflected this high-toned attitude.

Intelligent witnesses . . . set themselves to work to discover the source of the marvels they beheld. . . . the inquiry deepened into profound interest, and the phenomena of animal magnetism became familiarly known to the most progressive class of the community.

While many men like Brittan quickly embraced the new spiritual revelations, some harmonialists considered spiritualism vulgar. "Spiritual communications are numerous in proportion as the state of man is *low*," declared a Swedenborgian in 1853. Seances could only contact "abortions among spirits" that had been unable to pass peacefully into the spirit world. The Swedenborgian preference for introspection is apparent from the same writer's advice: "Let men look inward for spiritual communications, and listen to those 'rappings' that are more or less distinct, and more or less emphatic, according to the ruling love or feeling in the mind."[33]

Because of its middle-class respectability, harmonialism profoundly influenced the larger spiritualist movement. Spiritualism's attitude toward occult tradition is one instance of this influence. Spiritualists self-consciously distanced themselves from supernaturalism, presenting their discoveries instead as empirical data. We have already seen this tendency among mesmerists, who tried to duplicate the results they had witnessed or read about. George Bush, in his attempt to give an empirical underpinning to Swedenborgianism, used the mesmeric discoveries.[34] Also, spiritualism continued the stress upon personal harmony. Finally, although in some sense it offered healing, spiritualism continued the harmonial quest for wisdom through trance.

In matters of marriage, the harmonial influence was also important and perhaps decisive. After 1848 spiritualists accepted most of what Davis taught and, in some cases, went much farther than Davis in their belief that spiritual advice should control a decision as to marriage. Davis wrote in 1850 of loves that were "*innate affinities* which draw soul to soul; which cause the human mind to feel attracted to *corresponding* loves or *affinities* which draw soul to soul."[35] What Davis or Brittan had referred to as "elective affinity" became "spiritual affinity" among spiritualists. The idea of spiritual affinities found support from Swedenborg's *Conjugial Love*, though it was a notion the Swedish seer would have rejected.

Much like perfectionists in the 1830s, part of the spiritualist movement embraced "the doctrine of special affinities between man and woman; affinities which imply a spiritual relation of the sexes higher and holier than that of marriage." One spirit told a group in 1850, "Man and wife are not connected? [*sic*] if their spheres are not harmonious. Those whose spheres are harmonious are attracted, and they have an existence together." Another spirit reported in 1851 that "the minds of two discordant spirits must inevitably invite misery, when legalized together. . . . There is no husband and no wife in such covenants. They are null and void of all the essentials of wisdom and happiness." Relationships given institutional sanction and physical consummation were considered irrelevant: "It is erroneous to suppose that because a man is the husband of a woman in this world that he will be so in the Spirit-world."[36]

Since many spiritualists believed that affinities could be discovered in life—with enough careful searching and some help from the spirits of the dead—spiritualist doctrines often appeared to encourage divorce and even promiscuity. "One of the things which a man in the Spiritual circles thinks himself most of all free to do," commented William Dixon, "is to fall in love with his neighbor's wife." A less moderate critic claimed that spiritualism caused "the casting off of the legal wife for whoever inspires a stronger lust." By the early 1850s it was common for spiritualism to be linked with free love, an idea readily encouraged by free lovers but vehemently denied by most spiritualists. "It is true that a few of those who call themselves Spiritualists have professed to give their adhesion to the doctrines of Free Love," admitted a midwestern spiritualist editor, "but it is equally true that there is no known case where practices have failed to conform to the strictest rules of chastity and conjugal fidelity." Spiritualist editors probably protested too much. Affinities offered many unhappy husbands and wives the moral authority to end their marriages.[37]

Although there was a relationship between spiritual wives and spiritual affinities, it would be a mistake to see the spiritualist view of marriage as merely an extension of the perfectionist. Both spiritualism and perfectionism attacked marriage; both sought unions of men and women that were purer and more genuine than those available in society. Perfectionists, however, were much closer to the revivalist roots of Protestant heterodoxy and looked to the regeneration of the individual as the means of purifying marriage. Spiritualists, who began their movement only after the establishment of the Oneida community, maintained the distance from the revival that had been typical of the harmonialists. They elevated the middle-class ideal of love into a force ("affinity") transcending both society and death. Spiritual experience did not transform the sinner but showed how to follow the true life.

In addition to arriving later than perfectionism, spiritualism also attracted a different following. Women preachers, such as Lucina Umphreville who first prophesied a new marriage in the day of grace, had addressed rural women. Spiritual affinities, on the other hand, appealed to urban middle-class women who had already become thoroughly indoctrinated with the new standards of family life. They accepted the views of marriage idealizers like William Alcott who placed marriage at the center of life. Spiritualists extended this marriage into the infinite future, giving it a transcendent dimension and at the same time insisting that not everything with the name of marriage in this life was a true marriage. This vision could empower women whose marriages fell short of the loving ideal pictured by the marriage idealists and who were thus trapped and subordinated in an institution considered holy, permanent, and inviolable by church, state, and public opinion. Spiritualism, like perfectionism, offered sanctions formerly reserved to the churches. If marriages proved to be bad bargains, however, it was not because of personal transgression but because of mistaken understanding of spiritual affinity.[38]

During the 1850s harmonialist ideas about marriage persisted not only in spiritualism but also in middle-class radicalism and free love. Since many radicals and free lovers espoused spiritualism, it is easy to see them as merely extremists within the larger spiritualist movement. Free lovers, however, would accept only those aspects of spiritualism that agreed with their conclusions about marriage. Furthermore, like harmonialism, free love was a movement led primarily by men. Free love appeared in the 1850s in places where Fourierism had been preached and practiced in the 1840s. Many free-love leaders were former Fourierists, but these were always socialists who had accepted the necessity of harmonizing the society of the living with ideal, or spiritual, truths. It was probably within the harmonial brotherhoods that free love was first discussed and accepted, at least as an ideal for the future.

Middle-Class Radicalism

In America, harmonialism and Fourierism developed together. In 1844 Parke Godwin praised Swedenborg and Fourier as "the two commissioned by the Great Leader of the Christian Israel, to spy out the promised land of peace and blessedness." One of the American publishers of Swedenborg's works was also an ardent Fourierist. As we have seen, Henry James worked to spread the messages of both men. At Brook Farm, discussion of Swedenborg proceeded while the colony became a phalanx. The *Harbinger*, published at Brook Farm, took as its motto a quotation from Swedenborg and included articles on the Swedish mystic. The common interest in Fourier and Swedenborg seems to have arisen from the belief that Swedenborg provided a complete spiritual system to complement Fourier's comprehensive material system. This convergence of thought was expressed in a manner typical of the period by the collaboration of their ghosts. When A. J. Davis began receiving messages from the other side, he was contacted by both Swedenborg and Fourier. This is hardly surprising. Observers at Davis's 1846 sessions included both George Bush and Albert Brisbane.[39]

The synthesis of Fourierism and harmonialism was most complete among individuals who could not accept the evangelical Protestant version of salvation. One of the leading spokesmen for Fourier in the 1840s, and for spiritualism in the 1850s, was Warren Chase. Born in New Hampshire in 1813, Chase said later that his mother had made a mistake in bestowing her love; his father had deserted her before his birth. After his mother died five years later, Chase became the ward of various families until he turned twenty-one. His education had already led him in the direction of religious doubts, and his first visit to Boston in 1834, where he saw at firsthand the extremes of wealth and poverty, made him doubt the economic system and the politics that interested his neighbors so much. When his fortunes hit bottom, Chase abandoned his work as a farm laborer to move west. In Michigan he started his own book-selling business and married the sister of the woman with whom he was boarding. The book business failed, so Chase moved on to Wisconsin where he struggled to provide for his wife and three children on the small parcel of land he was able to purchase.

By the early 1840s Chase was already at the center of the fledgling reformism in his frontier community. Known as the town infidel, he studied phrenology and was becoming completely disillusioned with the system of land monopoly. In 1844 he met with others to experiment with mesmerism as described in LaRoy Sunderland's periodical, the *Magnet*. He read Swedenborg and followed the investigations of the Cincinnati Brotherhood. Chase also studied Fourier and took a leading role in founding a Fourierist society in his frontier community. He organized the stock issue for the formation of the Wisconsin Phalanx, or Ceresco, and became its leader. The settlement prospered for six years and realized a handsome profit on its 1,440 acres when the phalanx disbanded in 1850.[40]

Perhaps because of their jealousy of the phalanx's success, the colony's neighbors accused the Fourierists of tampering with marriage. This hardly seems likely. The annual report of 1846 showed that of 180 members only 80 were using the common dining table. The isolated family was predominant. Even so, Chase went out of his way to insist upon the rectitude of sexual relations in Ceresco. "The family circle and secret domestic relations are not intruded on by Association," he wrote in the first annual report. "The social intercourse between the members," he wrote a year later,

has ever been conducted with a high-toned moral feeling, which repudiates the slanderous suspicions of those enemies of the system, who pretend that the constant social intercourse will corrupt the morals of the members; the tendency is directly the reverse.

Eighteen years after the end of the community, Chase was still defending it. "Never had a case of licentiousness, nor a complaint of immoral conduct," Chase wrote of Ceresco. "Lived a strictly moral, honest, upright, and virtuous life, and yet was hated, despised, abused, slandered, lied about, and misrepresented, in all the country round about, —mostly by preachers."[41]

With his fellow members, Chase prospered from Ceresco's liquidation. He purchased the largest building of the community as his home and soon became a member of Wisconsin's territorial and state legislatures, where he supported woman and Negro suffrage. His life's work became clear to him, however, only when he discovered the works of A. J. Davis and learned of the Rochester rappings. He soon gathered a group of friends to conduct spiritual investigations, and by the early 1850s he became a traveling lecturer on spiritualism.

Whether Chase received new revelations concerning marriage is unclear. He attributed his insights to his abstinence from tobacco, pork, and coffee and to his studies of physiology. Chase spoke of recognizing the relations he bore to others and the higher heart-love, or pure affection, that was above sexual love. Scandal involving his relation with a woman friend emerged at this time and continued to reappear for years. Chase claimed that he and the woman met only publicly and with decorum, but others imputed base actions to him. Chase said that the new, purer relations he discovered were not shared by his wife until many years later. Apparently, these were bad years in their relationship. When his wife finally came to understand his views, "they met and lived on that plane of mutual love, mutual confidence, mutual purity, and mutual interest." They also found other couples who shared their attitude.

Chase, like James and Davis, believed that marriage as it existed in society was a disaster but that the institution could be redeemed.

Warren Chase (1813–1891).
Chase viewed marriage as a spiritual union but also believed that other relations between men and women could be intimate, though chaste. Not surprisingly, he was frequently labeled a free lover.

COURTESY OF THE LABADIE COLLECTION, DEPARTMENT OF RARE BOOKS AND SPECIAL COLLECTIONS, UNIVERSITY OF MICHIGAN LIBRARY.

Marriage should be either a civil or a religious contract; parties to the relation should hold property equally and retain the right to dissolve the union. Married couples should also continue to court one another after marriage.

True courtship, in or out of wedlock, would be somewhat different, but should never be so different as to prevent either from absolute control of person, nor should marriage ever give one party the right to dictate to the other, or compel, even by entreaty, any social or sexual relations not mutually desirable.

Like Davis, Chase recast marriage as a love union of equals who continued to seek the kind of intense attraction that they had known before marriage. Spiritual affinity implied for Chase "a spiritual relation of the sexes higher and holier than that of marriage."[42]

The stories of Warren Chase, Andrew Jackson Davis, and Henry James and the history of the Cincinnati Brotherhood suggest the personal sources of the emerging middle-class critique of middle-class society. Young men growing up during the 1820s and 1830s began to doubt the explanations that ordered the lives of their contemporaries. While rejecting evangelical Christianity, or at least doubting the Protestant dogmas of sin and salvation, they also became uneasy over the growing distance between the well-to-do and the poor. During the 1830s and 1840s, they became active, like other young men, in temperance or antislavery, but they also began a spiritual pilgrimage away from Christianity. This included experiments with mesmerism and the study of new ideas from Europe like phrenology, Swedenborgianism, and Fourierism. They formed or supported utopian colonies that attempted to overcome class conflict. When spiritualism opened the possibility of intensely personal and yet rational religious certainty, these men were prepared to become its disciples and prophets. Rather than the superstition of the churches, they put their trust in the ponderous pronouncements of Swedenborg or the insights of mesmerism. Rejecting the commercial system of the bourgeoisie, they believed that men could live without class divisions and trade without greed. And in marriage they rejected relations based upon law or scripture and insisted that love alone could guarantee "true marriage."

Middle-class radicals like James, Chase, and Davis refused to compromise the American faith in individuality and equality. Instead, they universalized these attributes of American society, making them standards for both this world and the next. The ideals of commerce among independent producers and of a society of equals shaped the social vision of the radicals. The free love movement was the epitome of middle-class radicalism, accepting both the worldly and heavenly reorganization first discussed by the harmonialists. If free lovers were more extreme, it was in their belief in individuality and their extension of it into marriage. Religious doubt and the rejection of orthodoxy would be as typical of free lovers as of harmonialists. For both, genuine spirituality meant purer relations between the sexes.

By turning to the early life story of an individual who became a prominent free lover, we can see that free love was simply one phase of middle-class radicalism. Stephen Pearl Andrews received early encouragement to recognize the danger to his immortal soul. The last son of a Baptist minister, Andrews, born in Massachusetts in 1812, began to learn minute distinctions of metaphysical beliefs when still a young child. Already at the age of eleven or twelve, he was hoping that the millennium would remove the necessity of death. His fear of death and hell persistently conflicted with his youthful exuberance, just as dogma had tempered the young Henry James's spontaneity. As an adolescent Andrews began to live a cautious and pious life, trying to conform his actions to a high standard of ethical behavior. Yet, in spite of his terror of eternal damnation, Andrews could never bring himself to publicly embrace Christianity because he dreaded public ridicule.

Andrews's pilgrimage away from Christian orthodoxy was much slower than was Chase's or James's. Stephen Pearl was able to attend Amherst Academy through the generosity of his brother Thomas. A prosperous lawyer in Clinton, Louisiana, Thomas returned to New England in 1830 and arranged for Stephen Pearl to go back south with him. Andrews had already begun to speculate on matters outside the scope of Calvinism. One of his mother's dreams, he recalled, accurately portrayed the great suffering that Thomas was experiencing more than a thousand miles away. In Louisiana, first as a teacher at his sister-in-law's female seminary and then as a clerk in his brother's office, Andrews observed a kind of evangelicalism different from what he had known at home. Baptist revivals in Massachusetts and New Hampshire had been solemn compared to the camp meetings in Louisiana. "Nowhere," he wrote in his autobiography, "are religion, amusement and business more successfully blended." Although the zeal of the gathering proved contagious, his "taste was offended, and I was led seriously to think whether this wild excitement could be religion" and if it benefited the character of the men and women involved.

During his years in Louisiana, Andrews frequently feared for his

life. Sick with fever at least once each fall for the first few years in the
South, he contemplated the sorry state of his soul. Also, Thomas was
involved in political disputes that put him at odds with many of the
local ruffians who called themselves gentlemen. After a vicious attack
on Thomas, Stephen Pearl gave up his teaching responsibilities to stay
with his brother and study law.

Night after night we lay upon our arms, a dozen or twenty of us camped upon
my brothers [sic] premises, with an equal or larger number of half-drunken
rowdies, raging through the town or howling round our quarters like so many
Savages or devils, threatening and endeavoring to provoke us to an open
encounter.

Andrews's autobiography repeatedly dwells on his fear that the southern code of honor and devotion to dueling would lead to his death by
violence.

For all his desire to extinguish the fear of death, Andrews was losing
confidence in religion. During an epidemic of congestive fever in the
late summer of 1832, he nursed many of the dying and found that few
sought the consolations of religion or seemed horrified by death.

I saw nominal Christians and confessedly good men dying along side of
professed infidels and profane heretics, and with no perceptible difference in
their mode of dying, or of feeling in the presence of death. I saw the ardent
philanthropist and the duelist and murderer, undergoing the same fate with
the same philosophical calmness, and giving his detailed instructions to the
notary with respect to his temporal affairs, and each alike unconcerned about
the affairs of his soul.

While his autobiography ends before Andrews brought to a conclusion
his religious speculations, it is obvious that he had come to doubt the
efficacy of religion and was prepared for the claims and proofs of
spiritualism, which he later accepted.[43]

As he moved away from orthodox certainty, Andrews also moved
in the direction of reform. While still a lawyer with his brother's firm,
he made a popular Fourth of July speech in favor of temperance. After
setting up his own practice in New Orleans in 1835, he represented
the Tappan brothers in a commercial suit and even endorsed the cause
of antislavery. It was also in New Orleans that he married Mary Ann
Gordon. The young man, who had so feared the scoffing crowd that

he could not confess his salvation, managed to find his voice after moving to Houston. In 1842 Andrews developed a plan for manumitting all of the slaves of Texas. Although the idea appeared to gain favor in Houston, Andrews's attempt to spread emancipationism to Galveston ended in his being politely, but firmly, ordered out of town by a citizens' committee. He later elaborated his plan to include compensation for the slaveowners. The slaves would be paid for by a loan from the British secured by land in Texas. He left Texas for New York and sailed for England in 1846 with Lewis Tappan, but he found British enthusiasm for his scheme diminishing and finally nonexistent. Texas was about to become part of the United States by joint declaration of Congress.[44]

When Andrews returned from England in 1846, well-established organizations dominated the reform movements. As an advocate of freedom for the slave, Andrews joined with Tappan and others in the antislavery societies. His fervent belief in the necessity of spelling reform, acquired in England, coincided with his vision of America remade along the lines propounded by Brisbane and Godwin. Andrews published a series of articles on spelling reform in the *Harbinger* and formed a publishing company with the associationist missionary Theron Leland.[45] Through the end of the 1840s the fervor of reformers like Andrews could find expression in abolitionism, associationism, feminism, and other groups. Individualist ideals seemingly harmonized with the demands of organization in the struggle to free the slave, empower the female, and develop human perfection. By 1850, however, such harmony as existed was being challenged and recast.

By the 1850s Fourierism was disintegrating due to its own failures and to sharper divisions between the working and middle classes. Growing confidence among the middle class in general contributed to an extensive reevaluation among middle-class reformers. Advocates of antislavery and feminism came to recognize by the late 1840s that moral suasion had failed. Like Stephen Pearl Andrews, who helped form the Liberty Party, many abolitionists turned to electoral politics, while feminists began to seek the vote. At the same time, slavery had come to appear more ominous. The American victory in the Mexican-American War gave slavery room to expand. As Congress tried to compromise the slavery issue out of existence during 1850, many antislavery activists abandoned nonresistance for political force. Angered that the Fugitive Slave Act made them potential slave-catchers, Northerners gave increasing support to antislavery.[46]

Consolidation did not so much unite as exclude. The return of ritual to the American churches tended to deprive women of both experiences and status that they had enjoyed in revival. Similarly, when middle-class reform turned to political solutions, many men and women found their most vital concerns ignored. Some nonresistants in the antislavery movement, for instance, continued to give priority to moral suasion, individuality, and millennial expectations. If the individual and the organization had been in harmony within associationism, these elements quickly separated as the associations failed. Spiritualists, nonresistants, and Fourierists all refused to compromise the most basic elements of their programs, holding to the fundamentals they had learned from the marriage reformers, the revivalists, and the utopian visionaries.

In religious terms these imperatives would have been called individual salvation, personal piety, perfectionism, and millennialism. But Andrews, Chase, and many others no longer accepted the religious structures or cosmologies that gave these terms meaning. Instead, they embraced the visions of Mesmer, Swedenborg, and Fourier and participated in the syncretic work of the harmonial brotherhoods. Excluded from, or hostile to, the reform societies of the 1850s, they began the work of remaking society in accordance with the needs of the individual and of ending the distinction between ideal conceptions of morality and the actual life of the individual. Both Fourierism and harmonialism had confronted the unhappy reality of marriage with an idealized and spiritualized marriage. As true believers from these movements coalesced in the late 1840s, they demanded that marriage either conform to an ideal version or that it be abolished so that purer forms could emerge. The networks that had grown up to spread Fourierism and harmonialism became the conduits for free love in the 1850s.

CHAPTER 4

Modern Times and the Emergence of Free Love

Free love grew out of harmonialist philosophies and Fourierist socialism. The first proponents of free love, however, preached from neither
Swedenborg's nor Fourier's texts. Instead, "individual sovereignty"
became free love's guiding precept. Even though its inventor refused
to apply individual sovereignty to marriage, by the 1850s marriage was
so important a topic—and criticism of it came from so many sources
—that a philosophy urging individuals to abandon all enslaving connections necessarily implied a new attitude toward marriage. Free love
first appeared in the community of Modern Times, where pioneers
had gathered to test individual sovereignty in a practical setting. By
examining Modern Times and its major ideologues, we can study the
culture of free love as it was being formed and understand what free
love meant to those who first embraced it.

The seance took place on December 6, 1850, at 233 East Broadway.
Acting as the medium of spirit communication was Edward Fowler,
brother of phrenologists and publishers Orson and Lorenzo Fowler.
Through Edward's voice came the words of J. P. Cornell, who had
recently died. Edward's sister, Charlotte Fowler Wells, kept a record
of the interview. In attendance were Stephen Pearl Andrews and
Josiah Warren. Andrews had an agreement with the Fowlers to have

them publish a series of works by authors whom Andrews considered especially worthy of note. At an earlier session Andrews had made arrangements with the ghost of Cornell to bring his friend. Twenty-five years before Josiah Warren had been the band leader at New Harmony. He had known Cornell during the 1840s, probably in Cincinnati where they both lived for many years. The two men had some differing opinions that death failed to reconcile:

Mr. Warren. Does Mr. Cornell understand my views more clearly now, than when I stated them to him while in the body?
Mr. Cornell. Yes.
W. Does he think them correct?
C. There are many good things; but they are not formed on the right principle.
W. What is lacking?
C. You must understand that there is a spiritual element upon which society must be formed. You have not that.

C. . . . The cost principle which you advocate is a good one, but a link is required to form harmony.
W. I do not expect that.[1]

Warren's reluctance to admit of any missing links rested on the careful testing and refining that his ideas had undergone since his residence at New Harmony. Warren believed that the garrulous residents of New Harmony had tested every possible form of organization, either in the many constitutions written and then discarded or in the various communities that had splintered from the major settlement. The obvious failure of the Owenite experiments weighed heavily upon the band leader who viewed Owen as the individual who had given his life value. Warren had been at the point of abandoning the ideals of reform "when a new train of thought seemed to throw a sudden flash of light upon our past errors, and to show as plainly the path to be pursued." The great error of Owen, Warren perceived, was making all property common and all individuals subject to the will of majorities.[2]

As early as 1833 Warren stated what would become the basic principles of his future system. The happiness of society could be insured by giving each person sovereignty over his or her own person and property, an equal share of natural wealth, and an equivalent whenever property was exchanged. Warren's beliefs slowly became more clearly and systematically articulated. In a journal he kept during 1840, Warren listed under *"New Social Arrangements, Intended to gradually restore the Natural Liberty of Mankind—To render to Labor its just reward . . ."* at least thirteen essential changes in society. The list shrank in later, published works and can be summarized in the two leading principles for which Warren was known: the cost principle and sovereignty of the individual.[3]

According to Warren, society required some formula for establishing both prices and wages rather than leaving these to the vagaries of the market. "The most successful speculator," he wrote, "is he, who can create the most want in a community, and extort the most from it. This is civilized cannibalism." "Cost the limit of price," or the cost principle, was the system Warren devised for reconciling producer and seller. Since labor created wealth, only labor costs should be added to the price of a product. If this were done, each producer would be equitably paid and become the partner of all others.

Costs being made the limit of price, every one becomes *interested* to reduce costs,—*to lighten each other's burdens!* Then, every man's hand acts *with* instead of 'against every man,' and HUMAN INTERESTS ARE HARMONIZED[4]

The cost principle worked in concord with sovereignty of the individual. Reacting against the excesses of New Harmony's democracy, which allowed the lazy to live on the labor of others, Warren intended to enforce individual responsibility by making everyone sovereign over his or her person, time, and property. Nothing hindered an individual from working with others on projects of common concern, but nothing coerced anyone to do so. Warren thus retained the equality preached by Owen while discarding the community of property favored by the factory owner.

Unlike his Fourierist contemporaries, Warren tested the practical applications of his ideas before publicly recommending that society be reorganized by what he called the equity movement. In his Time Stores in Cincinnati and later at New Harmony, Warren priced every item at cost plus 5 percent for rent on property. The only value added above that was the price of Warren's time in serving the customers. He kept a clock in his store and timed each transaction, adding about five cents for each minute. Customers quickly realized the value of not wasting the shopkeeper's time, and Warren's success forced down the prices in competing stores. He also experimented with the cost principle and sovereignty of the individual in education. During 1831 he reorganized a private school by requiring that the labor of the students be exchanged for the instruction they received. The labor of women and children was purchased at the same rate as for men. In 1840, while living again at New Harmony, Warren began a seminary upon his principles. Although he had only two students, and one of those was his son George, he instructed the two boys in the cost principle and sovereignty of the individual and followed their progress in both learning and living by these ideas.[5]

The ultimate test of the principles began in the late 1830s when Warren first attempted to establish functioning communities. Malaria ended his first community, Equity, in Tuscarawas County, Ohio, after only two years. Ten years later Warren made a second effort to launch his equity movement. After the failure of the Clermont Phalanx near Cincinnati in 1846, Warren helped some of the members reorganize. While the central land and buildings were used for the cooperative sponsored by the Cincinnati Brotherhood, Warren worked out an agreement with the owner of the easternmost acreage to divide these into quarter-acre parcels and to fix the price of the lots for three years. Families took up the parcels and repaid the seller with their labor. Within a few months, six families had houses and lots all paid for. One colonist, who had lost everything with the failure of the Clermont Phalanx, borrowed twenty-six dollars to begin again. In one year he paid back the loan, had a house, and thirty dollars over. The residents renamed their community Utopia. Even though the cost of land in the surrounding area rose too fast for them to expand their agricultural base, some members of Utopia still remained in 1872.[6]

Soon after helping to reorganize Utopia, Warren left for Boston where he met Stephen Pearl Andrews. The two men formed what would be a fruitful partnership for both. Sovereignty of the individual and the cost principle remained central to Andrews's thinking throughout his long career as a reformer. It was probably Andrews who convinced the free-thinker Warren to investigate spiritualist phenomena. About 1849 Andrews also convinced Warren to move to New York City, where both the short and single-minded Warren and the tall polymath Andrews taught the equity gospel. Andrews was familiar with the city's reformist social gatherings and organizations, which by 1850 were quite willing to consider Warren's system. While the Fourierist agitation had convinced thousands of the possibility and necessity of reform, the associational failures disenchanted many with the Fourierist joint-stock approach to community. Warren's lecture notes show that he would ask his audiences how many of those present thought that a change in society was necessary. Presumably many would agree with this proposition. He then went on to explain that while needs and sympathies drew people together, individuals still required both freedom and room for difference without antagonism.[7]

Among the Fourierists who made the transition to sovereignty of the individual was Theron Leland, one of the earliest associationists and a lecturer throughout upstate New York. "Socialism as announced by Fourier was my first love," he wrote many years later. During the 1840s Leland worked to build the movement both as a missionary and as a colonist, visiting every phalanx in New York and acting as a director at two of them. As the associations failed, Leland found such external excuses for their downfall as fire, disease, or bad debt. After the movement completely disintegrated, he admitted that the failure of the phalanxes had been inherent in their organization. In 1852 Andrews, with whom Leland had been working for seven years in the cause of spelling reform, introduced Leland to a new philosophy. "It seemed to me a total reversal and upsetting of all I had previously thought and taught. I scouted it as the same old 'perfect-the-individual' argument which I had so many times knocked down and riddled in my lectures." In spite of his initial misgivings, Leland soon accepted much of Warren's teaching but combined individual sovereignty with his many experiences of community life. In 1876, for instance, he wrote that the Fourier associations had failed because they had not instituted community of property and because they lacked competent leaders. Both of these views would have been anathema to Warren. Other Fourierists would also accept Warren's principles only to form their own systems.[8]

By 1850 Warren and Andrews felt that it was time to carry their movement beyond recruitment. When he sought the advice of Cornell's spirit, Warren was interested both in gaining wider recognition

Stephen Pearl Andrews (1812–1886).
After he met Josiah Warren in the late 1840s and converted to individual sovereignty, Andrews never doubted that marriage was badly flawed. His personal influence contributed as much to free love as his public statements and theorizing.

for the equity movement and in forming a new community. As with their discussion of the cost principle, Cornell and Warren could not quite agree about these matters. Cornell encouraged Warren and Andrews to form private circles to spread the principles. "Does Mr. Cornell think public lectures the best mode of introducing my views?" asked Warren. "No! Form a private circle." Cornell either did not know, or did not approve, of Andrews's lectures on "Social Science" that winter at the Mechanics Institute. Warren asked about the progress at Utopia. Cornell said that it was doing well enough but that it lacked the spiritual principle. Disagreements between Warren and his departed friend were most pronounced over the development of a new community.

C. Why do you not commence operations?
W. We have commenced.
C. More fully?
W. We always work up to our means. Every dollar is employed.
C. Dollars are not all that is required.
W. No, but we have got every thing *but* the dollars.
C. Not everything.
W. What else is wanting? We have all the disposition, and we wait for the means.

Cornell believed that Warren was mistaken in trying to interest the public rather than individuals only. He also told Warren that his views and experiments would be more successful in another part of the country. "They will succeed best where it is newly settled, where society is first forming." Cornell warned Warren that he would still face opposition. "I think my trials are passed," said Warren. "Not if you do your duty," rejoined Cornell.[9]

The give and take of the spirit interview was typical of Warren's single mindedness and his practicality. Like many reformers, Warren listened to the spirits for advice and encouragement about his projects. He accepted the advice that commended itself to his judgment, but his own plans for a new community were settled. Already searching for a suitable site, Warren and Andrews inspected a large tract in the pine barrens forty miles east of New York City only a few weeks after Cornell told them to go where society was first forming. They had the land surveyed, laying out seven streets running east and west and alleys running north and south. They called their new "city" Modern Times. One-acre town lots were priced at twenty dollars each, a maximum of three per purchaser. Acreage for farming was available outside the town at the same rate. Andrews hoped to interest enough workingmen to make the village industrially self-sufficient. Warren later remembered the beginning of settlement as being fully in accord with individual sovereignty.

One man went to the ground alone and built a shanty ten or twelve feet square where there was not so much as a cow-path in sight. He was joined in a few days by two others, and they built the first house. . . . More pioneers arrived, and soon the houses went up, apparently without means.[10]

Josiah Warren envisioned Modern Times not as a beachhead in the assault on marriage but as an economic experiment. Like Owenism, Warrenism sought to unburden society from the inessential or harmful accretions of superstition, authority, and custom. Once reduced to its fundamentals, society would then function smoothly. As a resident of Utopia had said of Warren's principles, "the subject once stated and understood, there is nothing left to talk about; all is action after that." Josiah Warren believed that society should insure equity to all, a vision attractive to an aspiring middle class that believed economic and social status should be rationally awarded. Warren himself was the quintessential Yankee bourgeois—an inventor of lamps and printing processes, diligent, thrifty, and successful at most of the projects he turned his hand to.[11] His conviction of sovereignty of the individual reduced the middle-class ideal of independence to its economic nucleus and then universalized it. For Warren, the basic reform was to build a functioning equitable economy on a small scale.

As an economic trial, Modern Times was a modest success. Most of the town lots had been cleared by 1853, and Warren had already built his brick "college" where he taught trades without apprenticeships and conducted his time store. Labor notes became the circulating medium at Modern Times, so that each individual could issue his or her own currency. For instance, the time store sold nails, molasses, and cloth for notes promising so many hours of carpentry or blacksmithing. Although the community was always short of hard cash, the labor notes and cost principle reduced the amount of cash required for many

Josiah Warren (1798–1874).
Warren's ideas became articles of faith for free lovers, who believed that marriage should be subjected to the same kind of "disintegration" that Warren recommended for other social institutions. Warren never entirely agreed with this, although he admitted the need for some changes in marriage.

projects. At first the location lacked a water supply, and the sandy soil needed clearing and fertilizing to make it suitable for farming, but by 1854 most of the thirty-seven families had truck gardens and a fruit-tree nursery was beginning. Villagers planted cherry and apple trees along the streets as windbreaks and to provide food for travelers. One man opened a dining saloon, labeling each can and utensil with the name of the person who used it and fixing prices according to the cost of the item and labor so that everyone paid less. During the panic of 1857 the village managed to survive with relatively little hardship because of its separation from the larger economy.[12]

Along with the cost principle, the doctrine of individual sovereignty organized life at Modern Times. This would have made the village remarkable at any time once news of its existence spread widely. The country abounded in cranks who irritated their neighbors at home; when they heard of a community where "nothing was in such disrepute as sameness; nothing more applauded than variety, no fault more venial then eccentricity," many found its attraction irresistible. Warren believed that an article about Modern Times in the *Tribune* precipitated

. . . a rush of people, ignorant of the principles upon which the enterprize [sic] was projected: among these were some that were full of 'crotchets!'—each one seeming to think that the salvation of the world depended on his displaying his particular hobby.

These included a blind nudist, a man with three wives, and a woman who believed that her diet should consist of nothing but beans. Visitors from the city were either charmed or disgusted to see the women of Modern Times wearing Turkish trousers, short skirts with plain white stockings, or the costumes of stage peasants.[13]

More fundamental to life at Modern Times than the strange *couture* of its residents were the ideas expressed in the village's social gatherings and practiced in its cottages. Henry Edger, an early settler, wrote that "small as our numbers are, almost every Individual of us has his own private and particular social theory." Edger, for instance, was a Comtian Positivist who struggled to support his family on a small remittance and with the nursery he was patiently nurturing. At the same time, he worked to make converts to Comte's New Catholic

Church by establishing a reading room and study sessions to interest others in Positivism. He probably had little success at converting Dr. Newbery, an English dentist who claimed to have been visited by Christ and commanded to be perfect. Newbery developed a system of personal and social reforms intended to make perfection available to all.[14]

The wealth of idiosyncrasy at Modern Times provided the environment for the emergence of a new attitude toward sexual relations. In addition to Modern Times's tolerance for strange and dangerous ideas, it possessed other attributes that made it a congenial birthplace for free love. The community was near New York City, where the major radical groups of the day existed, and sovereignty of the individual attracted radicals who were suspicious of all institutions. Finally, criticism of marriage had reached a critical juncture just as the village came into being.

Individual sovereignty, which repudiated the authority of both state and church, strongly implied that all social institutions were null and void. Matters of taste, right and wrong, sanity and insanity were the business of the individual, according to Josiah Warren, provided the individual made decisions at his or her own cost. "It is in combination or close connection only, that compromise and conformity are required. Peace, harmony, ease, security, happiness, will be found only in *Individuality*."[15] Such premises for a man rooted in an older and more utilitarian attitude toward marriage would have resulted, as they did for Warren, in confining the direction of his reforms toward economic practices. At the end of the 1840s, however, the institution of marriage was a topic everyone, it seemed, was discussing and that many people had some doubts about. The view of marriage that had been developed in the harmonial brotherhoods and among spiritualists could be easily adapted to individual sovereignty. If an individual were to enter no combinations without explicitly limiting the extent of his or her obligations then marriage could include no legal or religious restrictions, nor could it be expected to be perpetual. Individual sovereignty implied that marriage, as it existed in society, was an irrational contract that limited the freedom of the male partner and made the female a virtual slave.

Stephen Pearl Andrews had already revealed the hostility of sover-

eignty of the individual to middle-class society and marriage in his
lectures during the winter of 1850 to 1851 at the Mechanics Institute
in New York City.

Protestantism, Democracy, and Socialism are identical in the assertion of the
Supremacy of the Individual,—a dogma essentially contumacious, revolutionary, and antagonistic to the basis [sic] principles of all the older institutions of
society.

He told his audience that this included the end, "under favorable
circumstances," of all legal interference in the relations of the sexes.
The tendency of individual sovereignty, Andrews assured his audience, was "not the disruption of relationships, but the creation of
distinct independent personalities between whom relations can exist."[16] Purging human intercourse of falsehood required that each
should meet all others on a level of equality and independence.

The appearance of free love at Modern Times in 1852 shows the
close relationship between the development of the theory of free love
and its practice. Early in 1852 the first free-love polemic against marriage appeared and quickly made free love an issue among advanced
thinkers. *Love vs. Marriage* was the work of an enthusiastic Fourierist,
Marx Edgeworth Lazarus. One of his friends described him as being
of medium height, slender and dark, "with features slightly marked
with the most refined and cultivated characteristics of the Hebrew
race, to which he belongs." Lazarus was an eccentric who might offer
a gift of a hundred dollars but forget to repay a small loan. Without
encouragement he would launch into a speech on subjects more ob-
scure and abstract than his unprepared listeners could follow. Lazarus's aunt considered him quite mad.[17]

Living in New York City during the 1840s, Lazarus became acquainted with Albert Brisbane and other leaders in the Fourier movement. His series of twelve articles for the *Harbinger*, with the general
title of "Society, An Aspiration," explained Fourier's vision of the
future, including the reorganization of relations between the sexes.
Among his other forty articles for the *Harbinger* were several under the
general title "Cannibalism," in which Lazarus argued for a vegetarian
diet. With the end of the *Harbinger* in 1849, Lazarus decided to take
his ideas before the public on his own. He hired the firm of Fowlers

and Wells to publish his first book, *The Trinity*.[18] *The Trinity* probably created no excitement since Lazarus's writing was little clearer than his conversation, and the book contained nothing more noxious to public opinion than had Albert Brisbane's articles in the *Tribune*.

Love vs. Marriage, published in 1852, also suffered from frequent Fourierisms, difficult passages, and extended portions in which the author merely translated writers such as St. Pierre and Goethe. In the midst of all the heavy and self-defeating prose, however, Lazarus managed to hammer home his major themes. For instance, he wrote that once a man and woman's conversation turns sentimental

> . . . this instantly awakens a woman's mind to that peculiar institution called marriage, and the chances of a one-and-one *arrangement for life* in the isolated household. Sentimental conversation and any show of affectionate interest, must either mean this, or mean a trifling flirtation, or mean seduction! . . . At once a fair girl is metamorphosed into a garrisoned citadel, armed for defense, or revolving terms of capitulation.

The isolated household had been a pivotal evil in the Fourierist system. Here Lazarus united it with marriage as slavery—"that peculiar institution." The existence of marriage, Lazarus argued, ruins any contact between men and women. Even boys and girls learn to examine the conduct of one another in accordance with the standard of marriage, making friendship impossible.[19]

The one relationship allowed between men and women is both incomplete and unfulfilling. "Natures the most gracious and spontaneous, in the limited freedom of relations they have enjoyed before marriage, become sour as verjuice, and thorny termagents, by the harassing routine of domestic trifles." The woman, Lazarus stressed again and again, loses more than the man. A girl before marriage may be admired by all, "but let the queen, the belle, the goddess marry . . . and her power and glory have departed." Once he possesses her, the husband feels less passion for the wife: "Men talk to everyone except their wives." Cut off from other contacts by marriage, however, both husband and wife will claim more exclusive possession of each other. What happens when a woman is deprived of affectionate attention and enters a life of monotony? "The same person, most pleasing and brilliant in one sphere or set of relations, is perfectly stupid and unhappy in another." Lazarus concluded that marriage was a "social vampire."[20]

Dr. Lazarus's prescription for the marriage ailment was, on the one hand, quite simple. He wanted society completely remade along the lines set down by Fourier. With his Fourierist hopes, however, Lazarus included a number of changes that might have depended upon the phalanx but were treated independently of it. Women should be able to make a living and children given occupations from an early age in which they can earn as much as they consume. One of the results of ending legal interference in matters of love would be to encourage women to become socially independent and equal. "Let woman make herself pecuniarily independent of man, and there will no longer be need of law contracts in regard to property." Lazarus believed that husband and wife would contribute equally to the support of a child if the man supplied more of the money and the woman more of time and trouble.[21]

Although the only practical reform that Lazarus suggested was more liberal divorce statutes, he was far from innocent of encouraging individuals to throw off their bondage. As proof of what he said about love relations, Lazarus appealed to "sincere experience; to the numerous love relations my readers have actually sustained" and to those they might have sustained. By personalizing his message, Lazarus made personal response more likely. He also praised those with courage to set aside convention.

I feel that in the absence of any *social* standard of truth, he or she is the truest benefactor to society, and the noblest person, who fearlessly and spontaneously exhibits his or her type of passional character, and creates from inward forces those relations which belong to it, leaving the fashions in morality, as in dress, to scold, and whine, and cringe, and finally follow in the wake of the victorious innovator.[22]

Calling upon individuals to take their passional fates into their own hands would hardly have made much difference if no place existed where they could do so without being opposed by all the forces of culture and society. By 1852 at least one such place existed. Lazarus gave a clue to those who might be seeking like-minded radicals, when he referred to "the principle of Self-Sovereignty or Individual Liberty" as a growing movement. In *Passional Hygiene*, also published in 1852,

Lazarus took specific note of the work of Josiah Warren.[23] By the time this second work was issued, however, the connection between Lazarus's theory and Modern Times was well known.

Henry James reviewed *Love vs. Marriage* in the *Tribune*. James approved of some of the book's barbs against marriage but insisted that the family, not the individual, was the nucleus of society. In line with his arguments in the *Harbinger* and his Swedenborgian beliefs, James wrote that in the present society true love could rarely be discovered. Consequently, he advocated less restrictive divorce laws to make affection the basis for marriage and thereby purify and elevate marriage.[24] James's moderate view received immoderate responses, first from the editor of the New York *Observer* and then from Horace Greeley, who stated that the bonds of matrimony were divinely instituted and so indissoluble. Greeley opened the columns of the *Tribune* to debate the question.

The debate took an entirely new direction when Stephen Pearl Andrews joined it. He damned James for allowing any interference on the part of the state in the relations of two people. According to Andrews, James was too ethereal and effete and Greeley too stupid to be capable of the work of reform. Neither man was thorough enough.

The fatal blunder is the assumption, as a starting-point, that there is something now existing which must not, in any event, be changed. To keep good this assumption, *nothing* must be changed, for when change begins it will not respect your bounds and limits.

For Andrews the debate turned on whether or not a person supported marriage. Even though he claimed to have "no special doctrine on the subject of Marriage," he had a number of pointed opinions. "I *charge* adultery upon nine-tenths of the married couples in this city, committed not out of, but within, the limits of their marriage bonds." Andrews defined sexual purity as a relationship that contributed to the fullest development of both parties. From this standpoint, marriage fell far short of fulfilling its goal, especially for women. "Our whole existing marital system is the house of bondage and the slaughter-house of the female sex."[25]

Andrews supported Lazarus's claim that marriage created an artificial relationship between husband and wife that bore most heavily

Henry James, Sr. (1811–1882).
James never doubted the essential value of marriage. When he suggested loosening divorce laws so that bad unions could be ended, both Horace Greeley and Stephen Pearl Andrews attacked James in print—Greeley feared that divorce would destroy marriage, Andrews that it wouldn't.

upon the wife. Within marriage the wife was isolated and often subjected by her husband to immoderate sexual demands that were phys-
ically harmful. Since adult men and women could become intimate
only by marrying, the institution cast its grim shadow over all relations
between the sexes. Both Lazarus and Andrews believed that the abolition of marriage had to be set within the context of a reform of the
entire society. "I regard Marriage," Andrews wrote, "as being neither
better nor worse than all other of the arbitrary and artificial institutions
of society." But where Lazarus looked to Fourier to explain society,
Andrews looked to Josiah Warren, "the Euclid of Social Science."
Much of Andrews's debate with James and Greeley, as well as the
tract he published of the debate in 1853, extolled Josiah Warren's
system—"principles which render the righteous organization of society as simple a matter of Science as any other."[26]

The *Tribune* debate publicly joined sovereignty of the individual to
a revolution in domestic relations. At least as early as 1852 colonists
began arriving at Modern Times who intended to free themselves of
the shackles of marriage and assume their own individual sovereignty.
Editor George Stearns, who moved to Modern Times in May 1852,
removed himself and his family by August. The reason, he revealed,
was that there was a conspiracy in the village to end marriage and
replace it "with an open and respectful sanction of promiscuous cohabitation." "*Wife* with them is synonymous with *slave*, and *monogamy* is
denounced as a vicious *monopoly of affection*." Modern Times's reputation as the workshop of individual sovereignty made it an obvious
haven for antimarriage radicals.[27]

From the very first, free love was both a theory and a practical
response to circumstances. Throughout the 1850s free love would
serve as a sanction for informal divorce. For instance, one couple,
arrived at Modern Times from the Hopedale community. The man
had been married to someone else when they met, and their growing
affection brought community reprimands. When they were finally
taken before the elders, they defended their actions on the basis of free
love and later left together for Modern Times. In addition to those
practicing informal divorce, there were settlers like Mary Chilton. She
had been married to a wealthy southerner who turned out to be a
tyrant. When she finally divorced him, the legal settlement gave her

children to the father. "Her own experiences," noted one of her visitors, "led her to sum up the chief evils of society in the one word, *marriage*."[28]

Another type of colonist at Modern Times had been involved in Fourierism or harmonialism, and by the early 1850s was studying marriage and concluding that major changes were necessary in the institution. With the confluence of Lazarus's and Andrews's writings and the availability of Modern Times, these advanced thinkers adopted free love out of conviction and moved to Modern Times to help create the social forms necessary for freer individuals. Theron Leland lived at Modern Times in the early 1850s. Probably by that time his thinking about marriage had moved in the direction taken by other Fourierists, though he expressed his views only years later when he criticized a writer who had rejected human breeding as a violation of established moral laws. Leland wanted to know what the writer meant, "because if he means no violation of the present marriage laws, which seem to be rather established, and which permit the practical ownership of the woman by the man, the proposition looks to me like a stultification in terms." Marriage had improved humankind "all the way down from the first chimpanzee to the last wife-killer that was ever hung." In another letter he spoke of sex as a topic that "is abroad in the land."

We have had enough of this implication that the great department of sex running throughout the whole universe of vital being is a mistake which we must hide, cover up, apologize for, and get along with the best way we can.

Leland, like others suspicious of the institution of marriage, came to terms with his own marriage. Theron Leland and Mary Chilton became husband and wife.[29]

For communitarians like Leland, commitment to community life led to a deep concern about social problems. James H. Cook had been interested in Fourierism in the 1840s and visited both the association at West Bloomfield, New York, and Brook Farm. Back in New York City, working for the firm of Fowler and Wells in 1849, Cook first met Stephen Pearl Andrews. One glance at Andrews's head convinced Cook to become a disciple and begin studying Warren's writings. In 1852, after the failure of a cooperative farm and school sponsored by John O. Wattles in Indiana, Cook moved to Modern Times for six months. "There were some noble men and women there," he recalled, "who suffered hardships and poverty for principle. A few of us had a cost boarding-house, and we were largely pervaded by and advocated the Community spirit."

Perhaps Cook's understanding of marriage was a distillation of the study he had begun in the 1830s by reading Noyes and others who wanted to apply Christianity to practical life. Even though he worked for the Fowlers, Cook later diverged sharply from the marriage ideal commended by them and other partners in the firm. The superior part of the brain, according to Cook was "divergent, diffusive, distributive, attractive, constructive, *free*." In fact, the higher brain was a "law unto itself." People with well-developed frontal lobes feel compressed with the degree of freedom allowed in society. Cook did not say so, but such individuals would undoubtedly have felt more at ease at Modern Times. He concluded that those with highly developed brains were naturally free lovers. "Free-love," Cook wrote, "when not perverted, is the highest, purest, holiest expression that ever was made."[30] While Cook's thoughts on free love took their form only after other communal experiences, he undoubtedly participated in the marriage discussions that took place during his stay at Modern Times. Soon after Cook arrived, these talks turned into bitter disputes that briefly divided the village.

At the center of Modern Times's free love controversy in 1853 and 1854 were Thomas and Mary Nichols. Mary Gove had been the first woman to lecture on physiology and health. Following her separation from her husband in the early 1840s, Mary Gove moved to New York City where she practiced water-cure and became acquainted with Albert Brisbane and Marx Lazarus. In 1848 she married Thomas Nichols, an editor and writer. Thomas returned to college to earn his medical degree so that he could aid his new wife's medical practice. In 1852 the couple moved their American Hydropathic Institute to Port Chester, where they planned to train young women in the proper care of their bodies and in the development of their spiritual capacities. Thomas continued to write, though now his topics were health and medicine and reflected the more advanced theories of marriage that New York reformers discussed in their parlors. In 1849, he wrote in *Woman in All Ages and Nations* that new forms of society would be necessary to bring about more harmonious relationships. When women became financially independent and in other ways equal to men, "the only tie will be one of mutual love—the condition of the happiest unions on earth." Thomas and Mary Nichols believed that the most basic emancipation for women was for them to regain their health through proper diet and exercise. Women also required more leisure, opportunities for exercising intelligence, and work that would give them equality with men.[31]

In 1853, with the publication of *Esoteric Anthropology*, Thomas Nichols established himself as an advocate of free love. Both of the Nicholses accepted the physiological theories of Sylvester Graham and emphasized the danger of sexual excess within marriage. Thomas set out in detail the life regimen required for health, including moderation in eating, adequate sleep, daily bathing and exercise, and limits upon sexual indulgence. For the Nicholses, this became a means of freeing women from the sexual demands of men.

It is for her nature to decide both as to whom she will admit to her embraces, and when; and there is no despotism on earth like that which compels a woman to the embraces of a man she does not love; or to receive the embraces of a man she does love when her nature does not require them. . . . If a woman has any right in the world, it is the right to herself; and . . . she has a right to decide . . . who shall be the father of her children. She has an equal right to decide whether she will have children, and to choose the time for having them.

True marriage, for the Nicholses, was the "union of two persons in mutual love," and adultery was any gratification of sensuality without love. Accordingly, "a true marriage may be what the laws call adultery, while the real adultery is an unloving marriage."[32]

By 1853 the American Hydropathic Institute had six teachers and twenty-one students. One class had already graduated and the school seemed successful. With the publication of *Esoteric Anthropology*, however, it was impossible to separate free love from the American Hydropathic Institute. By summer, one young woman had made this connection and shared it with five other students, all of whom promptly left the school. A resident of Port Chester wrote to the *Tribune* that young women were fleeing from the school because they had been indoctrinated with sovereignty of the individual as it applied to sex and that this was "given a personal direction and application to the parties addressed." "This is the philosophy of the brothel," concluded the writer, "and no other institution can grow out of it." Thomas Nichols quickly replied that the few women who had left the American Hydropathic Institute had been deluded by a single upset woman who, in turn, conspired with the manager of a rival water-cure establishment. He further said that no one could accuse him of immoral conduct and that he would sue anyone who did. Finally, he wrote, the American Hydropathic Institute was leaving Port Chester not because the students had abandoned it but because it was moving to a better location —Modern Times.[33]

The Nicholses had probably known Stephen Pearl Andrews since the late 1840s when all three lived in New York and associated with the same reform circles. Andrews's book *Love, Marriage, and Divorce* was used at the Port Chester school as a textbook, and he had been the commencement speaker for the first graduating class. Andrews probably introduced Thomas and Mary Nichols to sovereignty of the individual. Thomas Nichols's book on *Women* was reissued with an introduction by Stephen Pearl Andrews, and the Nicholses adopted the language of sovereignty of the individual in the publications they issued after 1852. Very likely the idea of moving the water-cure establishment to Modern Times had been discussed by the Nicholses and by Andrews for several months. With the outbreak of trouble at Port Chester, the attraction of the new location must have been great. In October 1853 the Nicholses purchased a lot in Modern Times where they intended to build their school of life.[34]

In October 1853 the *Nichols Journal* announced the plans for a new institute to be named Desarollo. The large building projected for the school, as well as the life at the new institute—with its work groups, parades, and festivals—sounded distinctly phalansterian. For example, "Some of the work, in farm, garden, and printing office will go on without cessation, when requisite, but it will be done by relays of volunteers, working in shorting sessions and attractive groups." In November Mary Nichols wrote more about the school, pointing out that many women would leave unhappy marriages if they had the means of supporting themselves and their children. Desarollo would not only teach skills but become "a home where men and women, and children shall learn what constitutes a true life and true holiness, and shall live this truth."[35] Desarollo never rose among the cottages of Modern Times. The Port Chester incident undoubtedly damaged the Nicholses' reputation sufficiently that most students in the New York City area were reluctant to enter any school associated with the couple. Certainly the Nicholses lacked the wealth to construct the great edifice they envisioned, and the residents of Modern Times lacked the means to support such a grand scheme.

Perhaps even before the Nicholses moved to Modern Times in 1853 they became involved in the discussion and active promotion of free love, not just as an option for colonists of Modern Times but as the central feature of the community. The *Nichols Journal* was published at Modern Times, promoting sovereignty of the individual as the basis for the relations of the sexes and inviting those who would throw off the shackles of married conformity to join the Nicholses in their bold experiment. Some of the later numbers of *Nichols Journal* harshly attacked marriage. Thomas wrote that "it is by marriage that the great evils of civilization are produced and perpetuated. Marriage enslaves men and women, annihilating their individuality, and converting their very virtues into sources of misery." He claimed that marriage caused more misery than slavery. During their stay at Modern Times the Nicholses wrote their most substantial attack on marriage, a book published after the couple moved to Cincinnati in 1854. "Ours is a Declaration of Individual Independence and Sovereignty," wrote Thomas in *Marriage*. The law of morality that he propounded was "written in the constitution of each individual, and demanding liberty, for its development."[36]

Twenty years later Josiah Warren, apparently recalling Thomas Nichols, bitterly complained of an imposter who claimed to have founded the village and "put forth such crude theories, especially with regard to Marriage, that his audiences were disgusted, not only with him, but with what they supposed the village to be." Incensed at seeing his community turned to purposes he could not condone, Warren printed a broadside decrying the confusion of his theories with those of the Nicholses. Some of the community's neighbors, already appalled by the Nicholses work, slammed their doors in Warren's face when he came with his handbills.[37]

Warren's circular insisted that no newspaper or journal be considered a statement by him without his signature endorsing it. "I have a right to be the maker of my own reputation." Warren complained that "an impression is abroad . . . that the Equity Movement is necessarily characterized by an unusual latitude in the sexual relations." He protested that individual sovereignty could as easily support the present relations as change them. Furthermore, "I find no warrant in my 'sovereignty' for invading, disturbing, or offending other people, whatever may be their sentiments or modes of action, while they act only *'at their own cost'*." Josiah Warren made it clear that he would have preferred that his principles be reserved to causes other than marriage reform:

But for myself, so far from proposing or wishing to see any sudden, unprepared changes in the sexual relations, I am satisfied that they would be attended with more embarrassments and more disastrous consequences than their advocates or even the public generally are aware of; and further, I wish to have it understood, as a general rule, that I decline even entertaining the subject, either for controversy or for conversation.

Warren, like Owen, believed that the great social problems were the just reward of labor and the proper basis of community life. Having discovered the solutions, he was chagrined to learn that reformers were caught up in other issues—slavery, diet, marriage—to which his principles could be applied with unsettling results. When Warren established Modern Times, the intensity of debate over marriage was greatest. During the 1850s sovereignty of the individual became the standard for marital reform.

In her reply to Warren, Mary Nichols clearly showed the reorientation of reform since Owen. "Every function of the human being has its laws," she wrote, paraphrasing Sylvester Graham. The sexual hygienists and marriage reformers of the 1830s and 1840s had invested the individual, the married couple, and finally the family with the millennial hopes of the country. These experts had taught that purity, sexual continence and moderation, married love, and healthy offspring would redeem society. Where Warren wanted to reestablish the economic links among all people by abolishing those that constrained and undermined the laborer, the reformers of the 1850s sought to reconstruct personal behavior within the family. When Mary Nichols wrote, "we hold that the theory and practice of society is all wrong," she

referred not to the major institutions that Owen had believed determined human development, but to the most intimate of relationships.
For "the proof we point to [society's] miserable results," she continued,
listing "satiety, disgust, misery; sickly and short-lived, bodily-de-
formed, or soul-perverted offspring." [38]

The greatest value of free love, according to Mary Nichols, would
be the improved health of those who would practice it. In part two of
Marriage she went into many records of marital disaster that led to
nervous disease. Nine-tenths of the children born in marriage, she
claimed, were not desired by the mothers and many not by the fathers.
Civilization undermined the desire for children in women and even
robbed them of their sexuality. "The apathy of the sexual instinct in
women is caused by the enslaved and unhealthy condition in which
she lives." Healthy women would desire sex as much as men. [39] The
agenda that Thomas and Mary Nichols always insisted upon was for
women to gain their health and then claim their individual sovereignty.

The Nicholses also owed a great debt to Fourier, as would the free-
love movement throughout the 1850s. "The marriage of civilization is
the most infernal of all its despotisms," wrote Thomas. Fourier had
shown that the isolated household depended on marriage and was
productive of monotony and waste. Marital rape, prostitution, disease,
and crime all supported marriage, Thomas Nichols continued, harking
back to Hennequin's polemic in *Love in the Phalanstery*. In *Marriage* the
Nicholses stood squarely on the side of variety in love and sexual
union without external constraints, both ideas that Fourier had favored. Nature gave men and women "the power, and consequently
the right, to love more than one person at the same time—to have and
enjoy a succession and a variety of passions." The relations of the sexes
should be based upon the individual sovereignty of both man and
woman, "each independent of the other, and drawn together solely by
the charm of a mutual attraction, coming from a mutual fitness and
adaptation to the spiritual and material loves, or passional desires of
each other." [40]

Perhaps the final debt to Fourier was the pivotal importance of
marriage to civilization. "Of that system of superstition, bigotry,
oppression, and plunder, which we call civilization," wrote Thomas

Nichols, "the monogamic, indissoluble marriage is the center and the soul." Consequently,

If marriage is false it must be destroyed; and the social system that rests upon falsehood, must be false, as every one sees and feels society to be—false and rotten to its heart's core. . . . Let it be destroyed; the sooner, the better.

From the ashes of civilization would arise a society which, in its general features at least, resembled Modern Times.

The society we want, is men and women, living in freedom, sustaining themselves by their own industry, dealing with each other in equity, respecting each other's sovereignty, and governed by their attractions; no one presuming to interfere in the delicate, the private, and personal matters of the affections.

Such a society would be "a perpetual school of intellectual and moral improvement, in which men and women will grow every day more brilliant, more excellent, more estimable, more adorable."[41]

Even after the Nicholses left Modern Times in 1854 Josiah Warren considered their influence malignant. Part of Warren's purpose in beginning his *Periodical Letter* was to assure those interested in the equity movement that the Nicholses did not represent him or his views. Their journal, he assured a correspondent in Boston, was not an official organ of the community. "Whenever it is clearly understood abroad as it is here that Mr. and Mrs. Nichols represent only Mr. and Mrs. Nichols, there will be no ground for disturbance between us." In a short review of *Marriage*, Warren admitted that the book contained many useful statistics, but it also "contains an astounding amount of wild, undigested statement and delusive reasoning, which if accepted or trusted to by the inexperienced, might lead them into the most embarrassing and disastrous positions."[42]

In spite of Warren's opposition, free love remained a fixture of Modern Times even after Thomas and Mary Nichols departed. "Well, our people examined the subject, each according to his or her own ability and came to such conclusion as seemed just but varying according to each ones [sic] point of view," recalled Charles Codman who arrived three years after the Nicholses left. Since the individual sovereigns came to the colony intending to follow their own roads to truth without interfering with others', they made no attempt to dictate any form of marriage. "But agreed," continued Charles Codman, "that all views should be recognized as each ones [sic] right. 'Twas a fruitful topic for discussion."[43] Two of the fruits of these discussions were the change in Josiah Warren's views and the structuring of the first free love community.

Warren never idealized marriage in the manner of the marriage advisers of the 1830s and 1840s. Perhaps as a result of eighteenth century or Owenite feminist writings, Warren always accepted the equality of women. In 1831 he asserted that women and children should receive the same pay as men, and his earliest formulation of individual sovereignty gave women equal rights to person, time, and property. Warren's own marriage exhibited both a strong respect for his wife and his pragmatic attitude toward marriage. Josiah Warren married Caroline Cutter in 1825. She accompanied him to New Harmony the following year and retreated with him during his period of disillusion and illumination. Warren shared his discoveries with his wife and she fully accepted the principles of equity and individual sovereignty. After they returned to New Harmony, Caroline Warren settled down to raising their children, gardening, and taking care of her concerns in the community. Josiah Warren was soon traveling again to promote the equity movement, leaving his family in Indiana. By the late 1840s husband and wife were rarely together, and even though Warren later encouraged her to join him, she demurred. For years, she told him, he had receded from her views and habits. Although she still bore great affection for Josiah Warren and respected his opinions, she believed that their personal propensities and their separation had truly individualized the two of them.[44]

Although Warren always repudiated any suggestion that the relations of marriage and family be altered, his thinking on the topic changed during the 1850s, probably as a result of the continuing debate inspired by the free love counterculture and the investigation of the subject at Modern Times. In 1860 Warren wrote a manuscript, apparently intended for publication, called "Coversational Development." The discussions recorded in the journal purportedly took place at Modern Times and may have been based on actual conversations there. The book explained Warren's principles as they applied to specific circumstances. One of the speakers, for instance, said that individualizing interests would not work with drunks since sots act not at their own cost only but at the cost of their wives and children. Warren replied, "There should not be a *communism* of property between them"—that is, the wife and children should not be dependent upon the alcoholic husband. On the matter of marriage, Warren advised somewhat cryptically "that the deciding power, whenever vested should be individual not communistic like the joint ownership of the house." Fortunately, he explained himself at length a few pages later. In fact, the section on marriage took up a large portion of the manuscript and obviously formed an important element of the work.

He began his talk on marriage by dissociating "Individuality" from free love. He went on to say that the subject was so complicated that he never discussed it

. . . in a few off hand words, in conversation for fear some of them may not be well chosen, or may not be understood as I intend them, and yet we *must meet* this great subject and see it prospectively[?] harmonised with other great interests before we can think that true progress is fairly begun.

Warren already had departed a long way from his policy of never even talking about marriage. What followed departed even further. Rather than insisting that the present institution be left alone, Warren stated that it was a mistake to think that either nature or God had provided the truth on the subject of the relations between the sexes. He explained what these relations should be in light of individual sovereignty.

The sexual relation is founded on the affections *only*. No property or other interests are mixed up with it. Two persons of opposite sexes understand between themselves, *without any public notoriety*, that they will be the particular individual companions of each other in that particular relation, for a *certain specified time:* at the expiration of which time, the arrangement is positively to end—to be renewed, of course, if each prefers it—both being perfectly free. And that either party may put an end to the arrangement at any time—but if no notice is given to that effect each is assured that the arrangement is still preferred.

Warren even discussed some of the details of his plan. A small token might be exchanged between the signatories of this agreement to make public their relation. Both parties would of course still be affectionate to friends. Finally, to the objection that an agreement did not need a specific ending date, Warren answered that such a clause respected the law of change. Although Warren persistently condemned free love, his unpublished plan was free love in everything but name. It was only in the year before his death that Warren published a work that suggested a one- or two-year contract for marriage. By then, in 1873, he was thoroughly identified with the opposition to free love, an identity he preferred.[45]

Warren's "Conversational Development" represented not only the fruit of his own thought but also the actual practice of free love as it existed in Modern Times. In accordance with Josiah Warren's description of his system, Modern Times provided those escaping or eschewing marriage both room and freedom. Room meant both proximity and distance, so that love radicals could find sympathetic fellows while avoiding irritating contacts with enemies of free love. Freedom of discussion, as well as action, encouraged debate on free love and contributed to the growth of free love ideas; these ideas, in turn, influenced individuals who rejected marriage. Among the villagers who came seeking refuge from the marriage laws of civilization there developed informal practices that gave the first expression to the counterculture of free love.

"Freedom in love without the necessity of underhand intrigues and duplicity of conduct," Marx Edgeworth Lazarus predicted in *Love vs. Marriage*, "can exist only when public opinion is liberal and courteous, and demands the combination of persons prepared for nobler and more delicate relations than those which now obtain." The individual sovereigns of Modern Times were certainly liberal minded and were open to all ideas, since even a "creed overflowing with error" might contain a "single grain of truth." One visitor recalled a Sunday afternoon meeting for conversation where the topics ranged from law, sex, and marriage to trade and politics. The colonists exchanged no sharp words and accorded respect to each individual's opinion. Social life in the colony was apparently rich and created among the inhabitants "an easy, cordial frankness and simplicity of intercourse, which gave assurance that they were held together by a genuine attraction, and sustained by mutual sympathy."[46] Residents of Modern Times must have approached as near as any group could to the liberality and courtesy

required to prepare individuals for "nobler and more delicate relations."

An element necessary for the practice of free love that Lazarus had
not stated explicitly was respect for the privacy of others. One attack
leveled against Modern Times was that the houses were built far apart,
presumably so the dwellers could sin with impunity. While the place-
ment of houses was as much a product of the size of the lots as of a
quest for privacy, the people of Modern Times practiced, as far as
they could, the principle that "each person shall mind his or her own
business." One resident reported, "Well, folks ask no questions in
regard to *that* [marriage] among us. . . . We don't interfere; there is no
eaves-dropping, or prying behind the curtain." Henry Edger compared the women of Modern Times favorably to those in civilization,
saying that in Modern Times there was far less "scandal and backbit-
ing." Moncure Conway, who visited the village in 1857, found that
respect for privacy served those who departed from conventional marriage and parentage: "it was not considered polite to inquire who might
be the father of a newly-born child, or who the husband or wife of any
individual might be."[47] The open-mindedness of the residents of Modern Times and their respect for the privacy of one another allowed
those who wished to ignore marriage to do so. They were limited only
by the imperative of individual sovereignty—that they act at their
own cost.

Outsiders and residents held different views on the results of Modern Times's reorganization of the sexual relations. John B. Ellis, an
opponent of free love, wrote in 1870 that during the free love agitation
of the 1850s, "partners were changed with frequency." He told the
story of a Miss Smith who, during less than two years in the village,
had borne a child by one man and went on to live with eight others
before leaving. While Ellis apparently visited the community in the
late 1850s, it is very unlikely that he obtained his information about
"Miss Smith" while there; residents who lived through the period
never mentioned any woman acting with such sensual abandon. Henry
Edger wrote in 1855 that stories of "habitual inchastity" at Modern
Times were the products of "impure imaginations" and that those who
damned the community were lost to their own degraded vices: "Habitual companions of common prostitutes could not of course conceive of

the co-existence of opinions favoring the largest liberty with the constant prevalence of chastity, virtuous and modest conduct."[48]

Although some people at Modern Times, Edger admitted, practiced marriage without priest and divorce without magistrate, most obeyed the civil laws and were legally married. Discussion in the community, both among the living and with the spirits of the departed, had taught them that love was not a matter of whim but a necessity. "Love, it seems, is the gift of God: it is profanity to attempt to thwart it." Nor did the colonists of Modern Times attempt to thwart it. Among the most primary rights, taught by the Nicholses and consistent with individual sovereignty, was the "Mother's choice of Paternity of her child." This was upheld by many, recalled Charles Codman, but he claimed " 'twas a theory hardly ever put into practice." He mentioned only one woman who "yearned for the joys of Maternity and with intent chose an intelligent, upright and healthy man as the father of her boy and was always proud that she had done so. And she lost no credit among our people."[49]

Apparently the aboliton of marriage at Modern Times proceeded with caution and moderation. "Now in point of fact," wrote Codman, seeking to redeem Modern Times from the reputation of licentiousness that still clung to it in 1906,

despite the Notoriety and bad names which were given to Modern Times, there were very little changes among our people—the married remained in the bonds of matrimony and the unmarried did not drop into imorality [sic]. All carried themselves as selfrespecting men and women

Rather than anarchy in love and sex, there arose at Modern Times a system of informal marriage and divorce. Edger's mention of marriage without priest indicates that when a couple came to feel themselves truly in love, they could become intimate. Another resident admitted that there might be some who were not legally married.

A man and woman may meet in the cars in the morning, come here and buy a house and go to housekeeping in the afternoon, without ever having seen a clergyman or a magistrate, and, so long as they were quiet and peaceable, honest and industrious, no one here would say any thing against them.

Moncure Conway found that individual sovereignty was carefully followed in marriage.

The arrangements of marriage were . . . left entirely to the men and women themselves. They could be married formally or otherwise, live in the same or separate houses, and have their relation known or unknown to the rest of the village. The relation could be dissolved at pleasure without any formulas. . . . Those who stood in the relation of husband or wife wore upon the finger a red thread; and so long as that badge was visible the person was understood to be married. If it disappeared the marriage was at an end.[50]

The testimony of both residents and visitors shows that free lovers who put their convictions into practice did not abandon marriage for promiscuity. Ideologues like Stephen Pearl Andrews and the Nicholses remained married after their conversion to free love but redefined their relationships, asserting that they remained faithful out of love rather than coercion. For them, free love was an expression of the highest ideal of middle-class marriage. On the other hand, free love allowed those who had abandoned unhappy marriages to salvage the bourgeois ideal of marriage by building new relationships upon affection and interest, or what they would have called affinity. By stressing the affection at the core of these relationships free love bound these couples to the most elemental form of middle-class marriage.

Modern Times probably remained a haven for those who wished to set aside social conventions until well after the Civil War. As early as the mid-1850s, however, the community settled into a quiet nonconformity. In 1857 a group from Boston, many of them coming with Charles Codman, moved to the village and soon became some of the village's most solid citizens. During the Civil War the village reorganized as the town of Brentwood, named in honor of Henry Edger's home town in England.[51] As time passed and free lovers left, made happy marriages, or died, the town's radicalism became more moderate and discreet, changing the town from a bastion of radicalism into a sleepy village with a shady past.

The contribution of Modern Times to free love reform in America was considerable and can only be appreciated when it is set in the context of the movement. Modern Times was an important symbol of radicalism in the minds of conservatives and radicals alike. "The appropriateness of its name," Henry Edger wrote, "arises from the fact that it is a sort of distilled essence of modern opinion, a summary and condensation of the most remarkable peculiarities of modern society."

Josiah Warren represented a transformed Owenism and Theron Leland had been among the most committed Fourierists. Henry Edger
brought with him the new philosophy of Comte, and James Cook
brought the science of phrenology. Stephen Pearl Andrews represented so many reforms that he summed up many of the fervors of the
period. Everyone, it seems, practiced spiritualism. The community
showed that the practice of free love could be a living reality, thereby
giving others the courage to attempt similar experiments. Modern
Times also gave the counterculture of free love its basic ideology.
Throughout the decade, sovereignty of the individual would remain
the rationale for the society envisioned by those who rejected marriage.
Even equitable commerce would reappear in the writings of other free
lovers.[52] Finally, Modern Times was the beginning of a free love
network that spread throughout the North during the 1850s.

CHAPTER 5

The Free Love Counterculture, 1853 to 1860

During the 1850s a network of communities, reform organizations, and periodicals supported a new vision of American society. Advocates of this vision often perceived different details—some, for instance, favored phalansterian associations while others preferred individual sovereignty. In general, however, they agreed that commerce founded in selfishness, government based on force, and religion without proof destroyed social harmony and degraded the individual. These visionaries called themselves radicals, consciously separating themselves from bourgeois illusions and compromises. At the same time, radicals, as middle-class intellectuals, feared artificiality and believed in the individual, private property, and true love. The radical network formed a counterculture ineluctably bound up with the dominant culture's values, forms, and assumptions. The ultimate expression of middle-class radicalism was free love—the repudiation of any relations between man and woman that violated the individual sovereignty of either.

Free love shaded into other ante-bellum reform movements in many characteristics. Free lovers called for the immediate end of African slavery as well as for the end of married slavery. They expected woman to gain her equality with man only after she gained economic rights and freedom from possession within marriage. Vegetarianism and teetotalism were pervasive among free lovers, and both were part of the personal rehabilitation expected of those who sought more elevated sexual relations. Like less comprehensive reformers—and like their evangelical opponents—free lovers built their hope on individual regeneration. Although free lovers distinguished themselves from feminists and abolitionists by their attitude toward marriage, they shared a similar view of sexual relations with other reformers and with a broad range of thinkers within the middle class. They viewed love as an ungovernable force, a passional affinity that two people could not create where it did not exist, could not hold where it had disappeared. Within a free relationship, they expected sexual intercourse to be less frequent because both partners would be free of the lusts engendered by the artificiality of marriage.

The distinction between free love and other opinions about marriage reform appeared in a controversy between two abolitionists, Henry C. Wright and Francis Barry. Henry C. Wright's idea that love created marriage came very close to the free love understanding, though Wright rejected free love. He drafted and pushed through a resolution that condemned free love at a spiritualist convention at Sheboygan Falls in June 1856. Spiritualism, according to Wright, advocated exclusive marriage. Francis Barry, an abolitionist in Ohio who was a spiritualist and free lover, took Wright to task for his views.

I am aware that you and others advocate a system that you call marriage, in which *love* is an essential feature. I confess I see no propriety in applying the term "marriage" to such a system. . . . The term "marriage" has, by common consent, been applied to a system of which love forms no necessary part—a system essentially like chattel slavery.

Wright answered that he knew that some free lovers actually followed free lust, while other free lovers recognized that true love could exist only between two persons. Barry shot back that those who believed in exclusive attachments were a minority and were barred by their theory from following their attractions.

Free lovers demand perfect freedom and unconditional freedom for love as a right . . . and they are perfectly willing that the heart shall decide for itself whether it will have one or more objects . . . they believe . . . that variety in love is not only natural, but in the highest degree promotive of purity, happiness, and development.[1]

Although some free lovers would have considered Barry too extreme in his statement of free love, most would have agreed that marriage had to be abolished and replaced with purer relationships based upon affection and freedom. Thus, as an extreme statement of the free love doctrine, Barry's definition allows us to distinguish free love from other views of marriage.

Criticism of marriage appeared in the writings of feminists, spiritualists, and other reformers during the 1850s. Many feminists of the prewar decade came close to being love radicals. In 1853, the first issue of the women's rights journal the *Una* contained an attack upon the domestic confinement of women. A. D. Mayo wrote that women are as confined by the household as men would be were they forced to remain there. "Either can live exclusively in it, but only by the same process; by a systematic treading down of a whole scale of the nature." During its three years of publication, the *Una* persisted in questioning the limitations of marriage. E. H. W. regreted the fall of primeval marriage into sensuality and male domination. A trusting girl now binds herself to bitter servitude and, after years of grossness, is bruised, without accomplishments, and unable to support herself. "With this state of things who can say that marriage, as it now exists, is aught but a marred and imperfect institution?"[2]

The *Una*, edited by Paulina Wright Davis, represented many of the most important women's rights leaders in attacking marriage and demanding changes in divorce laws. At a convention in 1860, for example, Elizabeth Cady Stanton called for more liberal divorce laws. The harm done by the wrong choice of business partner, teacher, or minister, she said, was limited by the freedom to end contracts. This should also apply to the choice of a spouse: "the dictates of humanity and common sense alike show that the latter and most important contract should no more be perpetual than either or all of the former." Ernestine L. Rose, who had come to America in 1836, supported Stanton's resolution.

But what is marriage? A human institution called out by the needs of social, affectional human nature, for human purposes, its objects are, first, the happiness of the parties immediately concerned, and, secondly, the welfare of society.

As though speaking from an eighteenth-century text, Rose pictured marriage not only as an institution with objective attributes but as an institution that had individual and social functions without reference to religious ends.[3]

One of the most radical feminists of the 1850s was Hannah F. M. Brown. She contributed to the *Una*, made lecture tours, and edited her own journal, the *Agitator*. In 1859 Brown discussed marriage in a pamphlet on social freedom. In the pamphlet, Brown stated that men marry to obtain various goals—someone to cook, higher status and wealth. "The woman is often regarded as a sort of appendage to the goods and glory." Men refuse to learn the law of soul-marriage, while women are forced to marry from material necessity. "What are the results of uncongenial marriages? Ask the murderer. . . . Ask the suicide. . . . God has visited the sins of the fathers upon the children." Indeed, she went on, "there is no vice, no crime that is not the legitimate offspring of men-made marriages. Pauperism in rags; red-handed war, and slavery with its iron heart, may with propriety claim kinship with unloving unions." Hannah Brown believed that true marriages could be formed and would result if women were allowed to choose freely.[4]

Although Brown defended herself against the charge of being a free lover by saying she never advocated the abrogation of marriage, she rejected the idea of perpetual unions. Instead, she believed in what she called both the "chainless marriage" and the "divine marriage," a system apparently based upon spiritualism. Warren Chase wrote in the *Agitator* that only when marriage became a true union of harmonizing pairs would it be worthy of the name marriage. For Warren Chase, as for Hannah Brown, the redemption of marriage required a lot of work, including the purging of the institution that was then called marriage. "How strange," Chase wrote, "that seduction should be counted no crime when permitted by a priest or magistrate under the name and sanction of marriage." Mrs. Brown also opened her columns to many who forthrightly wanted to abolish marriage. "For one," the *Agitator* quoted Stephen Pearl Andrews, "I reject and repudiate the interference of the State in my morals, precisely as I do the interfer-

ence of the Church to prescribe my religious deportment or belief."
George Roberts attacked both Henry Wright and Andrew Jackson
Davis as priests who built theories and then distorted facts to agree
with them. The progress of the race, predicted Roberts, would inevitably carry it beyond the present system of priest marriages. Hannah
Brown also planned to publish a series of articles by Marx Lazarus,
but this plan ended with the *Agitator* in 1860.[5]

Hannah Brown, Henry Wright, and Warren Chase agreed that
marriage required a new dispensation and that spiritualism provided
the necessary insight to inspire the new epoch. As we have seen, early
spiritualists quickly adopted the harmonialist idea that spiritual relationships were based upon affinity. Although denying that they were
free lovers, many spiritualists came very close to the free love attitude
toward marriage. Andrew Jackson Davis included marriage lectures as
he traveled to spiritualist gatherings. Bad marriages, he told his audiences, produced evil offspring, while heart marriages would give the
world beautiful and peaceful children. Warren Chase, after becoming
a lecturer on spiritualism about 1850, often spoke on marriage, opposing the legal power husbands then held over their wives and supporting changes that would allow the parties in marriage to dissolve the
contract.[6]

On April 5, 6, and 7, 1856, Warren Chase spoke at a spiritualist
convention in the "fogy town of Dayton." He was joined on the
rostrum by William Denton, an English immigrant who was then on a
lecture tour throughout the Midwest. William Denton and his sister
Anne had grown up in England, the children of strict Methodist
parents. In the course of their religious development both William and
Anne became first more extreme in their pursuit of piety, then slowly
realized the many shortcomings of Christian religion as it existed in
the churches. They became Barkerites, rejecting established churches
for informal Bible study groups and worldly pleasures for simplicity
in dress and possessions. Among the ideas their small group considered
was that the law of God was sufficient for the children of Jehovah. If
so, then God-given affection should be the basis of marriage. Anne
Denton claimed that thousands accepted this notion and practiced free
marriage. Such a union was proposed to her, but she declined. From
rejecting established religion, the Dentons came to doubt all of Chris-

tianity. Soon after the Denton family emigrated to the United States in 1848, William and Anne exchanged religious doubt for spiritualism.[7]

A temperance and reform lecturer in England, William Denton began traveling in his new country lecturing on phonetics, antislavery, temperance, geology, Bible questions, and spiritualism. His stop in Dayton was only one of many during his 1856 lecture tour. He spoke on theology, women's rights, and slavery in Ohio, Indiana, and Pennsylvania. In Richmond, Indiana, he shared the platform with his old friend John O. Wattles, one of the original Ohio Fourierists, who had started a school on reform principles in West Point, Indiana. William Denton did not believe in variety in love but preached that unions should be between two people only, be exclusive, and be based upon free affection. Such a viewpoint was free love in everything except the claim that love should be followed as it changed its object.[8]

The attitude of Anne Denton and of her husband, Canadian spiritualist Alfred Cridge, was even more radical. The Cridges believed that bad relations retarded spiritual progress. Consequently, uncongenial relations should be dissolved. Like many spiritualists, Alfred and Anne Cridge taught that the spirits practiced free love and recommended that the living emulate the departed by replacing marital and chattel slavery with sovereignty of the individual. Unlike more extreme free lovers, however, they believed that the institution of marriage could coexist with the freedom of individuals within marriage. "Whatever be the defects of existing marriage regulations," Alfred reasoned, "progressive people . . . must and will form conjugal relations more or less in accordance with the present social order." In an epistolary debate with John Patterson, editor of the *Social Revolutionist*, Anne Cridge admitted that their version of free love was not compatible with Patterson's. Nevertheless, she claimed that their marriage allowed them to be "copartners" and "equals in social and business relations" and that in spite of the limitations of marriage, in *their* marriage "affinity, attraction, freedom and individual sovereignty are the principles and rules, the alpha and omega, the beginning and the end, the first and last."[9]

During the 1850s the discussion of antislavery, women's rights, and spiritualism almost inevitably led to the problems of marriage. As an integral element of the middle-class identity formed during the early nineteenth century, marriage seemed to be the basis of the entire system of human relationships constituting middle-class society. Consequently, the shortcomings of society appeared to be bound up with marriage. The importance of the marriage question to virtually every reform became evident at the Free Convention at Rutland, Vermont, in June 1858. The purpose of the convention had been to provide an open forum for the discussion of the most advanced reform opinions. Beyond damning slavery and agreeing that women should have greater rights, the delegates had trouble approving resolutions. Henry C. Wright provided several addresses and was supported by Ernestine L. Rose and others when he condemned religion as a waste and a fraud. A. D. Mayo, however, received loud applause for his defense of Christianity and the Bible. Freethinking Ernestine Rose proved tenaciously skeptical, even of S. B. Brittan's "natural" evidence of spiritualism.

Even though the convention never endorsed marriage abolition, discussion of the problems of marriage took such a prominent place in the proceedings that the *New York Daily Times* and the *Tribune* dubbed it the Free Love Convention. Julia Branch delivered a strong attack on what she called binding marriage, examining in her talk the evils of the isolated household and the deformities created by this kind of marriage. Woman, she said, "must demand her freedom; her right to receive the equal wages of man for her labor; *her right to bear children when she will, and by whom she will.*" Julia Branch continued:

I believe in the absolute freedom of the affections and that it is woman's privilege—aye, her right—to accept or refuse any love that comes to her. . . . when the love has died out for the man who has taken her to his heart, she is living a lie to herself, her own nature, and to him, if she continues to hold an intimate relation to him.[10]

The resloution against marriage offered by Julia Branch received careful debate but far from unanimous support. Stephen S. Foster suggested the resolution be amended to call for marriage based upon full equality. Joel Tiffany objected that marriage must exist until people rose above their sensual natures. "Whatever abuses there may be in the marriage relation," he argued, "they are not created by the institution, but *notwithstanding* it." Ernestine L. Rose was impressed by Tiffany's description of conjugal love. "But," she went on, ". . . facts are stubborn things, and we have not only to look at and investigate what ought to be, but what is. And what is? Just what has been stated here this morning by a woman (Mrs. Branch)." Other speakers on marriage took the rostrum. A Shaker elder told the audience that the solution was not to purify the lusts but to crucify them. Another speaker invoked physiology to show that divorce should be made available. And Eliza Farnham asserted that women were superior to men but were taught to be inferior in marriage and were in other ways damaged by the institution. While the delegates reached no consensus on marriage, they discussed it from every viewpoint available to advanced thought.[11]

Although it seemed to merge with antislavery, feminism, and spiritualism, free love was more than just an extreme element within various reform movements. Free lovers edited their own journals and established their own organizations. In many respects the free love network emerged from the Fourierist network that was already in place, though in decline. Fourier's ideas appeared in new formulations in the writings of Thomas and Mary Nichols and Stephen Pearl Andrews. Former Fourierists like James H. Cook and Theron Leland joined in the call for marriage abolition, as would associationists across the country. In 1858 Albert Brisbane issued a manifesto arguing that women should be beyond the control of their husbands and have the privilege of changing companions when necessary.[12] New York City, the headquarters of Albert Brisbane and the home of the *Phalanx* during the 1840s, was the earliest center of free love thought in America. The first works on the subject were printed there, by the publishing house of Fowlers and Wells. Stephen Pearl Andrews recruited members for Modern Times in New York City. Ohio, which had more phalanxes than any state except New York, became the center of free love agitation by 1856. Apparently, the lines of communication among Fourierists also carried the radical gospel, so that those who had come to despise the isolated household under the tutelage of Albert Brisbane and Parke Godwin were most likely to call for its destruction when the Fourier movement no longer provided a less harsh alternative.

Like other middle-class reform movements, free love was carried across the country by lecturers and journals. William Denton and Warren Chase merely brought marriage into discussion—others called for its abolition. After his sojourn at Modern Times, James H. Cook lectured on "anthropology" in the Midwest. Traveling through Illinois he summed up what he considered the elements of frontier civilization: "Pork, whiskey, tobacco, drugs, bibles and Sunday-school books are the ways and means by which riches temporal and eternal are obtained." The content of his lectures may be inferred from a catechism he published in a free love journal. "What constitutes the TRUNK of the tree of Social Evil? Legal Marriage. . . . Is legal marriage a far greater curse than African slavery? Yes, by far." Francis Barry carried the message of free love during 1856 into Illinois, Michigan, and Ohio, where he found more radicalism, he reported, than he had expected. "I have taken the field," he declared, "and do not intend to leave it till God—that humbug of humbugs; and the huge hydra, hell begotten monster, Government; and Marriage, that abomination of abominations, shall no longer curse the earth."[13]

The reception accorded to lecturers on free love varied considerably. In some places they were clearly unwelcome—Cook reported meeting opposition from a local minister, and church leaders probably made efforts to protect their communities from the pernicious doctrines. On the other hand, where spiritualist beliefs, Fourierist doctrines, or concern over marriage had already become issues, the lecturers were welcomed and sometimes made converts. During the spring of 1857, a former Methodist minister, E. S. Tyler, lectured on spiritualism and women's rights in Skaneateles, New York. Some residents there had already adopted the ideas of free love and agreed with Tyler when he claimed that marriage stood in the way of the advancement of women. In the next world, Tyler told them, affections were followed rather than possessed. By the fall of 1857 there were twenty families, all wealthy or at least respectable farmers, who endorsed free love. During October Tyler convinced one of his converts, Mary Lewis, to accompany him to a free love colony in the West.[14]

Publications probably spread free love doctrines more widely than lecturers did. Two of the most important works of the decade that supported monogamous marriage—*The Great Harmonia*, volume 4, by Davis, and *Marriage and Parentage*, by Wright—appeared in 1855. Both

of these works taught that love was the sole basis of marriage and that
the absence of love meant marriage no longer existed. One free lover,
C. M. Overton, even claimed Wright and Davis as allies. During the
1850s seven books appeared that endorsed some form of free love. By
1854 Lazarus's *Love vs. Marriage*, Andrews's *Love, Marriage, and Divorce
and the Sovereignty of the Individual*, and Nichols's *Esoteric Anthropology*
and *Marriage* had all been published. In 1855 Mary Nichols published
her fictionalized autobiography, *Mary Lyndon*, and in 1856 James Clay's
Voice From Prison emerged. The last extensive treatment of free love in
the decade was Austin Kent's *Free Love; or, A Philosophical Demonstration
of the Non-exclusive Nature of Connubial Love*, which appeared in 1857.
During the 1850s the only limitations upon anyone's study of marriage
and love was the availability of these books and their cost.

Readers of periodical literature could fault neither their booksellers
nor their pocketbooks if they lacked material on marriage. We have
already seen that Horace Greeley, though opposing free love, debated
the topic with Stephen Pearl Andrews. Similarly, Adin Ballou debated
free love with Austin Kent in the columns of the *Christian Socialist*
during the early 1850s. Beginning in 1853, Paulina Wright Davis
published the *Una* in Providence, Rhode Island. Alfred and Anne
Cridge and William Denton began publication of the weekly *Vanguard*
in 1857, a publication concerned mainly with spiritualism. And about
1859 Hannah F. M. Brown began publishing the *Agitator*. In addition
to the journals discussing marriage and free love, there were other
journals that endorsed the abolition of marriage. The *Oneida Circular*
carried the Christian perfectionist message of John Humphrey Noyes
and called for the marriageless Kingdom of God. It began publication
in 1851 out of Brooklyn, and a subscription was free. The *Nichols
Journal* began in April 1853, six months after Thomas and Mary
Nichols found they could no longer publish their articles in Russell
Trall's *Water-Cure Journal*. Even after they moved west, the Nicholses
continued issuing periodicals, with varying titles and at changing inter-
vals, until 1857. During 1856 and 1857, the *Social Revolutionist* was
published by John Patterson, who had been associated with the Cincinnati Brotherhood. The subscription rate was only one dollar per
year. While the Nicholses periodicals were largely made up of writings

by Thomas and Mary, the *Social Revolutionist* opened its pages to all opinions on the marriage question. It was followed by the *Age of Freedom* in 1858 and *Good Time Coming* in 1859.[15]

The many books and journals reporting or advocating free love reinforce the impression that marriage abolition was widely discussed during the 1850s. As early as 1852 Horace Greeley complained that the "free trade sophistry respecting marriage is already on every libertine's tongue." We cannot assume, of course, that ideas widely known were also taken seriously. For example, Thomas Nichols claimed in 1853 that *Esoteric Anthropology* already had sold ten thousand copies. While many of those who bought the book must have taken to heart his injunctions concerning the marriage bed, a great many more probably wanted to find out how much sleep they should be getting and on what kind of mattress. Thomas Nichols also claimed a circulation for *Nichols Journal* of twenty thousand, which would have put it in competition with some of the larger newspapers of the day. That *Nichols Journal* attained this popular success only three months after it began publication made it all the more remarkable. We can have more confidence in the circulation figure for the *Social Revolutionist*, which was four hundred in 1856, mainly of enthusiastic midwesterners.[16]

The call for the abolition of marriage, no matter how horrifying to middle-class conservatives, could arise from far different sources and support much different visions of the future of society. As suggested in an earlier chapter, religious conviction could lead to despair of marriage as profound as that felt by the anti-Christian individual sovereign. The perfectionist followers of John Humphrey Noyes at Oneida regarded any "exclusive idolatrous attachment as unhealthy and pernicious, wherever it may exist." Their system of complex marriage was to keep the heart "free to love all the true and worthy." But even though the perfectionists condemned marriage, they equally rejected the replacement of marriage with a limited contract or unfettered love. Noyes believed that only the love of God would guarantee harmony among men and between man and woman. "The idolatry of affection is as bad as the idolatry of brute blindness and fear," he wrote. The kind of marriage envisioned by Henry Wright, "founded on extreme specialty of mutual affection, in which the parties are ready to swear themselves inevitably mated for eternity," rarely works out; "it somehow turns out after a little while that they find there was a mistake made, and that after all they had failed to get the right one." [17]

Noyes and the perfectionists also repudiated variety in love at the whim of the individual sovereign. Noyes commended Warren's philosophy for its "straightforward Yankee meaning" but pointed to the limitation that the individual sovereign act at his own cost only. Actions never terminate with the actor, wrote Noyes, so that all other persons are involved in the life of the individual. As one Oneidan put it, "the free relation of the sexes on the basis of individual sovereignty may be Free Lust, or Free Licentiousness, but it cannot be Free *Love*." Noyes summarized his vision of love in the term "ascending fellowship": love by those without sin and within God, to God and to one another. Christians living together first would love God, and their affections would seek those who had already gained greater spirituality. Love was thus a community matter, to be directed to the larger family rather than to exclusive unions, and it was free only within the community of the sanctified. Finally, the perfectionists never accepted the popular notion that love "is an inevitable fatality which must have its own course." Rather, like work, love could be managed by "enlightened self-control" for the good of the community. During the 1860s Noyes sought to distance his community from the free love movement. By 1870 he characterized free love as a "sect based on Josiah Warren's doctrine of Individual Sovereignty" that recruited mostly spiritualists. The Oneida Community, on the other hand, was based on Unity, the opposite of individual sovereignty, and was "heartily opposed to Spiritualism." [18]

The extreme free love doctrines of Barry and Cook separated free lovers from marriage reformers like Henry C. Wright, who wanted to save rather than abolish marriage, and from the Bible communists, who believed love could only be free in a community of the regenerate. These are valuable distinctions if we want to know what free love meant in the 1850s to those who considered themselves free lovers. At the core of free love was a fervent belief in the individual. Society came into existence as a result of the individual's decision to end his or her isolation and bind himself or herself to a spouse; social evils originated from the limitations placed upon individuals within marriage. Consequently, redemption demanded that marriage be replaced with an unfettered flow of affection, affinity, or love. Sovereign individuals would enter relationships with one another, always understanding that they acted at their own cost and were ready to realign themselves or to enter into new contracts with others when their passions dictated. C. M. Overton wrote that to be a free lover was "to believe that ATTRACTION, or natural law, should form the bond of union between conjugal partners." "The sexual relations," said Thomas Nichols, lecturing to an audience in Cincinnati, "like all other relations, have their own laws, and the freedom we demand, is the freedom to obey those laws."[19] Yet even among free lovers who accepted the primacy of individuality and variety in love there existed an important division, with the authorities cited above on either side.

Although Thomas and Mary Nichols had become interested in spiritualism in the late 1840s, they merely added spiritual affinity to their other ideas on marriage and confined their discussion of the spirit world to the last section of *Marriage*. By the fall of 1854, however, Mary Nichols had become a "subjected medium" and began to receive messages concerning the reorganization of society. Spiritual allies revealed to Thomas and Mary Nichols that a new society would be created by a small group of persons who first purified themselves by abstaining from unhealthy practices. Once purified, this group would establish on earth new social forms, including free love. Sovereignty of the individual, Thomas announced, was "the first necessary step in progress. The mistake is in thinking it the last."

Spiritualist experience thus coincided with, or led to, elaboration of the Nicholses' free love doctrines. They had always expected that freely acting affections would be temperate, but they proposed no other limits to their fulfillment. "Man's morality," wrote Thomas in *Marriage*, "his most perfect conformity to the law of God, is his fullest and most harmonious exercise of all his natural faculties, and the complete gratification of all his natural desires." Communication with the spirit world revealed a new element of free love to the Nicholses. While variety was certainly the shape of things to come, a man and woman were to refrain from intercourse (material union) except when they intended to have children.[20]

Soon after the Nicholses announced their "Law of Progression in

Harmony" others took exception. "Peter Socialist," writing to the *Social Revolutionist* from Boston, protested the Nicholses' exclusivism; they established a standard of abstinence, not of temperance, and judged others by it.

> If freedom for the affections is not to be installed till mankind may control the sexual desire, as they now control the desire to ride on horseback, or to travel in foreign countries, we who are fighting for it, may as well lay down our arms.

The writer insisted that health required more intercourse than allowed by the Nicholses' rule. Thomas Nichols defended his belief in the pages of the *Social Revolutionist* and was seconded by L. A. Hine who believed that free love, if it did not lead to children, was free lust. John Patterson answered Hine, saying that Hine assumed the continuation of the isolated household. If the philosophy of free love retained the family, which was allied to social despotism, "so will this philosophy be found waving its plumes in the popular war on social freedom." Francis Barry attacked the idea of purifying a small group in preparation for a better society. "We do not believe in getting ready to live;— we believe in LIVING."[21]

Such a controversy might have been interminable had not the Nicholses abruptly halted it. In 1857 they announced that revelations from the spirit world by St. Ignatius Loyola and St. Francis Xavier led them to the study of Catholicism. In March they were baptized at St. Xavier's Roman Catholic Church in Cincinnati. "Whatever in our writings and teachings, and in our lives," stated Thomas in their recantation of former errors, "has been contrary to the doctrines, morality, and discipline of the holy Catholic Church, we wish to retract and repudiate, and were it possible, to atone for." To Alfred Cridge this seemed a fitting conclusion to the Nicholses' thinking. "Those who believe in CRUSHING, instead of DIRECTING and admitting of wholesome and spontaneous activity, would confer a benefit to the cause of Reform by leaving its ranks, and going where they belong, as Dr. and Mrs. N. have done."[22] Thanks to the Nicholses' defection from the ranks, the question of authority and social harmony was removed from the free love debates; free love was tied firmly to individual sovereignty.

Even if many people sympathized with the ideas of free love during the 1850s, reading, studying, debating, and promoting ideas make up only half of the process of conversion. As the author of the epistle James wrote, "faith without works is dead." Free lovers faced several problems in practicing their beliefs. For most Americans free love was anathema, not to be tolerated in family members or neighbors. Free lovers also probably suffered from confusion as to what, exactly, a life of free love meant. Thomas Nichols and Francis Barry offered different ways of realizing individual sovereignty. Perhaps the greatest problem faced by those who wanted to be free lovers was the need for contact with other free lovers. In a large country where most free lovers had to be discreet about their beliefs, separation from congenial radicals might have destroyed aspirations to practice free love.

The Free Love Club in New York City was a conscious attempt to forge connections among those interested in marriage reform. In 1854 Stephen Pearl Andrews, Albert Brisbane, and other advanced thinkers in New York began meeting at Andrews's house for tea and talk. The circle grew so quickly that by 1855 a league had been formed, holding its meetings in rented halls. According to a *New York Daily Times* reporter who infiltrated the Free Love Club, the meetings attracted about 150 men and women twice a week. The entrance fee, to pay for refreshments, rent, and utilities in the hall, was twenty-five cents per person or ten cents apiece for a couple. "They danced;" wrote the correspondent, "they made merry; they took part in plays of whist and chess and backgammon," and they discussed such radical literature as Mary Gove Nichols's autobiography. The reporter assured his readers that nothing licentious happened at these meetings; in fact, so innocuous did the Free Love Club prove to be that the only thing he accused it of was plotting to establish free love in American society. Harmless or not, the Club aroused enormous interest in Manhattan. A crowd showed up at a meeting one week after the *New York Daily Times* article appeared. The police soon arrived and closed the meeting down. Smaller groups continued to meet, however, and social freedom was a lively topic among liberals and free thinkers in New York until late in the nineteenth century.[23]

In the great distances outside of America's few cities the creation of networks among marriage radicals became the business of the journals.

Readers of the *Social Revolutionist* not only could follow the debate over Progression in Harmony or learn the latest communications from the spirit world on free love, they could have their names added to the list of variety free lovers. For nine or ten cents to cover postage, their names would be sent to everyone on the list and they would receive the list themselves, thereby allowing possible affinities to contact one another. "Let radicals make themselves known to each other," read the announcement. Alfred and Anne Cridge opened the columns of the *Vanguard* to advertisements for "congenial relations." For a nominal fee men and women could publish anonymous descriptions of themselves and have interested parties contact them through the periodical.[24]

A far more elaborate network was the Progressive Union, developed by Thomas and Mary Nichols as the basis for their harmonic society. Mary Nichols's contacts in the spirit world, including J. P. Greaves and Henry G. Wright, two of Alcott House's founders, revealed that they belonged to a spiritual league called the Spiritual Body or Heavenly Unity. They directed the Nicholses to form a Progressive Union for the development of higher spirits on earth. Beginning in 1854 or 1855 the Nicholses distributed a pamphlet describing the goals of the Progressive Union and requesting those interested to contact them. As with the variety list, members would be put in touch with one another. The Progressive Union, however, required that its members prepare themselves for harmonic society by quitting tobacco, eating only pure food, improving their manners, and saving their money to help establish the envisioned society. Progression in Harmony—that is, sex only when child-bearing was desired—was enjoined upon all members of the Union. "Friends," Thomas urged, "begin today. Do the first duty. Free yourself of any discordant or repulsive habit. Correct the first error."[25]

In 1855 Thomas traveled throughout Ohio and Michigan promoting the Progressive Union. "The men and women who are its members," he reported, ". . . are persons of great honesty and devotion; of moral worth, and, in many cases, of intellectual culture." He had been surprised to learn that many were wealthy. One member, a Baptist for twenty-five years, wrote from Wisconsin that "the last eighteen months have worked a revolution in my mind and enabled me, as I hope, to sail on the clear sea of Individualism." Thomas Nichols's own name stood at the top of the Progressive Union list, followed by Stephen Pearl Andrews's and several hundred other names of people who had devoted themselves to spiritual and physical purity.[26]

While networks established contacts among prospective free lovers, radicals could realize their agenda only by living together. The Nicholses intended the Progressive Union as a way of recruiting colonists for their community of Memnonia, to be established in Yellow Springs, Ohio. Yellow Springs was also the home of Antioch College, whose president, Horace Mann, viewed the coming of a free love community with alarm. Mann gathered considerable resistance to the Nicholses' venture, even after the School of Life was dedicated in April 1856. During June, however, a spiritualist ally of the Nicholses, J. B. Conklin, arrived in Yellow Springs and began holding seances and converting many of the town's residents. Soon many in the community sided with the Nicholses. Mann left for vacation that month, and the Nicholses took possession of their school in July.[27]

As should have been expected of the authors of Progression in Harmony and the founders of the Progressive Union, the Nicholses established a regimen at Memnonia that was far from giddy. Among the twenty residents were some water-cure patients and some students at the School of Life. All had to follow a strict diet. Those who wanted to attain harmony had first to practice continence during their ninety days of probation. Students practiced mutual criticism, discussed the great utopian writers, and attended Mary Nichols's daily seances. Also, in order to establish harmony at Memnonia, Thomas and Mary instituted a temporary despotism. "There must be, in the preparatory condition," Thomas explained, "the power of preventing or removing discord." In 1857, of course, the Nicholses joined the Roman Catholic Church, thus ending the short career of Memnonia.[28]

The structured life of Memnonia contrasts with what we know of the few other free love communities. Some of the members of the Wisconsin Phalanx had remained at Ceresco and continued to study radical doctrines and follow cooperative living, thereby making Ceresco "notorious as a centre of infidelity to fogyism in all its forms." James H. Cook moved there and helped run a boarding house on the cost principle. By 1856 residents planned to build a "Unitary Edifice" as a means of further combining their commercial interests. The community at that time rejected religious sectarianism, held seances, and recognized the sovereignty of each individual. The teachings of reason led them to believe "that entire affectional freedom with the elevation of woman to an equality with man is the natural safe and only exodus out of the evils consequent upon the present unhappy and repugnant relations of the sexes." Another resident agreed. "The legalized marriage institution is directly antagonistic to individual freedom, and those who submit to its yoke, can, at best, but be FREE IN PAIRS." He asserted that only social, political, religious, and affectional freedom could make a social experiment successful. These very attributes seem to have inspired intense hostility among Ceresco's neighbors, some of whom attacked the community at night, smashing windows and doors. Many of the community members left to protect their lives and property.[29]

The *Social Revolutionist*, which contributed so much to the western free love network, was the work of the Rising Star Community. This group began in 1853, apparently without commitment to any particular form of community life. "We hold to the doctrine of self-sovereignty in fraternal relations, with respect to property and the struggle for life," they announced in the first issue of the *Social Revolutionist*. At that time the group numbered only thirteen, including five children. They were farming 110 acres and owned four town lots in Stelvideo, Ohio, with a two-story frame house and a large steam mill. Each new member was expected to invest everything in the business; the original sum was guaranteed to the new member, but with no interest. Board was available at cost, and parents were responsible for their children. Only the community's equalitarian sentiments suggested official changes in marriage: "No distinctions are made between the sexes but such as spontaneously arise." John Patterson, writing from the community, explicitly linked the true freedom of women with the destruction of the "triple bulwark of despotisms": "The God-despot of the sects must be hurled from his throne; the superstitious rule of the bible must be set aside; and the despotism of marriage must be utterly extinguished."[30]

By the time the *Social Revolutionist* began publication in 1856, the Rising Star group was already considering forming a larger community with other free lovers in the Midwest. Communities congenial to free love were being organized in southern Minnesota and in Texas by

1855, but the advocates of a site in Ohio soon dominated the discussion. From perhaps as early as 1854, Francis Barry encouraged other radicals to join him in Berlin Heights, a township forty-five miles west of Cleveland originally settled by New Englanders. Berlin Heights had an active spiritualist group and opened its public hall even to radical lecturers. One resident of the village remembered Barry as "an oily, plausible fellow, who had some good points about him." As it became clear that the newcomers advocated beliefs that the townspeople both hated and feared, tension arose between the two groups. "Marriage, they said," reported an eyewitness, "was a fraud, and the cause of all the unhappiness in the world, and we were great fools for clinging to it."[31]

The eyewitness may have been understating the language used by the free lovers who came to Berlin Heights. "Marriage," wrote Francis Barry, "we shall destroy. We shall then obey our attractions." Very likely he minced few words in his lectures or in conversations with his neighbors. We have already heard Barry thundering against both God and government. One of his companions at Berlin Heights was equally forthright in his atheism and anarchism. "Atheism," wrote J. K. Moore, "is the system of ATTRACTION—of supply and demand. Godism is the CLAIMING, FORCING system. Marriage is a branch." One wonders if he discussed topics with his neighbors as freely as he did in the columns of the *Social Revolutionist*. If so, we can imagine a talk concluding in this way: "Now, bigot, conservative, what have you to fear? Only that you can't be scoundrels, monopolists, libertines, oppressors, aristocrats, and perpetuate your vice. Farewell God."[32]

Late in 1856 radicals gathered at Berlin Heights to discuss the prospects for a free love community. One group purchased ninety acres, where they established a farm. Both James H. Cook and Thomas Wright moved to Berlin Heights from Ceresco. Although in 1857 the free lovers purchased the hotel in town and used it as a common home and visitors' inn for other free lovers, they never viewed the former Davis House as a substitute phalanstery. The Berlin Heights settlement coalesced around the ideas of individual sovereignty, equitable commerce, women's rights, and free love. There was no attempt to order the lives of the colony according to any master plan. "In regard to organization," Barry insisted, "the less the better." In addition to the group at the farm, smaller groups purchased separate lots and followed their own paths to individuality and spirituality. The Berlin Heights free lovers rejected marriage as simply and completely as possible. "Believers in marriage . . . will not come among us," Barry wrote, "for fear of losing their 'property'." He continued with a challenge: "Those however who have faith, that the 'one-love' will be secure where attraction is recognized as law, we shall of course, welcome. But I warn them that 'variety in love' will be the result."[33]

The first convention at Berlin Heights alerted the more conventional residents that not only were radicals among them but that their numbers might soon grow. A meeting was held at the Presbyterian church to denounce the free lovers. Joseph Treat arose to reply on behalf of the free love community to the charge of licentiousness. "I am thirty years old," he concluded his short speech, "and I have never yet carnally known a woman. Can anyone of you, who persecute me, say as much?" The meeting quickly turned into a debate on the merits of free love, with those believing in fair play happy to leave the marriage radicals alone. S. J. Finney, a spiritualist lecturer, turned the tide in favor of respecting the free lovers' rights: "so long as they obey the laws, their opinions are their own."[34] This split between the opponents of free love and those who believed in tolerance would persist in the community for years to come.

A second free love convention in August 1857 (also in Berlin Heights) seems to have cemented the decision on the part of the Rising Star group to move to Berlin Heights. For some of the town's monogamous residents, this was too much. They convened a second meeting to oppose free love, and this time barred the free lovers from attending and blasted spiritualism as well as free love. Free lovers had no moral right to be in Berlin Heights, the meeting declared, adding that the radicals labored "under a state of partial insanity, caused by disappointed hopes and blasted expectations, by an inordinate love of notoriety and other causes unknown or unnecessary to mention." Children of the free love community were barred from the township's school, forcing the free lovers to form their own school.[35]

Those who opposed free love were ready to do more than merely condemn it. In November several free lovers were arrested for immorality; among these were E. S. Tyler and Mary Lewis. Sheriff's depu-

Davis House Hotel.
Radicals attending the 1857 free love convention in Berlin Heights packed the
hotel, where Sophronia Powers acted as hostess. Two young lawyers from a
nearby town arrived to have a look through the rooms, hoping to witness free
love rites or to find temporary companions. Sophronia Powers confronted
them on the upper landing, telling them that they were invading the privacy
of her guests. When they offered to pay for accommodations and companionship, she said, "You infernal fools, get out of here. I am not furnishing
company for idiots." She grabbed their collars and threw them down the
stairs. The hotel was later purchased by E. S. Tyler, but his scheme for a
water-cure establishment fell through.

QUOTE FROM ALVIN WARREN, "REMINISCENCES OF BERLIN HEIGHTS," Our New
Humanity 1 [JUNE 1896]. PHOTO COURTESY OF THE HAYES PRESIDENTIAL CENTER
CHARLES E. FROHMAN COLLECTION, FREMONT, OHIO.

ties took the free lovers to the county seat in Sandusky. They were
allowed bail and lived comfortably at a local hotel during the weeklong
trial. The conclusion of the case involved several different judg-

ments. Five of the free lovers were released on their own recognizance when they promised to leave the county. Tyler was required to give a quit-claim deed to the Davis House and was allowed to return to Berlin Heights only long enough to finish his business. Mary Lewis was returned to her husband. The press of the *Social Revolutionist* was to be removed from the hotel. And the farm, where many of the free lovers lived, was foreclosed and put up for sale by the sheriff. The obvious intent of these judgments was to force the free lovers out of the community. "The Free Love organization of Berlin," reported the Sandusky newspaper, "may therefore be regarded as essentially defunct. We heartily congratulate the people of that township on the result. They are relieved of a monstrous nuisance, and shocking social enormity." [36]

The Sandusky paper underestimated the free lovers. The radicals stood fast and even printed a November issue of the *Social Revolutionist* on the press, which had been moved to the farm. The radicals, it seems, had underestimated the antipathy toward them in Berlin Heights. Frank Barry took the papers into town to mail. As Barry hitched his horse, two men took hold of him, as a "gang of infuriated women, hissed on by their owners," seized the packages on his wagon and made a bonfire of them. [37] By the end of 1857, the free lovers in Berlin Heights had thus faced both legal and informal violence. Without property or much sympathy in the village, some of the radicals decided to leave. They had not, however, been defeated; they merely staged a strategic withdrawal.

During the winter and spring of 1858 the free lovers slowly returned. They leased and then purchased a water-cure site and grist mill; others came to live at the water-cure establishment, and the group was soon milling wheat. By summer they had built two or three houses and were buying more land. Ready cash seems to have calmed the scruples of those they did business with and undermined a plan to force them out by isolating them. One of the leaders of the opposition, for instance, abandoned the isolation plan when he found that the free love flour was cheaper than competing brands. Other opponents of the free lovers advocated violence, and rumors of mobs from Huron, Sandusky, and Norwalk circulated during the summer. The radicals had learned their lesson. They set up a system of signal guns to warn of an approaching attack and began making preparations to meet force with force. C. M. Overton issued a stern warning that attacks on free lovers "will be the precursor of certain death to some of our enemies as well as to us." Even peace-loving Francis Barry bought a shotgun, "and for the first time in his life, set himself to work investigating the philosophy of its construction and the mode of its operation." This time no mobs appeared.[38]

Although the Berlin Heights free lovers established their community in spite of the hostility of their neighbors, they still faced difficulties. The Cleveland *Herald* reported in 1858 that the fifty to sixty free lovers in Berlin Heights were becoming bolder. A small group of them enjoyed swimming naked, a practice that brought down the censure of both neighbors and fellow radicals. Charles Latchar, a young man who worked on the *Age of Freedom*, committed suicide. He left a note that cursed marriage, religion, and "God, the Father-Master." "The poor wretch was undoubtedly in a morbid state of mind," commented the New York *Herald*, "produced by the wild vagaries of the Berlin Heights people."[39]

Occasionally a wife or husband who had abandoned a husband or wife sought refuge in the community. Two such incidents were reported in the Detroit *Free Press*, revealing something of the practice of free love at Berlin Heights and the relationship between free lovers and their neighbors. In one story, a man discovered that his missing wife had gone to Berlin Heights and immediately set out after her. The woman returned willingly, stating that she was "disgusted with the scenes enacted in that abode of wretchedness." Another woman saw this article and wrote to the *Free Press* that her husband had left home three years before and "roamed around in search of free-love companions" with whom he went to live in Berlin Heights. Apparently, free love at Berlin Heights, as at Modern Times, served as an informal divorce. Husbands and wives who despaired of their marriages could invest their hope in the free affection that purportedly existed on the shores of Lake Erie. Merritt Hunter told his wife he was leading a pure life at Berlin Heights. The wife who had left her husband had a different experience, reporting that she was subjected to "low-bred familiarities with vulgar, fanatical men . . . and a close familiarity with a brutish, criminal, enjoyment, which was the highest sphere aimed at in this delectable community."[40] It also seems that the authorities made no attempt to invade Berlin but allowed husbands and wives to work out their own problems and establish their own separations.

If the enforcers of middle-class culture left the Berlin free lovers alone, they had reasons other than providing a last resort for hopeless marriages. The free lovers worked hard and seem to have slowly established good relations with their neighbors. Free love author and editor James Clay built a store where free lovers came to dance and talk on Sundays. The grist mill, box factory, and fruit business operated by various free lovers all prospered.[41] One Berlin Heights resident recalled many years later:

As a matter of fact, the members of the community though dreamers, were conspicuous for intelligence, industry and good citizenship. They were men who read and thought and gave consideration to the possible improvement of the present state of society. In their hands the waste places of the town became its garden spots. They were the pioneers in various industrial enterprises. They were quiet and law-abiding; and not least among their virtues was their capacity for thinking well of others and minding their own business.[42]

A story that is even more revealing of the convergence of middle-class values with the free love viewpoint concerns a social occasion. The musicians who played for the free love dances invited a group of marriage radicals to a dance in nearby East Townsend. Aware that free lovers would be attending, many who felt particularly hostile to the radicals stayed away. Among those who came, however, were some men who believed that they could woo the free love women. "Conspicuous among them," recalled a free lover, "were the representatives of a class who always on such occasions carry a bottle of whiskey in their pockets." For a time the free lovers, "by their dignified and prudent behavior," managed to avoid any unpleasant incidents. When drunkenness finally overcame the meager scruples of one of the sports, he introduced himself to a free love woman "and began abruptly making familiar advances to her." She immediately called for her wrap and announced to her friends "that they had gotten into bad company, and the thing to be done was to get out of it." The entire free love group departed together.[43]

Like their neighbors, the free lovers demanded respectable behavior, individual responsibility, hard work, thrift, and privacy. Those who violated the decorum expected of the middle class lost status both in the dominant culture and among free lovers. The free lovers, it seems, were good bourgeois in everything except their attitude toward society and marriage.

Free lovers in the early 1850s who had inherited the vestiges of Fourierist and harmonialist organization began to establish their own social and cultural forms. The vigorous polemics of these years helped develop a free love ideology and to define its separation from middle-class culture. This ideology attacked evangelical Protestantism, government, commerce, and marriage, while the networks and communities that carried and promoted these ideas built alternative forms of social interaction. Spiritualism or agnosticism replaced the Christian denominations; sovereignty of the individual redefined republicanism; equitable commerce made capitalism irrelevant; and free love repudiated marriage. By the end of the 1850s, with substantial communities at Modern Times and Berlin Heights and a network that carried the debates and news of the marriage abolitionists, free love constituted a small, but vigorous, counterculture within American society.

The counterculture not only existed within a context provided by the dominant culture but expressed itself most forcefully in ways that it either derived from or shared with the dominant culture. Middle-class reformers, like those who met at Rutland, Vermont, in 1858, generally disapproved of free love. However, they saw it as a topic emerging from the comprehensive reform of society, and one that needed to be carefully discussed even if eventually rejected. Conservatives might be more intemperate in their damnation of free love, but they shared with free lovers the belief in uncontrollable passion. For most Americans free love was a legitimate, if horrifying, topic for discussion. The means of discussion proceeded in ways familiar to Americans, such as lectures, journals, conventions, and correspondence to newspapers and periodicals. The institutions of free love—networks based upon the journals, clubs, and communities—all existed within American society. The counterculture, then, depended upon the dominant culture for the forms that expressed it. For their part, defenders of the dominant culture could hardly unite to demand the extirpation of groups that so frequently mirrored American society.

CHAPTER 6

Free Love Portraits

Free love was an attack on the middle-class ideal of marriage. Whether it was expressed in the words of Fourierism or of individual sovereignty, criticism of marriage shaped every aspect of the free love ideology. While free lovers gained allies in the women's movement and spiritualism, their insistence upon the abolition of marriage also separated free lovers from other reformers. This chapter will examine the lives of several free lovers to determine what personal experiences led to an overriding commitment to the destruction of marriage.

The story of free love at Berlin Heights offered two complementary pictures of the relationship between the free love counterculture and the dominant culture. On the one hand, the two groups traded attacks. According to the respectable citizens of Berlin Heights, free lovers suffered from licentiousness and insanity. Free lovers, for their part, saw the defenders of monogamy as fogies, bigots, and libertines. Such sharply divided opinions, however, obscured the capacity of the two groups to live together. The free lovers, like many of their neighbors in Berlin Heights, valued hard work, respected independence, and paid their bills. The tension between free lovers and their opponents involved both repulsion and attraction—both sides saw in the other something horrifying and something desirable.

We catch a glimpse of this double vision in the *New York Daily Times* exposé of the Free Love Club. The reporter who infiltrated the Club described both the free love man and the free love woman. The free love man was hairy and bearded, was dressed carelessly, but had clean teeth and bathed frequently. Though often learned and well-spoken, a free love man was inevitably a "rabid socialist." The woman dressed simply, without lacing and with little makeup. She was strong-minded, enjoyed the company of men, and knew something of phonography, Swedenborg, and spiritualism. Like her male counterpart, she was clean and tidy.[1] Although these descriptions carry a sarcastic tone, they conform to what we know of individual free lovers—the man described could have been Francis Barry or Stephen Pearl Andrews; the woman might have been Mary Gove Nichols. Whether the reporter's impressions were accurate or merely stereotyped, what he saw when he looked at the free lovers were people who had adopted the dress reforms and personal hygiene preached by Graham, Alcott, and other hygienic reformers. The women displayed the independence of thought and life that women's rights advocates promoted. The topics they discussed frequently found their way into the parlors of businessmen. In almost every respect, free lovers represented elements of middle-class culture that had developed during the early nineteenth century.

An equally interesting exercise is to recall how Thomas Nichols described the members of the Progressive Union whom he recruited during 1855. He claimed that they were men and women of honesty and devotion, "or moral worth, and, in many cases, of intellectual culture." He even found that many were wealthy.[2] While we can be no more certain of Thomas Nichols's claims than we can be of the reporter's, this free love self-portrait suggests the middle-class aspect of the movement. Nichols expected members of the Progressive Union to be highly virtuous and to purify themselves—or, in other terms, to build character. The goal of the Union was to establish in Ohio the ideal society, including the perfected sexual relations that many Americans—Fourierists, health reformers, and spiritualists—had so far sought in vain.

Examining the lives of several prominent free lovers will add detail to the free love portrait. Four men—Stephen Pearl Andrews, Marx Edgeworth Lazarus, James Arrington Clay, and Austin Kent—played important roles in articulating and spreading the free love ideology.

After examining these four men and developing some insights into their relationship to middle-class culture, we will consider the problem of women in the movement by looking at the life of Mary Gove Nichols. In this way we can see in particular instances how elements of middle-class identity could be transformed into a free love identity.

Andrews, Lazarus, Clay, Kent

The two men who first made free love an issue provide interesting contrasts. Stephen Pearl Andrews was one of the oldest free lovers, born in 1812, the son of a Baptist minister in Templeton, Massachusetts. After attending Amherst Academy, Andrews went south to teach Latin and study law; he was a successful lawyer in Louisiana and Texas before becoming involved in antislavery work. Marx Lazarus's father Aaron was a wealthy Jewish merchant in Wilmington, North Carolina. Lazarus, born in 1822, was one of the youngest of the prewar free lovers. Lazarus studied at the University of North Carolina in 1838 then traveled north to Philadelphia to study medicine. In the North, Lazarus was swept away by the ideas of Fourierism. He lived at the Brook Farm Phalanx while working on the *Harbinger* with George Ripley and made a will directing that his estate be administered for the advancement of association. Since both Lazarus and Andrews participated in the Fourierist and reformist circles of New York City during the 1840s, they undoubtedly knew one another.[3]

We know much less about the backgrounds of James Clay and Austin Kent. Kent was born about 1811, probably in upstate New York. Trained for the ministry, he became an activist for both antislavery and nonresistance during the 1830s. In 1852 he observed that a large and growing number of people opposed dual marriage and that they were just now gaining the liberty to speak. At the beginning of a series of letters advocating free love during 1854, Kent called himself "one of the oldest believers of the main principle of the Free-love doctrine." Kent's free love had grown partially out of his study of phrenology, which revealed to him the higher levels of the human mind. In addition, the New Testament doctrine of "love your neighbor as yourself" had guided his researches. "It was in sounding this to its deep, full and universal or *unlimited* meaning, that I was converted to my present view of Christian Chastity." All sexual love, he concluded, that elevated the mind and affection was pure and chaste. It seems that Kent took seriously his own beliefs. He wrote to the *Social Revolutionist* in 1857: "I have had some experience as to the workings of freedom in love." That same year his book *Free Love* appeared, setting out in detail his arguments for free love.[4]

Kent's 1857 letter also included warnings against the kind of permanent community that the *Social Revolutionist* editors were promoting. James Clay, on the other hand, was a committed communitarian. Clay was born in 1814 and grew up in Gardiner, Maine, with such bad habits as hard drink, tobacco, and eating meat. He received an education only to the age of fourteen, when he had to go to work in a tavern. Clay gave up his vices in the course of his spiritual development and also adopted the practice of bathing daily. A student of reform and a believer in association, Clay edited two periodicals, *David's Sling* and *Eastern Light*, while he searched for a suitable community. His wife, unfortunately, had no desire to leave her home to live with strangers, and James Clay reluctantly abided by her decision. Clay came to believe that government based upon force was evil. Only by life in association, in which wealth was roughly equal and each possessed his own land, could harmony be created. Whether or not he was inspired by Warren, his thinking was in many respects identical to Warren's. "Absolute, individual, perpetual freedom from any external statute law," wrote Clay in 1856, "is my unalienable right, more sacred to me than my material life."[5]

More than just an extension of his anarchist beliefs, free love for James Clay was the basic reform that would end inequality in wealth because charity would be extended to all. "Freedom in love is to result in the universality of love, and a community of love, which is to be followed by a community of property, which is to be founded in truth, on a community of interests in each other's life and happiness." Like other free lovers, he believed that all relations between men and women could be purified by freedom from the compulsion to marry. Just such a purified relationship sent him to the Augusta town jail. Clay discovered a passional affinity for a young woman, Maria Cole, and the two were soon living and sleeping together. Not surprisingly, Clay's wife left him; what is surprising is that Clay and Cole never had sex.

Arrested and tried for adultery, Clay was exonerated when an examination showed that Maria Cole was still a virgin. The local authorities persisted, however, charging both with lewd and licentious conduct. Although Clay paid Maria Cole's fine, he served out his own sentence of six months, assuring his accusers, "I know and obey a higher law than your smoky volumes have record of, or your smoky men of courts can understand." In prison he wrote *A Voice from Prison*, making a sustained case against government and marriage. After his release Clay lived at Modern Times for several years before moving around 1860 to Berlin Heights.[6]

Even these brief biographies suggest interesting relationships between free lovers and the developing middle-class culture. Three of these four men would have been young adults (and the youngest a child) in 1830. They grew up during the period that Whitney Cross characterized as the triumph of ultraism. Antislavery was coming under the influence of Garrisonian immediate emancipation, temperance reform was turning into teetotalism, and health reform was spreading ideas of sexual continence and personal purity. The reform movements that were essential to the emerging middle class in these years were formative influences for free lovers and became important elements of their personal identity. All four aspired to positions in the new middle class, working their way into the four liberal professions: Andrews the lawyer, Lazarus the doctor, Kent the minister, Clay the editor. The brave new bourgeois world was not foreign to them but something they helped define. At least until the 1850s, the future free lovers probably felt that they were not attacking but helping to perfect society. The consolidation of the middle class after 1848, including a return to orthodox Protestantism, confidence in the state and economy, and a more pragmatic attitude toward reform, suddenly left the radicals in the margins of a culture they had formerly led.

Attitudes toward reform during the prewar years were essentially religious. Young Jacksonian evangelicals identified both their own internal chaos and injustice in society as sin. In personal and social reform they could objectify sin and attack it. Conversion also brought them into Christian denominations, where sin was a cosmic problem with the cosmic solution of the final destruction of evil on the Day of Judgment. Free lovers entered reform movements early in their lives and worked enthusiastically for reform, following the path of many who rose into the middle class. But reform implies that limited social change is desirable and possible, a faith that many found less persuasive during the 1840s. Like perfectionists, frustrated radicals came to recognize that many desirable changes were impossible without a total reorganization of society, beginning with its most basic elements. Where most members of the middle class accepted these imperfections and turned their energies to other reforms or to private life in the 1850s, free lovers adopted systems that set them at odds with the middle class. This was because free lovers found reform without conversion; they discovered sin without grace. Consequently, in confronting the evils of society they found that American society could not be saved.

Evangelical Protestantism had touched every one of these free lovers, yet none of them accepted the Christian solution to sin. Though an ordained minister, Kent spoke of Protestantism as a desirable social movement. "Protestants profess to believe," he wrote, "in leaving every man's religion—whether pure or impure, true or false—*free*, except when and where it trespasses on a like freedom in others." For Kent, Christianity was an ideal social state in which all people and both sexes would be "equal, free and independent." Clay claimed to be a Baptist, but Christianity appealed to him not because of his faith but because it conformed to philosophical principles and the laws of nature. He certainly would have had trouble finding other Baptists who agreed with what he called his religious sentiment, "which is love, free and universal, and . . . extend it to the sexual relations with such 'bonds' as I choose to place myself under, or no bond, whatever . . . other than those He who creates all life places me under."[7]

The two free lovers whose early lives we know best both struggled with and rejected evangelical conversion. Andrews's father taught his youngest and favorite son the fine points of philosophy and metaphysics, and the entire family urged and prayed for his conversion as he grew older. By the age of eleven or twelve, Stephen Pearl hoped for the millennium to remove the necessity of his dying. Again and again he felt that he was undergoing conversion, but he failed to present himself for membership in the church for fear of the ridicule of his friends. Aware of the grave consequences of denying Christ, Andrews spent his nights "given up to tears and suppressed wailings over my terrible and hopeless condition." His desire for conversion continued until the end of his youth, when events took his life in another direction. Andrews never completed his manuscript autobiography, but he hinted at the sources of his disillusion in speaking of the excesses of the Methodist camp meeting he attended in Louisiana and of the meager comfort derived from religion by those facing death during an epidemic of congestive fever.[8]

It is not clear what finally decided Andrews against accepting salvation according to the evangelical Protestants with whom he lived and in whose culture he was immersed. Andrews, like Kent, spoke glowingly of Protestantism, but Protestantism as a political movement like democracy and socialism—"identical in the assertion of the Supremacy of the Individual." Andrews's references to God abstracted the notion of deity from Christian dogmas such as the Trinity, incarnation, and atonement. On the other hand, Andrews was profoundly affected by his struggle with conversion. Recalling his adolescence, he wrote:

I was myself deeply penetrated by the spirit of Christianity, had earnest wrestlings of the soul for forgiveness, which were at times terrible, I still can say that my constant feeling was one of deep gratitude to Almighty God for all the blessings with which my life was crowned.

Such intense emotions would be unlikely to disappear even if their initial object were rejected. Andrews testified to the importance for his later life of this inner struggle:

I always confess that I look with a sort of pity upon those of my friends who have grown up among the influences of a more liberal . . . Christianity or among infidels, and who have thus escaped the terrible array of the forces of the mind in deadly conflict with each other as in [illegible] the young catechumen under the teachings of the older and sterner forms of the Christian faith.[9]

Although Marx Edgeworth Lazarus's parents were Jewish, his mother Rachel had converted to Christianity. Consequently, Marx's education included instruction in both the Jewish and Christian religions, with his mother (and her brother and sister after Rachel's death) trying to convert him. In a short sketch of his life written in the 1870s, Lazarus identified this conflict between the two traditions as the beginnings of his anarchism. He could never entirely accept either system but came to see the flaws in both. Like Andrews, however, Lazarus would ultimately reject Christianity but accept other elements of evangelical culture. Lazarus's first book, published in 1851, was divided into two parts. The titles, "Trinity" and "Incarnation," seem like recantations of his Jewish heritage. In these short works, Lazarus used terms that were unmistakably Christian: "that incarnation of the divine nature once fulfilled in Jesus Christ," the "Divine Spirit poured out at Pentecost," and "Atonement." Yet placing these terms into context reveals the object of Lazarus's devotion. The incarnation once fulfilled in Jesus, Lazarus wrote, "must receive a collective and social fulfillment in Christian societies, wherein we shall all be truly members, one of another." At Pentecost thousands were converted "to the truth, filled with the spirit of fraternity, reciprocity, voluntary association." [10]

Lazarus had converted not to Christianity but to Fourierism and to middle-class culture. In becoming thoroughly enamored of and integrated into the reform subculture in Philadelphia, New York City, and New England, Lazarus adopted the language, perhaps even the beliefs, of a kind of generalized evangelicalism that used Christian theology to comprehend social evil. Like the transcendentalists he admired, Lazarus's theology encompassed all religious symbols that showed mankind's need for harmony. He spoke of the "sublime worship of Mithraic Christianity, which adores the Soul of Nature and sees in the Sun the Spherical Chief, and in Christ the Solar Man." In the Combined Order of Fourier's vision, he predicted, all will know the Lord. Nearly thirty years later Lazarus spoke of Jesus as the first anarchist. [11]

To the extent that free lovers had any kind of religion it was spiritualism. For some it was simply an interesting phenomenon; for others it was the fount of all truth. Marx Lazarus agreed that spiritual affinities reigned in the next life but recommended that we leave the "supramundanes to fight their own battles and make their own laws." His manuscript autobiography recalled walks during his youth when he wished to meet spirits. He never met any. Austin Kent, on the other hand, claimed to have been a spiritualist from the early 1840s, probably referring to experiments with mesmerism and clairvoyance, and to have communicated with the dead from the late 1850s. After the Civil

Marx Edgeworth Lazarus (1822–1895).
Although Lazarus saw his writings on free love as extensions of Fourier's ideas, by the time he wrote the book that ignited the first public free love controversy, Fourierism was rapidly dwindling in importance. Lazarus had little connection with the free love network of the 1850s.

COURTESY OF THE LABADIE COLLECTION, DEPARTMENT OF RARE BOOKS AND SPE-CIAL COLLECTIONS, UNIVERSITY OF MICHIGAN LIBRARY.

War, Lazarus contributed to anarchist journals while Kent wrote for spiritualist papers.[12]

Although none of these four free lovers was an atheist, several prominent free lovers were, and it is essential to briefly discuss them. The radical's rejection of social sham grew primarily out of religious experiences and retained a fervor that simple intellectual conviction could never match. From Andrews and Lazarus, we can see that free love was one possible result of the inner struggle over religious questions; atheism was another. In his recent work on the emergence of unbelief, James Turner has identified the religious roots of agnosticism, showing that men and women of the second half of the nineteenth century progressively rejected the contradictions between their understanding of morality and the character of God as portrayed by church leaders and the Bible. Speaking of this contradiction, James Clay wrote, "Many are so unwise as to think, if we reject one part of the Bible, we also reject the simple truths of nature which are recorded in another part of the book." Clay still believed in God, but men like Francis Barry, Joseph Treat, and J. K. Moore took rejection of Protestant orthodoxy further. Treat wrote that he knew "no greater truth, than for men to be told, there is no God." Yet nineteenth-century atheism was a distinctly religious attitude, as Turner has shown, and would have required intense soul-searching. Treat, for instance, seems to have been a Christian perfectionist in the early 1850s, thus making his pilgrimage to atheism and free love simultaneous, if not identical.[13]

Most free lovers simply reconstructed God, placing him further out of the picture and making priestly duplicity the enemy of both reform and true divinity. C. M. Overton, for instance, blasted "the great conservative institutions of the age—Marriage, Slavery, and Brimstone." But he did not reject God simply because the churches had painted a picture of Him as a slaveholder, aristocrat, and tyrant. As the Creator of movement from primal nonexistence, God was the first radical and reformers needed to recapture this understanding of Him from the church and from its child, the state. "The gods must be regenerated," declared Overton, "before men can be!" One of the small groups at Berlin Heights was led by C. M. Overton and was devoted to religious exercises in order to overcome accepted notions about God and the Bible: "The Christ *principle* was the Christ with them."[14]

There is no record of their relationship with the atheist circle around Francis Barry, but it was probably warm. All free lovers seem to have been earnestly seeking religious truth. As children growing up during the Second Great Awakening, they would have been unusual if they had not. What was unusual is the result of their search.

Rejection of evangelical Christianity separated free lovers from the bourgeois self-definition that they had helped shape. Free lovers absorbed ideas of hygiene and purity and worked to build the ideal of true love and social harmony. Like their contemporaries, free lovers valued character and feared the spread of artificiality. But unlike reformers and conservatives, free lovers lacked a cosmology that resolved the contradiction between desired ideals and present evil. The convert to evangelical Protestantism could accept profound flaws in society, knowing that these would be swept away in heaven or in the millennium. Free lovers relied more upon the socialist rhetoric of Owen and Fourier that pointed to the kind of practical transcendence that a Berlin Heights free lover declared near the end of the century: "The kingdom of heaven is already within the grasp of any who are fitted to appreciate it." [15] As the Fourier movement fell apart and the division between the ideal and the reality of social reform became more apparent during the 1850s, free lovers abandoned American society, damned it as artificial, and called for the end of the immoral world of ante-bellum America and for the creation of a new order. This transformation of the free lovers' religious values into social visions and personal disciplines is clear in the areas of artificiality, purity, and courtship.

Middle-class Americans in the 1830s and 1840s struggled to determine what was genuine because they sensed that disharmony resulted from falsehood. Soft money robbed the country of prosperity; demagogues snatched political rights from the farmer and mechanic. In the same way, counterfeit people, whether rakes or gold diggers, devalued social relations and snapped the bonds of personal reliability. In Mary Gove's story "The Artist," Sophia Wilton replies to her mother's comment that Mr. Montague "bears an excellent character," by saying, "So may anyone who goes to church and is able to pay for private apartments to drink and gamble in." Montague endangered polite society and virtuous people by appearing to be what he was not. This fear of the artificial sent young men and women to the bookshops for manuals on etiquette to learn unaffected behavior and how to detect falsified respectability.[16] Their evangelicalism augmented their fear of artificiality. The tendency of Protestantism had been to eschew form and artifice in religion for direct experience. Evangelical conversion made mere appearance seem contemptible.

For free lovers, artificiality was so grave a problem that it caused them to despair of society. Stephen Pearl Andrews wrote, "If the close combination of interests is artificial or forced, then the parties exist toward each other in false relations, and to false relations no true principles can apply." This meant that all of society was irrational. Andrews agreed with Greeley that government had to forcibly restrain lunatics and criminals, but only "as the temporary necessity of a false and bad social system, which *makes* such characters, and must, therefore, take care of them." This same conspiracy of lies made marriage in its image. "The laws," wrote James Clay, "not only endeavor to hold together what God has not joined, but put asunder what he *has* joined."[17]

Lazarus came much closer than other free lovers to formulating the central problem of society in terms of alienation, which for him was the separation of the individual from the life of the instincts (or passional affinities, in Fourier's terms). The resulting social forms kept the malfunctioning and malformed individuals in line and in their place as they were used for society's own purposes. In 1851, Lazarus wrote:

Cities act as social and industrial maelstroms, absorbing from a periphery of hundreds of miles the number of beings necessary to be used up in factories and workshops, and then deposited in warehouses, or folded away on shelves in the shape of lead, glass, cloths, knives, and various fabrics, traceable through every step of the transformation from the raw human material.

Marriage was fundamental to social disorganization. "Civilization," Lazarus wrote in his Fourierist terminology, "is a state of permanent conflicts, an organization of civil war, and its pivotal character is marriage, which *aims* to abstract at last one element of life from the general shock and wreck of individual destinies."[18]

The heightened sense of social falsehood and disharmony that free lovers expressed points directly to the source of their separation from the middle class. For Theodore Weld or Horace Greeley, society contained grave flaws that required strong measures. During the 1840s

Lazarus and Andrews, along with Brisbane and the Fourierist establishment, believed that industrial associations would gradually redeem
American society. By the 1850s the free lovers had so lost faith in
American society that remedial measures seemed futile; the entire
system had to be remade. It was at this time that the insights of
individual sovereignty offered the simplest and most comprehensive
solution to society's malaise. Evangelicals, transcendentalists, and marriage advisers already viewed society as collections of married couples
and families struggling to save their souls and reform their lives.
Reformers with such preparation readily perceived the utility of what
Warren called "disintegration," the ending of all nonvoluntary relationships. Stephen Pearl Andrews believed that men naturally loved order,
justice, and harmony and that this was the reason they put up with
government. Similarly, they naturally loved their children and sought
unions of true affection, so they put up with marriage and the family.
Austin Kent insisted during the 1870s that "only Free-Love . . . can
save our civilization from its sexual corruptions, its rottenness, and its
horrible running sores, both in and out of marriage."[19]

Kent's plea for the genuineness of free love also included his assumption that artificiality led to sexual excess. Purity was essential to social
harmony. Clay believed that free love would "teach purity of person,
and the race are to be taught the legitimate uses of the sexual organs,
of which they are now so misinformed." Lazarus expressed the search
for purity in its most cosmic form. "Health," he wrote, ". . . is something more than a dietetic code of rules for private use; it is the entire
harmony of man with his planet and his universe; not a scheme of
individual evasion, to dodge the common evil, but a theory of integral
or social redemption."[20]

Personal cleanliness was a matter of morality. Honesty, benevolence, industriousness, and economy were important virtues, wrote
one radical author, but "these qualities will not make life happy, unless
there be added to them a deportment at once dignified and unobtru-
sive, and a freedom from noisy, dirty and disagreeable habits." He
went on to recommend bathing the whole body (including the parts
covered by clothing), brushing teeth, and quiet and orderly conduct.
The connection between personal cleanliness and virtue grew out of
middle-class health reform. Water-cure enthusiasts had popularized

the belief that bathing cured most sickness, so that many doctors recommended cold or tepid baths and water-cure health resorts became an important industry. Bathing, like other activities recommended by early nineteenth-century medical advisers, required a discipline that would order the individual life.[21] And the ordered life was the virtuous life.

Bathing implied more than merely physical health. Young bourgeois must have connected bathing with the discipline of sexual continence that required a careful scrutiny of all one's thoughts and desires. Bathing also resembled the ritual of baptism, the sacrament that first joins the individual to the Christian faith. James Clay, for instance, called himself a devout Baptist, though this might have been a pun about his daily bathing. He was quite serious, though, in claiming that daily bathing prepared one for spiritual rebirth. Stephen Pearl Andrews thought that free love resulted from the development of truly religious natures, not through the exhortations of preachers but through natural developments. Those who became capable of free love experienced a second birth. Surely Andrews's use of the evangelical term of rebirth resonated with Jesus's words that those who entered the Kingdom of God must be born again through water and spirit.[22] Free lovers seem to have had strong religious convictions without religion. Consequently, they tended to move from one spiritual verity to another. What remained constant was their belief that purity of person—outer purity in cleanliness, personal purity of action, inner purity of thought —was essential to salvation, that is, to a higher development of life and thought.

Perhaps the crisis of conversion explains not only the eventual repudiation of the compromises of society and marriage but also the form of relationships that free lovers prescribed. Both Lazarus and Andrews indicate that the confusion they felt over religion was related to their developing understanding of sexuality. Andrews recalled that at about the age of sixteen he virtually worshiped one of the girls in his father's congregation. When she converted and began urging him to confess Christ, his feelings as both her admirer and an infidel were excruciating. Clearly courtship and conversion were joined in Andrews's mind. Lazarus went into no such details of his own life. As he grew older, however, his religious doubts were never resolved until he recognized that he could direct his adoration toward women; then religion rushed upon him.[23] For both men, frustrated religious longings led to an increased idealization of women. The concurrence of the spiritual crisis with the beginning of adolescent courtship provided the occasion.

This may explain the continuing importance of courtship to adult free lovers, who believed that those in love must be constantly courting one another. Warren Chase, for instance, felt that after marriage husbands and wives should continue courting. Those who admitted to being free lovers merely removed the necessity of marriage. A writer in the *Social Revolutionist* thought that men who were free would be more completely satisfied and so continue to court their wives throughout their lives. "All of our affectional needs should be supplied. What one cannot give, it is not only our right, but our duty, to seek in another." Another writer referred to the period of courtship as the time when love blossoms, and to marriage as the time when it fades. Stephen Pearl Andrews recalled that as a young man he noticed how marriage put an end to romance. "Many times as a boy I experienced sensations of sadness when an attendant on weddings, far more depressing than those which occurred to my mind when present at funerals." Even John Humphrey Noyes believed that in his perfectionist communities courtship should be the model for all sexual relations. James Clay's free love relationship, one of the few we have any details about, suggested the rural bundling of early nineteenth-century courtship rather than marriage. Clay asserted that he rarely found anyone who answered "no" when asked, "were not your days before marriage the happiest you ever experienced?" "Then love was enjoyed in freedom," Clay explained, "there were no bonds; and no little acts of kindness or courtesy, that would render each other more happy, was [*sic*] overlooked. Alike might be the result throughout life in freedom."[24]

It is hardly surprising that the period of courtship should be fondly remembered. For those who reached adulthood in the early nineteenth century, adolescence was a time of great freedom in relations between the sexes, especially for women. While young people in the cities and towns had largely abandoned bundling by the 1830s, couples still sat up together until late at night or until early morning at the girl's home. American girls were noted for having several beaux and for shame-

James Arrington Clay (b. 1814).
Clay disrupted his marriage and scandalized his home town when he took a young woman into his home and apparently into his bed. Clay insisted that their love was pure. Since a court-ordered examination showed Maria Cole to be a virgin, the relationship between Clay and Cole was probably chaste.

FRONTISPIECE, JAMES A. CLAY, A Voice From Prison [1856].

lessly flirting. Presumably, the men willingly went along with this. Also, during courtship affection seems most overwhelming, thus providing the model of true love that was widely accepted by both middle-class marriage advisers and free lovers. Finally, the intoxication of affection and the limits placed upon actual intimacy allowed a couple to cherish idealizations about one another, thus giving the relationship a spiritual character. After marriage, man and wife typically moved into their separate spheres and began dealing with all the shortcomings of their partner; relations with others of the opposite sex were narrowly governed by fear of scandal. Free lovers who called for courtship to be extended sought to rekindle the affection that the unwed couple experienced for each other—the only kind of affection they believed was genuine. This also would free men and women to pursue other intergender relationships, not necessarily of a sexual nature.

Free lovers viewed sexual relationships much differently than had the eighteenth-century feminists. Mary Wollstonecraft, who believed that love was too unruly a passion to be the basis of any lasting union, recommended friendship as the basis of marriage. More than fifty years later, the middle-class ideal of marriage had made love the core of the married relationship. Free lovers concluded that marriage could never coexist with true love—that is, the kind of love that flourished during courtship—and so marriage should not exist at all. Rather than friendship as the basis of a sexual relationship, free lovers insisted upon infatuation. This maintained the distrust of physical intimacy and the spiritualization of marriage typical of middle-class marriage advisers. It is no wonder the most consistent free lovers endorsed variety, since only multiple relationships corresponded to the adolescent model.

If courtship with its emotional intensities and idealizations were the model for free lovers then we can more clearly understand their attitude toward marriage. They could find confirmation for their outrage not only in divorces and unhappy marriages, but even in marriages that gave no public evidence of being inadequate. Stephen Pearl Andrews remembered his brother Thomas as one of the most impressive men he had ever known, a lawyer whose success gave him a position of prominence in Clinton, Louisiana. Thomas's bride, Louisa, was stunningly beautiful and, though the daughter of slaveholders, became an ardent abolitionist. After marriage Thomas took less interest in his business and preferred to spend time at home with his wife and children. It would seem from these circumstances that Thomas and Louisa enjoyed one another and their family life together. Andrews drew much different conclusions. Citing Louisa's poor housekeeping as proof of her low level of development, Andrews went on to lament Thomas's

> . . . sinking from year to year more and more into the mere uxorious drudge, conquered into the common-placeness of domesticity, losing his ambition, losing his industry, losing his interest in life, except in the petty affairs of his badly managed and unfortunate household.[25]

Marriage was not the high road to happiness but the slough of despond.

In this context it is important to bear in mind that crusaders for the abolition of marriage were virtually all married. Alfred Cridge had pointed out that in spite of the "defects of existing marriage relations, progressive people . . . will form conjugal relations more or less in accordance with the present social order." Their actions show that radicals, in spite of their rhetoric, believed that spiritually complete and happy unions could be consummated on earth. Not only were Andrews, Kent, and Clay married, so were Francis Barry, Joseph Treat, and John Patterson. Andrews remarried after his first wife died. And Clay, whose wife had abandoned him during the Maria Cole incident, either remarried or became reconciled to his wife after he moved to Berlin Heights. One memoir of the free love movement even claimed that two free lovers who never found loves committed suicide in frustration and disgust with the world. It was not specific marriages but the institution of marriage that had to be destroyed. Idealization, whether of the loved one, of the married state, or of marriage itself, always pervaded the social thought of free love. The abolition of marriage, like marriage, was a spiritual matter.[26]

For the evangelical, the pivot of spirituality was his or her conversion experience. Typically this occurred in adolescence or early adulthood, at a time when the young man or woman was struggling to establish a respectable character. The convert became part of a church and a community that defined his or her behavior in relationships with others. While those who struggled with conversion but rejected it gained independence from some forms of social domination, they were left with the need to construct their identities from other materials in the culture. They possessed the heightened sense of sin and fear of artificiality characteristic of evangelical converts, and they responded to this by projecting sin onto society and by adopting forms of personal discipline and purity. Both of these responses were typical of evangelical reformers who, nevertheless, retained the promise of eventually overcoming both sin and death. Free lovers, with no such certainty, believed they had to overcome the sinfulness of society and defeat the death of the spirit. Their conversion struggle gave them the fervor and strength to lead a religious life without the religion offered by society.

Mary Gove Nichols

Free love demanded equality and freedom for women in every aspect of life. Like activists in the women's rights movement, free lovers recognized that the separate spheres touted by marriage advisers and literary pundits trapped middle-class women, leaving them at home without occupation or confining their activities to charity and church work. Supposedly queen of her household, the wife took a secondary role when the king (or oracle, as Sophia Ripley put it) returned from work. Separate spheres offered women agency within home and church but only as deputies of husbands and ministers, while the doctrine gave men actual agency everywhere else. Of the ante-bellum movements that challenged separate spheres, only those that projected the destruction of marriage promised real power to women. The Shaker leadership, for instance, included both elders and eldresses. Only free love, however, demanded the destruction of both marriage and separate spheres for all of society.

Paradoxically, the free love call for the freedom of women seems to have been made mostly by male voices. There were a few prominent free love women, especially at Berlin Heights. Mary Hall taught the school there, and Sophronia Powers managed the Davis House. Even so, as late as 1857 Minerva Putnam wrote that "in the discussion of free love, no woman has attempted to give her views on the subject." Although women contributed to and helped edit both the *Social Revolutionist* and *Age of Freedom*, until late in the century the only book supporting free love written entirely by a woman was Mary Gove Nichols's fictionalized autobiography *Mary Lyndon*.[27]

The appearance of a woman's liberation movement with few women leaders may be an artifact of either the culture or the sources. Perhaps, on the one hand, both men and women were so accustomed to having male leaders that men naturally took command of the movement. Though free lovers condemned marriage, most were married themselves. Wives might join husbands in repudiating male domination, even though they personally adopted a subordinate role. This undoubtedly helped shape the power relations in the movement, but free lovers had examples available to them in the women's rights movement and in spiritualism of women presiding over conventions and assuming leadership in organizations. On the other hand, women may have been more prominent in conventions and in lecturing than in journalism. However, reports of lecturers in the field from the *Social Revolutionist* seem to undermine this. The few women mentioned in the field were usually not radical enough to be free lovers.[28]

A more basic reason for the lack of prominent women free lovers was that free love appeared a far more ambiguous blessing to women than to men. For men, free love was one more manifestation of individualism. Men who rejected free love believed that marriage offered the best environment for the unfolding of individual virtue. Men who embraced marriage abolition, on the other hand, felt that the sacrifice of individual limitation was too great. For women, however, free love promised to lift the burden of male domination and simultaneously threatened the status and security they gained from marriage. To women who endorsed free love the suffering of women seemed far more pronounced than the benefits of marriage. Minerva Putnam, who had convinced her husband that only complete liberty could ensure their love and happiness, attacked marriage for making "woman the property of man, and she MUST submit. There is no use of quibbling in the matter, of attempting to cover from sight those loathesome ulcers on society which are bred by marriage, and which nothing but its abolition can heal."[29]

Those women who felt the limitations of the married sphere less poignantly could hardly rejoice over a reform that threatened to deny them the prestige and protection that marriage ideally gave them. A husband converted to free love might leave to roam the land, searching for free love mates. It is no wonder that a mob of women attacked Francis Barry and burned the *Social Revolutionist*, since his movement potentially deprived them of their families. "A true-hearted woman," writing to Adin Ballou's *Practical Christian* stated the problem succinctly: "The man who, 'in ultimating his passional attraction', becomes the father of twenty or twenty-five children in the course of a year, cannot feel any particular affection for his numerous progeny, nor the responsibility which devolves on the author of their existence." Freedom would not only sever the father from the care of his children, but also end the love of husband for wife. "A man would never feel any especial obligation to sustain and cheer the mother of his child, when she might with equal propriety depend upon the sympathies of other men, with whom she had held the same relation." Ballou's correspondent believed that true love was not free but exclusive.[30]

If the evils of marital subordination were more real for women, so were the risks of free love. Without her husband's support a woman embracing free love cast herself into society's outer darkness. A cultural predilection for seeing women as passionless made women seeking freedom seem unnaturally lustful. Women could more safely find comfort in spiritualism, which offered women more power while largely accepting the relationships dictated by ante-bellum society. Free love demanded changes in society that would deprive women of both familiar relationships and comforting regimens. An unrepresentative sampling of the leaders of the free love movement suggests that women confronted inner doubts and external hostility greater than that experienced by men. James Clay pursued a life of free love at least into the 1860s, when information on him ends. Andrews, Kent, and Lazarus all supported some form of free love until their deaths late in the nineteenth century.[31] Mary Gove Nichols, the most prominent woman free lover of the 1850s, abandoned the movement by 1857. Her life can show us a great deal of the woman's experience of radicalism and free love.

Soon after the publication of *Mary Lyndon*, the *New York Daily Times* devoted three and three-quarters columns on its second page to a review of the book, entitled, "A Bad Book Gibbeted." It was not only the book that the reviewer attacked. To the *Times* writer, Mary Gove Nichols embodied the personal vices of free lovers:

She was naturally, as we judge from her book, a woman of strong intellect, coarse tastes, violent passions and unbounded self-conceit. Her experience of

life has sharpened her intellect, exasperated her temper, inflamed her sensual
appetites, augmented vastly her self-esteem, and made her ten-fold more the
"child of hell" than she was before. She has written this book apparently . . .
for the purpose of convincing the world of the advantages of hydropathy, the
abominations of Christianity, and the reforming influence of fine art and
fornication.

According to the reviewer, Mary Nichols's sensualism, egoism, and
connection with Fourierism formed the basis of her attack upon marriage. The danger of books like *Mary Lyndon* was that they could fall
into the hands of some of the tens of thousands of men and women
who lived in unhappy marriages, many of whom might be weak-
minded or reckless enough to "make their own passions or their own
wishes the sole law of their future conduct."[32]

During the late summer and fall of 1855, the *Times* explained free
love as the monstrous work of weak, deluded, or bad people tempted
into folly by the gaudy fantasies of French socialism. People like Mary
Gove Nichols—advanced thinkers, reformers, faddists, or pushy
women—were the targets and then the agents of a socialist conspiracy
that had already weakened the divorce statutes in Ohio, Illinois, and
Indiana and had led to many of the elopements, desertions, adulteries,
fornications, and divorces in the country's higher circles.[33] From the
perspective of conservative opinion, the bond between Fourierism and
free love served an important purpose. If questioning marriage was
identified with socialism, Americans could view free love as an unwanted foreign import, like the Irish and cholera. Obviously, the only
people who would embrace such doctrines were those with grave
character flaws.

Mary Gove Nichols fit the free love stereotype perfectly. She was
the first woman to speak on physiology; by the early 1840s, she was a
famous "lady professor" lecturing to mixed audiences of women and
men. As she revealed in her autobiography, Mary Gove left her husband and later kidnapped her own child. While separated from her
husband, she had a love affair with an English communist. A novelized
biography of her, published in 1853, insisted that she had seduced
several men with her powers of spiritual vampirism. That she should
embrace Swedenborgianism, spiritualism, and free love seemed to her
detractors congruent with her personal shortcomings. Aggravating Mary

Nichols's perversity was her association with the literary and reformist demimonde of New York, a hodgepodge of questionable characters, such as Stephen Pearl Andrews, Edgar Allan Poe, and Mary's future husband, Thomas Nichols. The *New York Daily Times* commented that Thomas's early literary works "were simply licentious and immoral, and belonged to that class of writings of which the police claims a much more rigid supervision than it exercises." Within the context of the *New York Daily Times*'s 1855 crusade against free love, the worst influence in New York emanated from Albert Brisbane and the circle of committed Fourierists. Mary Nichols recalled that she was among several Fourierists at the water-cure boarding house she ran.[34] Although to defenders of monogamous marriage, Mary Gove Nichols's free loveism appeared both horrible and inevitable, her ideas emerged from sources familiar to the middle class and highly valued by those who set the moral tone of the period.

Born in 1810 in Goffstown, New Hampshire, Mary Neal grew up at a time when conversion, marriage, and reform provided the elements of identity for young people moving into the new middle class. Mary Neal sought to transform her own life with the chemistry of the time, but for her the elements made a peculiar compound. Perhaps the most important distinction between the set of beliefs embraced by Mary Nichols and that which came to characterize the middle class in America was a difference in religion. At the age of fifteen Mary Neal experienced conversion in a revival and joined the Presbyterian church in her small New Hampshire town. When she wrote her autobiography in 1855, Mary Nichols attributed her willingness to convert to sickness. This may well have been the case, though it is far more likely that ill health only contributed to the many conflicts she faced. Her family had moved to the village a few years before, so Mary may have still felt lonely. As she approached adulthood, she probably became anxious over the prospect of marriage and confused as to what kind of life she wanted to lead. And, since she found her father a far more sympathetic figure than her mother, Mary Neal may have desired to emulate his role in the world rather than her mother's role in the family.[35]

Conversion served purposes other than calming adolescent anxieties. Particularly in the early nineteenth century, revival religion offered young women the opportunity to participate more fully in the world of their mothers, sisters, and friends. Within the church they became agents of Christianity, joined with others—mostly women—throughout the country and the world who contributed their money and time to civilize and Christianize the American wilderness and the heathen jungles. If Mary Neal found this sense of purpose attractive, she shared her enthusiasm with many girls. Unlike most girls, however, Mary's father was the town skeptic, and Mary received no support from her family for her religion. In addition, an argument with the Presbyterian minister's wife soon ended her relations with that church. However, Mary Neal's brush with religion was more than a passing adolescent fancy since her repudiation by the Presbyterians led her to Quakerism.

There were no Quakers in the town where the Neals lived. As a result, Mary was able to idealize the followers of Fox. She assumed the simple dress and archaic speech of the Quakers, whom she read about, and practiced a personal and independent piety. Quaker religion must have given Mary some satisfaction beyond reinforcing an adolescent sense of uniqueness since she continued in the sect for seventeen years, long after discovering that her ideal of a people consecrated to simple living and genuine piety was an illusion. Her uncle introduced her to Hiram Gove, a Quaker twenty years her senior. For reasons not entirely clear, Mary Neal married Hiram and went to live with him in Weare. There she found her Quaker neighbors narrow-minded, moralistic, and bigoted. Her husband combined with these traits his brutality, meanness, and business debts.[36]

While piety and conjugal love proved disastrous for her, Mary Gove began to establish her own identity with the restoration of her health. Frequently sick from childhood on, Mary Gove endured four miscarriages after the birth in 1832 of her daughter Elma. In despair she turned during the mid-1830s to the study of physiology and attended the lectures of itinerant experts such as Sylvester Graham. Grahamism, she believed, gave her back her health, and Sylvester Graham's theories of physiology became the center of Mary Gove's life. She later wrote, "I regard Mr. Graham as one of the greatest benefactors the world ever had." By 1837, with the help and encouragement of William Alcott, she started lecturing on physiology for women. This proved so successful that by the early 1840s she had carried her message of physiological salvation to cities throughout the eastern United States.[37]

Graham's theories organized the descriptions of anatomy and physiology in her lectures and determined the advice she gave to her women listeners on healthful living. Disease, crime, and wretchedness, she told her audiences, resulted from ignorance. "Many seem to have no idea that there are established laws with respect to life and health, and that the transgression of these laws is followed by disease. In this sense disease is a visitation of the almighty." She warned against quacks and allopathic medicines and included good advice on dress and exercise. "A majority of the present fashions are an outrage on humanity, and many of them as repugnant to health as they could well be contrived, even had the contrivers sought after the most deleterious mode." She urged personal reforms in diet, such as meat in moderation and the elimination of spices, coffee, tea, and alcohol.[38]

The regimens recommended by Mary Gove and Sylvester Graham offered plans for young people to build their characters at a time when traditional institutions were losing coherence and new forms of social status were emerging. As men and women from rural areas or the working classes moved into new neighborhoods and new occupations, they searched for ideas that would make sense of their lives. Basic to the construction of middle-class reality was a vision of society in which isolated individuals and families struggled to improve their economic lot and perfect themselves. In such a world diet, exercise, hygiene, and purity would not only save the individual from both disease and personal disorder but would also provide the basis for a harmonious social order.[39] Physiological salvation, however, had different meanings for men and women. For men seeking to become masters of their own fate, physiology reinforced their individuality and their need for control. For women, physiology had importance for their role in the family, where they had learned to look for their destiny.

Mary Gove advocated Graham's controversial views on sex and probably attracted more animosity than Graham since she was a woman speaking to women. She was among the very first to condemn masturbation as a grave evil for young women. Girls, like boys, endangered their sanity as well as their health and life when they began self-abuse.

In addition, she warned, "There is reason to believe that in nine cases out of ten, those unhappy females who are the tenants of houses of ill fame, have been the victims of this vice in the first place." As with Graham, Gove's strictures against the solitary vice were only part of her campaign for sexual purity. Both Graham and Gove deplored immoderate sex within marriage: "The fact that the ceremony of marriage has been performed, will not save people from the consequences of venereal excesses." Women who engaged too frequently in intercourse subjected themselves to nausea, uterine diseases, miscarriages, deformed children, and hysteria.[40]

For women, sexual purity probably carried far more attraction than it did for men. A young woman taught to believe that she lacked animal lusts would likely receive little sexual information from parents and may have remained innocent of informal instruction from friends and siblings. If the reinforcement for passionlessness approached the pervasiveness necessary for the doctrine to seem viable, then women would fear those sexual desires present in themselves and be disgusted by the desire of others. One consequence of this would have been to make intercourse even in marriage seem horrible. Even if the couple had intercourse infrequently, these experiences might have been traumatic for the wife. Sexual self-control allowed women to determine the frequency of intercourse. Mary Gove, with other reformers, believed that when wives lacked control over the married couple's sexual behavior physiological vengeance followed. As an example, she claimed that gestation and parturition were as natural as digestion and in a healthy state would be accompanied with little or no pain. "But," she continued,

the healthy tone of the nervous system is destroyed. Diseased, convulsed, and erratic action is established by the various abuses of civic life, and the most tender and endearing of all relations becomes a terror and a curse.[41]

Grahamite sexual purity would become integral to Mary Gove's free love. Her lectures and writings consistently carried the message that women should determine the frequency of intercourse and the number of children within the marriage. "Licentiousness," Mary Nichols wrote in 1849, "is the same with or without the marriage sanction." In *Esoteric Anthropology* (1853), Thomas Nichols expressed his wife's opinion that it was for woman to decide "whom she will admit to her embraces, and when. . . . She has an equal right to decide whether she will have children, and to choose the time for having them." Govism, like Grahamism, gave women their physiological right to health and attacked the presumed sexual prerogatives of men. Both health reformers offered complementary elements in the middle-class search for standards of behavior. The free love version of this middle-class ideology would condemn domination by the man and the gratification of his lusts in marriage and call for relationships based upon equality and companionship.[42]

Just as sexual purity was far less abstract for women than for men, so was the suffering that could result from a bad marriage. Mary Gove's life with Hiram Gove taught her that matrimony could be a terrible trap. Hiram collected all of Mary's earnings as a lecturer and limited her social life to a narrow circle of unsympathetic Quakers. In 1842, having endured her husband's tyranny for ten years, Mary Gove fled with her daughter Elma to the protection of her father's home. A short and happy period followed, during which Mary found true love outside of marriage with Henry G. Wright, the English communist who taught her about water-cure. Gove's happiness ended in 1844 or 1845; Wright died of consumption, and, soon after, Mary's father died. Hiram took Elma away, forcing Mary to kidnap the child and flee to New York City.[43]

Throughout her early life, Mary Gove found frustration and heartache where her culture claimed women would realize happiness. Her conversion turned sour, and marriage, purportedly the foundation of society, had proven a fraud. But, while Mary Gove found the promises made to women were empty, she also received little encouragement to pursue other ideals. Even as a successful lecturer she was bound to her husband and compelled to support him. Forced to rely on her own resources, she was still surrounded by the demands of marriage. Consequently, the personal and intellectual problems that would concern Mary Gove were the limits placed upon women who sought to realize their individuality and the necessity for individuals to find some way of stepping beyond their individuality.

In 1842 Mary Gove's personal dilemma encouraged her to adopt a pessimistic attitude. "There is no doubt in my mind that society as it is, is radically and fundamentally wrong; but we must make the best of it." After moving to New York City, Mary Gove became acquainted with the latest ideas and nostrums and with many of the thinkers and quacks as well. She met Marx Lazarus, who financed her water-cure boarding house where Albert Brisbane paid frequent calls. Conversations with these and other radicals helped Mary Gove develop her own understanding of the contradictions of American life. She had adopted the Fourierist equation of "civilized" with "artificial" by 1842 as she urged readers of *Lectures to Ladies* to live "in a less artificial manner" so that they would not "suffer the penalty of violated laws, as do our victims of civilization[.]"[44] During the 1840s Mary Gove believed that the reconstruction of marriage and of society began where the falsehood in the relations between men and women ended.

Throughout the 1840s Mary Gove wrote fiction that criticized various aspects of American society. In virtually every piece, she showed that the results of substituting false objects for genuine ones leads to ill health or death. Sophia Wilton in "The Artist," for instance, glimpsed her true nature in her attraction to Gilbert Ainslie during a trip to Niagara Falls, but her mother refused to allow Sophia to be seen with the penurious artist. Although Sophia might have risen above these prejudices, "she had returned to fashionable society, where the dazzling brightness of wealth and fashion had so blinded her that she had no perception of the good and the true." Sophia marries wealthy Mr. Montague, and so incompatible are they that they destroy one another. She gives birth to an idiot child and dies in obscurity soon after Montague's bankruptcy and suicide.[45]

In Mary Gove's first novel, *Agnes Morris*, we meet poor Mr. Morris. As a young man he had loved another but had gone to Philadelphia, where he "was dragged into fashionable life, because he was too weak to resist." His punishment was Lydia Mason.

He remembered that she dazzled him greatly, but why he should find himself married to her, as a penalty for all this, he could not understand. Beauty, novelty, wine, witchery, and a weak man!—other people saw in these the solution of the mystery.[46]

Lydia Morris is completely devoted to fashion, which in her case includes being an invalid and taking fashionable medicine. Her death,

Mary Sergeant Gove Nichols (1810–1884).
By the time she opened her water-cure boarding house in New York City in
the late 1840s, Mary Gove already held radical views of marriage and society.
Her beliefs led her, during the 1850s, to advocate free love, sexual temperance,
spiritualism, and, finally, Roman Catholicism.

COURTESY OF THE BRITISH LIBRARY.

near the end of the novel, is the inevitable consequence of her devotion
to false ideas.

If marriage sealed a false relationship, it became a trap. Those with
insight enough to marry wisely, however, made the institution the
basis of lifelong happiness. In "Marrying a Genius," Horace Simmons
learns that a good housekeeper can be a boring wife. When his wife
dies after ten years, he meets and marries Eliza, a literary woman of

talent. In another story, "The Evil and the Good," Mary Gove contrasted Florence Hastings to Sarah Lee. Sarah runs off to New York City with Florence's fiancé Herman Liston. He becomes a lawyer and lecturer, while she becomes the belle of the city. Soon, however, Herman is devoted to his own fame, and Sarah is disgusted with her life in the city. After eight years Sarah and Florence meet again. By this time Florence has married a hard-working printer and editor. For Florence, marriage is the realization of her high ideals about spiritual love.[47]

In a world of human sham, Mary Gove believed, genuineness existed in experiences beyond human manipulation. Middle-class theorists in the early nineteenth century proclaimed that love was a force of nature, inherent in the individual and outside of rational control. Phrenologists Orson and Lorenzo Fowler instructed their patients and readers on the latest discoveries from France and Germany of organs in the brain governing sexuality, the desire to have children, and the propensity to marry for life. Henry C. Wright believed true marriage was founded upon intrinsic spiritual qualities that would never vary: "A masculine soul and a feminine soul, in marriage, are absorbed each into the other." The word most commonly used to indicate the inner commands of the spirit was *affinity*. Fourier had spoken of passional affinities, a term his followers retained into the 1850s. From the end of the 1840s, spiritualists adopted spiritual affinities as a means of describing the organization of conjugal relations after death. Perhaps the best explanation of the workings of love, however, was in a short novel by Goethe, *Elective Affinities*, in which he compared the action of love to a chemical reaction. Two people whose inner beings held affinities for one another became bonded when they came into contact.[48]

By the late 1840s, theories about love took on specific meaning for Mary Gove. At a Christmas party in 1847 she met Thomas Nichols, and, in spite of their resistance, both were soon deeply in love and exchanging letters almost daily. Like others in love, Thomas and Mary were sure that their passion was rare, if not unique. Thomas believed that the spiritual gender of each would intermingle and refine the other. Throughout their correspondence they spoke of love as a force outside their control, a gift of God to them alone. "If our love make us one," Mary wrote to Thomas, "then we shall have one life only, and one life-impulse." She continued in the same letter, "I am almost frightened at my enthusiasm about you." A few days later Mary expressed the overwhelming quality of her emotion in even stronger language:

I love you with an infinite love. There is not the struggle, the unquiet, the hunger and thirst of a finite state. I am stilled in this love that wraps, and *is*, my being. I pause reverently before this almightiness of affection.[49]

Free love for Mary Gove became a question of faith. Marriage to Hiram had been destructive; but society bound her to Hiram Gove in perpetuity, thereby making marriage to Thomas impossible. "Alas, what a world!" she complained to Thomas. "Who can blame the good for wishing to leave it?" "Our holiness is impurity to the world, and freedom for us, except in spirit, is impossible. No—not so—all things are possible to our Father." Mary believed in love, and her ideal gave her a means of overcoming the demands of the world. Love, like the evangelical ideal of marriage, would redeem the world. "You do well to repose all faith in the omnipotence of love," Thomas wrote to her. In the end Thomas and Mary decided to live together; for them, as for many who became free lovers in the following decade, free love meant informal divorce and remarriage. The ideology affirmed what society condemned. By chance Hiram Gove had decided to divorce his wife at about this same time, so Thomas and Mary were able to marry within a few months.[50]

The horror of unloving or forced marriage was so clear to Thomas and Mary Nichols that when free love became a public issue they were among the first to endorse it. The Nicholses captured the radical limelight by 1853 with their American Hydropathic Institute at Port Chester, Thomas's book *Esoteric Anthropology*, and their journal published at Modern Times. "In our published works," Mary stated in her defense of free love, "we have endeavored to set forth the laws of the sexual relations, as revealed by science." Her position on the question was squarely on the side of Grahamite purity and opposed to the artificiality of American life.

It is our belief that four-fifths of all the disease, premature mortality, and general unhappiness of our race, is connected intimately with violations of the true laws of these relations. Truth in love relations brings health, vigor, long life, and happiness.

Although potentially healthy and loving, individuals suffered because the corruptions of society turned them aside from their true natures.

There is a true, genuine, God-ordained relation of the sexes, in mutual love, which is the real marriage; but all civilization is full of counterfeits, abuses, perversions, and falses, and not less filled with their consequences.[51]

Mary Nichols considered free love essential to men and women who wanted to lead healthy lives free from the snares of civilization. Women, she claimed, would overcome sexual apathy once they recovered their health. When women gained the right to choose who would be their lovers and who the father of their children, sexual union would begin to approach its true potential. The Nicholses' version of free love, however, was never frequent love. A man or woman might have many kinds of loves—friends, spouses, brothers and sisters, etc. Presumably, one individual would be fully united with only one other individual at a time. Also, Grahamite physiology taught that sexual intercourse was harmful, and the Nicholses never contradicted this. Mary expected that independent women would choose to have sex infrequently, while men rescued from civilized corruption would find this appropriate. By 1855, when she was being damned by the *New York Daily Times* for her sensualism, Mary had already received spiritual enlightenment concerning Progression in Harmony. Material union (intercourse) was prudent only as often as children were desired. She might have answered the *Times* reviewer as she had answered critics in 1853: "To those who would represent us as sensualists seeking a mere material liberty, I have only to say, 'You read your own lives into our movement.' You know nothing of the holy sacrament of a marriage of love."[52]

Mary Gove Nichols had been among the army of lecturers and writers who attempted to teach behaviors that would help the new bourgeois allay their anxieties at facing the state and the market alone and show them how to anchor their lives in what was genuine—love, marriage, family, God. For many Americans, some element of this middle-class culture failed and left them searching for substitutes. Converts who could not be satisfied with the blandness of church life very likely turned to Millerism or to spiritualism, or both. An independent artisan unable to compete and forced into factory work might turn to labor agitation, socialism, or sovereignty of the individual. Similarly, those seeking true marriage but finding themselves in something else, might demand the abolition of marriage. What is most unusual about Mary Nichols's development is not that she became a free lover, but where free love led her. Her struggle for genuineness and purity did not end with radicalism, as it did for other free lovers. As with her faith in free love, Mary Nichols's life followed a course laid out by religious desire.

Even though she abandoned sectarian Protestantism when she fled Hiram Gove and the Weare Quakers, Mary Gove retained her religiosity in an idealized version of heavenly order. "All this outward beauty," she has Florence Hastings tell Sarah Lee, ". . . speaks to my heart that there must be spirit beauty, for whence is all loveliness but from the ever-living, all-pervading spirit of beauty that lives in God, in angels and in man." In her love letters to Thomas, Mary expressed an earnest piety: "Our God and His angels will do all for us that we can not do. We are to have no anxious care but only faith and love, and a pure, heavenly obedience to our faith and our love."[53] Such raptures have a hint of transcendentalism, which was itself an extension of evangelical Protestantism.

Of the other heterodox versions of Protestantism besides transcendentalism during the 1840s, Swedenborgianism was probably the most impressive. During the late 1830s or early 1840s, Mary Gove requested the loan of Swedenborg's *Conjugial Love* from a New Church minister. Perhaps the minister knew of Mary's personal problems. He obviously realized that Swedenborg's teachings challenged the middle-class ideal of marriage. "Many are seeking to justify themselves in evils and lusts by New Church Truths," he told Mary. In spite of this setback, the Church of the New Jerusalem remained attractive to Mary Gove. At her marriage to Thomas Nichols in 1848, a Swedenborgian minister "read the beautiful marriage service of that denomination; and then he repeated the Lord's Prayer, as we knelt together, in deepest thankfulness, before our Father and his angels."[54]

Spiritualism also gave many Americans a path to religious fulfillment apart from the denominations. It provided a unifying vision of the universe and calmed fears of death. Both freethinkers like Robert Dale Owen and Warren Chase and renegades like Henry C. Wright found the combination within spiritualism of scientific proof and religious certainty deeply satisfying. While Mary Gove's attraction to spiritualism must have been enhanced by her own well-developed mesmeric powers, the importance of spiritualism to her was far more in its ideological function than in its practical results.[55] Spiritualism allowed her to comprehend the world in terms that were familiar. Spirits existed in a purified version of nineteenth-century America or Europe. The ideal forms of marriage and individuality, of economy and religion, so fervently sought and so obviously absent in antebellum America existed among the spirits. From the spirit realm came the message that we should conform our lives as closely as possible to higher levels of existence by becoming individual sovereigns, following passional attractions, and ignoring government.

While spiritualism became one of the most important elements of Mary Nichols's life, it only briefly satisfied all of her aspirations. Mary Gove believed that she was destined for greatness. Writing in 1839 to her cousin, John Neal, she referred to her work as a teacher of the Graham system: "The world misunderstands and abuses me but I shall yet have a *name* and a *place* among the benefactors of our race." In general, those women in Jacksonian America who caught the public eye had some religious occupation or, like Catharine Beecher, some quasi-religious occupation. Perhaps for this reason, Mary Nichols's vision of her own glory was always implicitly religious. The language she used shows that she continued to struggle with religious questions and to explain her life in religious terms even during her radical sojourn in New York City. To Thomas she wrote in 1848, "I am the Apostle of Health and the Illustrator of Health Laws. Health, physical and material, is another name for harmony and holiness." She went on in terms that reveal her desire for eminence: "I feel the worth of my work, and I have long been willing to be sacrificed, crucified in any way that should best serve God, for the health of man." Mary Nichols repeated her willingness to sacrifice herself in 1849, while describing the diseases of women displayed at Albany Medical College. "I felt then that I would lay myself on the altar, and be burned with fire, if woman could be saved from the darkness of ignorance, and the untold horrors of her disease."[56]

Mary Nichols's spiritualism became all-encompassing in 1854 when she began receiving messages from a society of spirits that instructed her and Thomas to begin an earthly association that would enable the higher society of the future to become present reality. At the same time, individuality began to recede as a concern for the Nicholses, and collective harmony became prominent. The Progressive Union served as a vehicle for Mary Nichols's ambitions, as did the community of Memnonia founded to gather the pure of the earth into a harmonious circle. At Memnonia, Mary Nichols held daily seances to instruct the remnant gathered around her, and she and Thomas established a temporary "despotism" to make certain that the Memnonians rose above their earthly condition.[57]

Emile Durkheim wrote of late nineteenth-century economic life that "the longing for infinity is daily represented as a mark of moral distinction." For Mary Nichols this longing went beyond economic matters. Like other spiritualists, she claimed actual conversation with the infinity of the afterlife but went farther by proposing to realize that perfect order among her disciples. The Nicholses, who placed themselves at the pinnacle of Harmonious Progression, accepted their longing for infinity as moral distinction. It also seems that they must have come to realize the hollowness of their own pretensions, what Durkheim termed "unregulated consciences which elevate to a rule the lack of rule from which they suffer."[58] Not only had the Nicholses cast scorn upon American society, they also claimed insights that set them apart from the free love network of their time. Mary Nichols probably felt the ambiguity of her position, preaching purity and calling for the end of the institution that was supposed to guarantee purity. At the same time that Mary's desire for religious eminence was expressed in her visions, her own connection with religious traditions and symbols became more tenuous. The tension she had felt between individuality and social harmony now appears to have become intolerable.

If Mary Nichols's communications with a spirit society were hallucinations, at least they conformed to her beliefs and desires. One of the spirits who appeared to her was her former lover, Henry G.

Wright, and the association projected by the spirits conformed to Thomas and Mary's ideas about love, marriage, hygiene, sex, and reform. In 1856, however, the communications changed dramatically. St. Ignatius Loyola appeared, telling Mary and Thomas to study Catholicism. As a tutor, the spirit of St. Francis Xavier soon appeared to guide the Nichols in their knowledge of the true faith. When they sought admission into the Roman Catholic Church in March 1857, John B. Purcell, the archbishop of Cincinnati, hesitated at accepting the "Mother Abbess of free lovers" into the Holy Mother Church. He insisted that the couple retract all of their former errors, thus ending their free love and radical reform work.[59]

Catholicism allowed Mary Nichols to resolve conflicts within her own life and thinking. Her search for ideal forms had led her first into health and social reforms and then into close communion with the spirit world. While she continued to believe that true marriage, true love, and true sexuality existed, her movement from reform to spiritualism represented a distancing of her ideas from ante-bellum America. Perhaps she recognized, in the end, that the Progressive Union and Memnonia would produce nothing closer to harmonial life than had her marriage to Hiram Gove. Within the Roman Catholic Church Mary Nichols could retain her commitment to health reform and to spiritualism (in spite of the condemnation of spiritualism by all orthodox Christian churches). She and Thomas lectured to religious orders on diet and exercise, and she practiced water-cure after they moved to England in 1861. The Roman Catholic Church also provided Mary Nichols with a limit on her desire for the infinite and a valid form of integration that included its own ideal forms of marriage, motherhood, sexuality, and love.[60]

Probably the most important ideal offered by the Roman Catholic Church was that of the ideal woman, the Virgin Mary. As early as 1849 in *Agnes Morris*, Mary Gove included passages about an Irish woman who was devoted to the Virgin. Mary Gove had apparently begun identifying herself with the other, transcendent Mary even earlier. Several of the heroines in her stories were named Mary. In "The Artist," the author took time to extoll the very name: "Mary—it was his favorite name. I hardly ever saw any one who did not love this name. A sweet poetess has said—'I begin to think that, as of old, the

Marys are ever nearest the Lord.'" Mary Nichols's biographer, Janet
Noever, has suggested that the Catholic exaltation of the Virgin as the
pinnacle of perfection must have appealed to Mary Nichols. Mary's
desire to establish a religious order that would combine education,
health, and childbirth, to be called "The Order of the Chaste Birth,"
shows that her desire to purify and perfect sexuality found expression
in Catholic terms.[61]

Mary Nichols's conversion, a year and a half after the *New York
Daily Times* accused her of spreading sensualism and atheism, provided
her with a foundation for her other reforms and gave her a community
and an ideology from which she could derive her sense of identity.
Writing to Paulina Wright Davis sometime after the Civil War, she
commended those working for women's rights, saying she claimed for
woman all human rights, "that she be free to obey the Divine Law of
her own life—that she be not subjected to the lustful despotism of one
man, or the selfish or unwise legislation of many." Mary Nichols might
have written the same lines in 1855, but not those that followed.

Those who have protested against the Church and separated from her have
carried with them little of the veneration for woman which has ever existed in
the hearts of true Catholics. The Church has placed no hindrance in the way
of woman, though individuals calling themselves Catholics may have done
so.[62]

She continued for three pages, listing the eminent women of Catholicism. For Mary Nichols the Catholic Church offered both present and
practical as well as eventual transcendence.

Like the male leaders of free love, Mary Nichols had experienced an
adolescent religious crisis that left her with an intense sense of social
wrong and artificiality but without fully converting her to evangelical
Christianity. Instead, Mary Nichols joined the middle-class avant-
garde, urging upon others and adopting herself new ways of dressing,
eating, and bathing. Just as Andrews, Lazarus, Kent, and Clay built
their social systems around the individual, Mary Nichols advocated
the entire freedom of women from socially imposed duties. The grace
of this system was love—the intense and volatile love of courtship that
free lovers raised to an ideal for all love. But for Mary Nichols,
infatuation and individuality proved incomplete. As a woman she
faced the realities of motherhood and had struggled with the limits

placed upon working women. Isolated and embattled in the mid-1850s, she finally found in Catholicism the network of support and the reliance upon faith that others had discovered in evangelical Protestantism. Yet by embracing ritual and obedience, Mary Nichols placed herself further from the ideal of the American middle class than when she had advocated free love. Catholicism was her final and successful attempt to make sense of her life and universe.

CHAPTER 7

Free Love Versus the Middle Class, 1865 to 1900

The years of Civil War and Reconstruction transformed the relation-ship between free lovers and the middle class. The first generation of marriage radicals continued to demand changes in the relations of the sexes, encouraging, inspiring, and instructing committed postwar free lovers. This consistency within the free love movement meant, how-ever, that it would be increasingly at odds with the American middle class. Personal liberty and sexual equality came to be defined by American society in narrower terms than during the 1840s and 1850s. As marriage took on the attributes of sexual respectability and as nationalism replaced the republicanism of the prewar years, advocates of individual sovereignty became more marginal to American society. By the middle of the 1870s, free love radicals had lost their connections with many of the more moderate reformers and found themselves faced with a middle class committed to ending discussion of marriage reform and sexual liberty.

The Civil War united most reformers in defense of the Union. Where formerly their loyalty had been to America as an ideal or vision of future harmony, the war demanded their loyalty to an American nation as defined by the government in Washington, D.C. Antislavery activists and radicals, who had been calling for secession from union with slaveholders, suddenly found the war for the Republic consistent, when not identical, with the struggle against slavery. Even nonresistant William Lloyd Garrison came to support Lincoln after the Emancipation Proclamation. Among the intellectuals who reconciled individuality with the war against secession was Henry James, the Fourierist and Swedenborgian. Our current political troubles, James assured his audience in Providence, Rhode Island, in an 1861 July 4th oration, were "the inevitable fruit of our very best growth, the sure harbingers . . . of the rising Sun of Righteousness." The coming war repeated the cosmic conflict between the human spirit, evidenced in the North, and animal passions as seen in the South. "This animating controlling spirit of our national polity, like that of our own private souls, is Divine." Consequently, the struggle with slavery opened for the nation the prospect of "the heaven of free spontaneous order, or the hell of enforced prudential obedience."[1]

Others who valued individualism as much as James joined him in finding the Republic a means to a greater end. The preeminent individual sovereign, Josiah Warren, suggested in *True Civilization* (1863) that the whole matter of slavery could be worked out (resulting in the freeing of the slaves) if only Northerners and Southerners would discuss the matter reasonably. That such a dialogue had long since ceased to be possible in the 1860s must have been evident to Warren; both *True Civilization* and his 1862 work, *Modern Government*, departed so far from individual sovereignty as to admit the need for some policing power—in this case, the military.[2]

Warren's grudging acceptance of government in the emergency of war was duplicated by other middle-class radicals. Stephen Pearl Andrews wrote his autobiography during the war years and recalled his experiences in the South. Slavery, he had discovered, united all segments of Southern society so that no amount of antislavery agitation would ever defeat it. Warren Chase viewed the war in much the same way as had Henry James. Inherent in the development of the United States, he asserted, was the extension of the rights of education, labor, and land to more and more people—a tendency at odds with the spirit and direction of the South. Several of the writers for the *Social Revolutionist* who had helped make Berlin Heights a center of free love in the 1850s became strong Unionists following the attack on Fort Sumter.

The periodical's editor, John Patterson, enlisted as a private in a Union artillery unit. James Towner became a captain in the Iowa Volunteer Infantry. And peace-loving Francis Barry, who had condemned government in 1856 as "the huge hydra, hell begotten monster," believed that the war emergency made "an imperative demand" for a "sublime, prayerful, determined, brotherly effort to save our beloved country."[3]

Perhaps the most instructive decision to support the war was Austin Kent's. As a young man in the early 1830s Kent had become both a fervent abolitionist and a nonresistant. Although in 1852 he looked forward to a time when even verbal and mental resistance would end, it was his commitment to the destruction of slavery that determined his actions following John Brown's raid on Harper's Ferry. Partially paralyzed and unable to bear arms himself, Austin Kent went along when his son was mustered into the ranks. In front of the recruit's captain Kent told his son to refuse to return any fugitive slaves. If the officer insisted, Kent continued, then shoot him.[4] For Kent and his fellow radicals, the energy diffused among many reforms during the 1850s was suddenly concentrated in the national crusade to end slavery. The dubious legitimacy of force and government became temporarily irrelevant.

Those among the radicals who refused to support Lincoln's call to arms illustrate the diversity of responses to the war. Thomas and Mary Nichols left for exile in England, claiming that they could not be loyal by edict as Mr. Seward demanded. Although attempting to paint their decision in terms of high ideals, Thomas Nichols undoubtedly had other considerations in mind. Thomas had been a Democratic activist throughout his adult life, and as Catholic converts, the Nicholses were at odds with the evangelical abolitionists and the anti-Catholic elements of the new Republican party. Also, Thomas never appears to have believed that slavery was a problem; in his 1864 travel account, *Forty Years of American Life*, he painted slavery as an unfortunate but somewhat pleasant manner of life for the slave. Marx Edgeworth Lazarus also failed to rally to the war for the Union. Instead, he remained in the South where he practiced medicine. Lazarus wrote later that what he saw of the Confederate government confirmed his disgust with all government.[5] As Lazarus and the Nicholses show, prewar loyalties could prove more important than hatred of slavery.

To examine ideological consistency we must introduce a younger radical. Ezra Hervey Heywood was thirty-three in 1862. As an undergraduate and then as a divinity student at Brown University during the 1850s, he became a follower of Garrison. Discussions with young women at his boardinghouse and in his Sunday school further broadened his ideas and led him to radicalism by the late 1850s. He told an audience at the Boston Music Hall in 1860 "that in proportion as institutions had declined, civilization advanced." When the war erupted, Heywood stood firm in his recently acquired principles and soon found himself in conflict with his abolitionist mentors. In 1863 he met Josiah Warren, whose philosophy of individual liberty Heywood adopted.[6] Ezra Heywood also became a leading advocate of free love and a leader and representative of the second, postwar generation of free lovers for whom ideological consistency meant personal hardship.

As is evident from Henry James's speech, many intellectuals expected the war to change the nation. While compromise of principle might be expedient for the greater good of ending slavery, reformers and radicals anticipated the realization of their treasured goals in the years following the war. By 1864 antislavery activists were pushing for the Fourteenth Amendment, while feminists demanded the extension of suffrage to women. "The great Anti-slavery movement having now run its race and come to a successful *denouement*," wrote a supporter of communitarian societies, "there are many signs that it is to be succeeded by a socialistic agitation on the largest scale." He cited several proposed or prospering communities and concluded, "But all these signs indicate that the oil of Socialism—of true union and brotherhood —has been struck, that the people believe in it, and that they are bound to have it." Warren Chase expected the war to usher in a new era in which the United States would enjoy unprecedented wealth and power. He warned, however, that this would be the time when "more than ever, we must guard the rights of the people against the encroachments of monopoly and combination. Every true democrat will then have duties and responsibilities requiring all the powers of mind and heart."[7]

Chase was prescient in realizing that a Union victory held both great promise and danger for the libertarian society he favored. Prewar radicalism, as we have seen, rejected institutions of all kinds, from

Ezra Heywood (1829–1893).
Heywood became one of the most steadfast defenders of free love in the post–Civil War era. With his wife, Angela, he edited and published the *Word* from 1872 to 1893. In 1873 he founded the New England Free Love League.

COURTESY OF THE LABADIE COLLECTION, DEPARTMENT OF RARE BOOKS AND SPE-CIAL COLLECTIONS, UNIVERSITY OF MICHIGAN LIBRARY.

legal marriage to government. In this respect radicalism expressed a suspicion of institutions that was widely accepted among the prewar middle class. Sectionalism weakened the central government, revivalism undermined church authority, and reform societies preached individual regeneration. For radical intellectuals, the war against slavery increased hopes for greater individual liberty. At the same time, however, war accelerated the consolidation of middle-class culture that had begun a decade earlier. The Civil War was a great crusade, in many ways the national revolution of the United States, binding the sections under a stronger federal government and creating a commitment to the nation that had not existed before. Congresses during the late 1860s and 1870s repeatedly denigrated the South's putative right of secession as they passed reconstruction legislation that was enforced by the president and the army.[8] Institutions and social control would become the agencies of civilization for the postwar intellectual mainstream.

Conservatives embraced the war as a means of imposing control upon social inferiors. Perhaps their greatest success was the Sanitary Commission that provided hospital care for wounded soldiers. Following the war, the lessons of the Sanitary Commission allowed conservatives to bring discipline to voluntary benevolence, so that organization and alliance with local and federal government would characterize much of postwar philanthropy and conservative reform. This contrasts markedly with the 1840s and 1850s when concern for the family, for instance, had taken the forms of medical and clerical pamphlets on secret vice and sporadic anti–free love rhetoric. During the postwar years, defense of the family became the basis for organized campaigns against vice. Moral reform in the late 1860s was quickly dominated by former abolitionists who saw the goal of reform as moral perfection. Consequently, they denounced measures that compromised with evil or policies that allowed unholy behavior to continue with impunity. The regulation of prostitution came under their attack in the late 1860s, and a national campaign against pornography was initiated by 1872.[9]

Ante-bellum physicians had denounced pornography mainly because they believed it led to masturbation. Following the war, obscene literature could inspire the same horror as masturbation had previously. A YMCA report of 1866 called pornography "feeders of brothels." The most implacable of smut destroyers wrote in 1880 that "this nefarious business . . . is, *the greatest curse to the youth of this country.*" Obscene literature, Anthony Comstock continued, "works beneath the surface, and like a canker worm, secretly eats out the moral life and purity of our youth, and they droop and fade before their parents' eyes." Comstock was a young veteran working as a dry goods clerk in New York when he began arresting smut dealers in 1868. By 1872 he had chased away, arrested, or confiscated the merchandise of four of the major dealers in the city and the next year went to Washington to lobby for stronger legislation against mailing of pornography. For Comstock, pornography was only part of the threat to youthful innocence and the sanctity of the family. Any discussion of sex might lead to lascivious thoughts, and any attack upon the family subverted Christian values.

While Comstock would prove the most important of the sex censors, he marched in step with, if somewhat in advance of, the nation's mores. Comstock submitted every case to his employer, the YMCA-inspired Society for the Suppression of Vice, before proceeding with it. Samuel Colgate presided over the organization whose sponsors included such noted philanthropists as William Dodge, Jr., Kiliaen Van Rensselaer, and J. P. Morgan. Private subscriptions provided the Society with ten thousand dollars per year for its work, from 1873 until after the turn of the century. At the national level, Congress passed postal legislation against the mailing of obscene material in 1868 and toughened the law in 1872. Comstock's law was combined with other proposals to extend the scope of the law and to close loopholes.[10] Thus by the early 1870s the national government and national organizations helped define and propagate a particular view of sexual relations.

Following the Civil War, American attitudes toward sex hardened into a dogma that excluded what had formerly been alternative conclusions growing out of the same assumptions. It was one thing when in 1860 Horace Greeley labeled Robert Dale Owen an exponent of free love because the latter favored divorce, then opened the columns of the *Tribune* to Owen to argue the merits of divorce; it was quite another thing when free discussion ended in a bill condemning Owen's tract on birth control as pornography and making the mailing of it a federal crime. The attitudes that historian Peter Cominos termed sexual respectability attacked both prostitution and the double standard and placed chastity and lifelong monogamy at the center of social virtues. Although many Americans assumed and preached these ideas during the early nineteenth century, their views often shaded off into opinions at odds with majority viewpoints. As contrary opinions became marginal to the mainstream of middle-class belief following the war, free love could no longer appear as a logical extension of what the middle class claimed to believe but only as a dangerous attack upon the most prized middle-class values.

One guide to the marginalization of free love is its divergence from the women's movement. During the 1850s, the differences between free love radicals like Mary Gove Nichols and women's rights advocates like Elizabeth Cady Stanton were small enough that they often seemed to be working for the same goals. Paulina Wright Davis, who edited the first women's rights periodical, considered Mary Nichols a co-worker, first in health education for women then in women's rights. After the war, Stanton, Wright, Susan B. Anthony, and other feminists formed the National Woman Suffrage Association (NWSA), headquartered in New York City, and demanded that woman suffrage be addressed at the same time that Negro suffrage was granted. This stand lost them the support of many former allies among the abolitionists and led to a split with the Boston-area feminists who were willing to allow priority to Negro suffrage. For NWSA activists, Reconstruction opened the way to either radical demands for major changes in American life or to a more moderate program of attempting to gain legal and political rights for women.[11]

The most radical visions of the feminists frequently found support from free lovers. "When women are no longer owned," Francis Barry wrote in 1868 to Anthony and Stanton's journal, *Revolution*, "when men are no longer slaveholders (and this will be when the *system* is abolished) then . . . will men be manly, and just, and women be recognized and treated as equals." Barry wrote a few months later that mistresses were less degraded than wives. Other journals expressed outrage, but Elizabeth Cady Stanton defended Barry by citing the marriage laws in various states: "In view of laws like these, is not Francis Barry fully sustained in his assertion?" When a reader wrote to ask if she opposed "the present legalized marriage relation," Stanton replied, "Yes, I am opposed to the present legalized marriage, and the marriage and divorce laws of most states . . . because they bear un-equally on man and woman." She assured her readers that she did not wish the abolition of marriage but its purification by the elevation of women. In 1871 Stanton called for reforms in the divorce laws of the nation.

From a woman's standpoint I see that marriage, as an individual tie, is slavery for woman, because law, religion and public sentiment all combine . . . to hold her true to this relation, whatever it may be, and there is no other human slavery that knows such depths of degradation as a wife chained to a man whom she neither loves nor respects.

As she had done before the war, Stanton demanded that marriage become a contract like any other, dissolvable at the will of either party. This would provide a remedy for mistaken choices, lead to greater domestic harmony, and allow marriage to realize its great potential.[12] During the early 1870s, middle-class feminists came as close as they ever would to marriage radicalism.

New York City during the late 1860s not only became the home of the NWSA but it again became the center of free love, through the work of Stephen Pearl Andrews and his newest discovery, Victoria Woodhull. Victoria Woodhull, born in 1838, arrived in New York in 1868, having moved there upon the advice of spirit voices. With her second husband, James Harvey (better known as Colonel Blood), she brought her mother Roxanna Claflin, sisters Tennessee and Utica, her two children, and various other family members. The Woodhull household included other residents, from time to time, like Victoria's first husband and Stephen Pearl Andrews. Apparently Woodhull had been indoctrinated in the tenets of free love by Colonel Blood during their premarital tour of the Ozarks as Dr. and Madame Harvey, fortunetellers. Certainly she agreed with, or at least went along with, Andrews's teachings about individual sovereignty. When Andrews and Woodhull met in 1869, she and her sister Tennessee Claflin were already notorious as the first women stockbrokers in New York City. A New York *World* correspondent predicted that she was "destined to act no inferior part in the coming conflicts and reforms in the country." By 1870 Woodhull had declared her candidacy for President of the

United States, and the sisters began publishing *Woodhull and Claflin's Weekly*. The paper, managed by the Colonel, opened its columns to every reform idea of the time.[13]

For two years Victoria Woodhull seemed destined to become the new heroine of women's rights in America. In December 1870, she testified before a congressional committee in support of her memorial on the legality of woman suffrage. Although the committee majority rejected the arguments Woodhull presented, a long minority report supported her. In May 1871 she appeared with Elizabeth Cady Stanton on the platform of the National Woman's Suffrage Convention where she foretold the great consequences to flow from gaining the vote. "The enfranchisement of ten millions of women, is a revolution such as the world has never seen, and effects will follow it commensurate with its magnitude and importance." Women, she warned, must begin immediately to decide what to do with the power about to be theirs. And if Congress did not enfranchise them, she called upon women to form a convention and frame their own constitution. "We mean treason," she assured her audience, "we mean secession."

Woodhull so electrified the 1871 convention that the delegates approved all of the resolutions sponsored by her (penned by Andrews), including the demand that government cease

. . . to interfere with the rights of adult individuals to pursue happiness as they choose . . . or with contracts between individuals of whatever kind . . . which will place the intercourse of persons with each other upon their individual honor.[14]

The wording of the resolution made it only slightly more radical than Stanton's demand for marriage as a free contract. However, Victoria Woodhull's more forthright declarations of free love principles convinced some feminists to begin distancing themselves from the free love movement's most important spokesperson.

Woodhull's speech on "Social Freedom" in November brought so many spectators to Steinway Hall that hundreds had to stand outside in the rain. Reading from a manuscript written by Andrews, Woodhull insisted that if all people have constitutional rights to life, liberty, and pursuit of happiness then the law can have no power over marriage. Love alone constitutes marriage, and love between two people neither appears nor departs by their volition. As Elizabeth Cady Stanton had done in May, Victoria Woodhull argued that marriage laws should operate as contract law did, protecting provisions freely agreed upon by the parties. Unlike Stanton, however, Woodhull construed this view of contractual marriage as the basis of free love. "Yes, I am a Free Lover," she proclaimed, suddenly departing from her text.

I have an *inalienable, constitutional* and *natural* right to love whom I may, to love as *long* or as *short* a period as I can; to *change* that love *every day* if I please, and with *that* right neither *you* nor any *law* you can frame have *any* right to interfere.[15]

Although feminists were still enthusiastic about Woodhull at their 1872 convention in Washington, D.C., by that time Woodhull was moving away from her middle-class allies and free love formed only part of her itinerary. With Stephen Pearl Andrews she became involved in labor organization, supporting the International Workingmen's Association, Section 12. In 1871 *Woodhull and Claflin's* published the first English translation of the *Communist Manifesto* to appear in the United States. Andrews and Woodhull also supported the Paris Commune. Only three months after her speech on "Social Freedom," Victoria Woodhull delivered a message in Boston on the "Impending Revolution." "Now, Christ was a Communist of the strictest sort," she told her audience, "and so am I, and of the most extreme kind." No doubt referring to her associates on the New York Stock Exchange, she said,

Since those who possess the accumulated wealth of the country have filched it by legal means from those to whom it justly belongs—the people—it must be returned to them, by legal means if possible, but it must be returned to them in any event.[16]

Moderate and radical opinion of Victoria Woodhull was already diverging. By May 1872 Susan B. Anthony had changed her mind about Woodhull and opposed the plan of other feminists to form a political party to support her candidacy for the presidency. Anthony believed that Woodhull's prominence in the women's movement was dangerous because she attracted cranks, communists, and free lovers. At the May convention in New York City, Anthony refused to allow Woodhull on the platform and stonily watched as Woodhull's friends

Victoria Claflin Woodhull (1838–1927).
Thomas Nast's picture of Victoria Woodhull, "Get Thee Behind Me, (Mrs.) Satan," appeared in *Harper's Weekly* in 1872. Woodhull inspired both her supporters and her opponents—though with different emotions. What she actually stood for, if anything, is more difficult to determine. Stephen Pearl Andrews and her husband, Colonel Blood, apparently wrote or edited most of her articles and speeches.

and supporters left the hall with their heroine. Barred from the NWSA convention, Woodhull called her own convention at Apollo Hall, where she was triumphantly nominated for the presidency. Moses Hull, a former abolitionist and rising star among radicals, nominated Frederick Douglass as Woodhull's running mate. The *Weekly* had already begun to attract letters and articles from prewar radicals, such as Warren Chase, Francis Barry, James H. Cook, and Hannah F. M. Brown. As controversy continued to heat up around Woodhull, Ezra Heywood defended her in his journal, the *Word*. In a pamphlet, Austin Kent argued that "Protestants profess to believe in leaving every man's religion . . . *free.* . . . Mrs. W. claims no more and no less for conjugal love." [17]

If preaching red revolution and the destruction of marriage strained Woodhull's relations with the respectable reformers, the revelation of Henry Ward Beecher's love affair with Elizabeth Tilton snapped the bonds of all such alliances. In November 1872, *Woodhull and Claflin's Weekly* published "Victoria C. Woodhull's Complete and Detailed Version of the Beecher-Tilton Affair." According to the article, Victoria Woodhull had first learned from Elizabeth Cady Stanton in 1871 that Beecher, pastor of the Plymouth Church in Brooklyn, was making love to the wife of Theodore Tilton, editor of the highly influential *Independent*. Tilton later confirmed this information, Woodhull said, and became a believer in many of her causes. Beecher was also a free lover, Woodhull claimed: "Mr. Beecher told me that marriage is the grave of love, and that he never married a couple that he did not feel condemned." She strongly implied that during the intervening months both Tilton and Beecher had become her lovers. Anthony Comstock had Victoria Woodhull and her sister arrested in 1872 for sending the paper containing the Beecher-Tilton article through the mail. The judge eventually dismissed the case, ruling that the 1872 law did not cover newspapers. By then Comstock had lobbied through his tougher law, but it was too late. [18]

Marriage radicals rallied to defend Woodhull and remained indifferent to intimations that she might become a disaster for their movement. The article revealing Beecher's folly contained language out of place in such an exposé, language that hinted at Victoria Woodhull's dangerous infatuation with herself. "I am a prophetess—I am an evangel—I am a Saviour, if you would but see it; but I, too, come not to bring peace, but a sword." [19] During the next few years free lovers generally approved of Victoria Woodhull's actions regarding the Beecher-Tilton affair. This was symptomatic of middle-class radicals' commitment to principle at a time when their principles had less and less relevance to American society.

The radicals would have profited by heeding the warnings of one of their fellows. In April 1873 Joseph Treat, a former *Social Revolutionist* contributor and Berlin Heights free lover, joined the staff of *Woodhull and Claflin's Weekly*. During the war Treat had left Berlin Heights for a medical practice in New York City. Far from abandoning reform, however, he continued to live by his principles. When his wife converted to Methodism, Treat announced that he had to part from her in order to remain true to Tyndall, Spencer, Huxley, and Darwin. Victoria Woodhull's proclamations and fearlessness in the face of public outcry over the Beecher-Tilton article so impressed Treat that he idolized her as the great hope of radical change in the country. Treat soon found his awe fading, however, and turning to disgust. It is true that Treat's disillusion with Victoria Woodhull caused him great anguish, and he may have actually been in love with one or more of the Claflin sisters, but his pamphlet on the Woodhull group was as much a product of Treat's devotion to truth as of his venom. [20]

Even though some of the evidence Treat presented is so circumstantial or unsubstantiated that it must be questioned, Treat's testimony in matters where he had firsthand knowledge is telling. Writing in the form of an open letter to Victoria Woodhull, Treat refuted the notion that she was the power and the genius behind the *Weekly*. "You write nothing, not even a word; Col. Blood pens your every private note, and signs your name to it." The Colonel also wrote Woodhull's speeches, which she often did not read until she delivered them: "you are utterly incapable of executing these productions which appear in your name." While these are the best substantiated of Treat's charges, his other revelations were far more sensational. Both Claflin sisters were gamblers, he insisted, and he named their bookie. The sisters were also prostitutes, having slept with wealthy brokers for large sums of money, and they had procured customers for their sister, Utica, who died of a sexual disease. Treat even claimed that Roxanna Claflin, Colonel Blood, and Stephen Pearl Andrews were all involved in illicit sex.[21]

Radicals who embraced free love could hardly damn Victoria Woodhull for prostitution, even if the charges were true, since they had always claimed that marriage was far worse than prostitution. Austin Kent asked why there was such concern about the Claflin sisters' morals when reformers often united with men of questionable morality. "The fact is," Kent wrote, "very few radicals are half saved from this unjust prejudice against women." Ezra Heywood, in the *Word*, also attacked Treat, but the doctor was defended by his old fellow lecturers William Denton and Francis Barry.[22]

For her part, Victoria Woodhull moved on to other matters. Lecturing across the country to large audiences, she offered her own interpretation of scripture and claimed that the human body was immortal. The *Weekly*, apparently mismanaged, lost many subscribers in the years before its final demise in 1877. Radicals might defend Woodhull's right to say what she pleased, but they equally claimed the right not to read what they considered nonsense, such as Woodhull's claims about the immortality of the flesh. Woodhull also broke with Colonel Blood. Irritated that the Colonel had helped his ex-wife, Woodhull trumped up a charge of infidelity against him and won a divorce. In 1877 the Claflin sisters, their parents, and their children sailed to England. Both sisters would marry into wealth and gentility, living down, if not suppressing, their free love past.[23]

Victoria Woodhull's notoriety added to the public reputation of free love as a sinister movement and hurried the end of the free love movement's cooperation with the women's movement. Organized feminists already confined their discussion of domestic reform to demands for freer divorce laws and increasingly concentrated their efforts on the struggle for suffrage. By 1890 the NWSA activists merged with their moderate sisters in Boston. In addition, as feminists became involved in work for moral purity they came into conflict with marriage radicalism.[24] Woodhull's actions probably did nothing to discourage those who were already committed to free love, but the defection of its colorful standard bearer appears to have demoralized the New York–based movement. Free love existed in the postwar era, as it had in the 1850s, as a network. When New York ceased to define the movement, leadership passed to the anarchist circles in Massachusetts and the West.

Changes within the free love network often reflected shifting personal relationships. In Ohio, for instance, Francis Barry left Berlin Heights and moved first to Cleveland and then to Ravenna where he established the Western Reserve Woman's Emancipation Society in 1873, with the object of overthrowing marriage. The Society's 1874 convention condemned the half-hearted language of Warren Chase and Victoria Woodhull and invited these moderates to engage in "an unqualified and persistent demand for the immediate and unconditional abolition" of marriage. It was easier, read the convention report, to speak of "true prostitution" than of "true marriage," and it was better for women to become prostitutes than to become wives. Those free lovers who remained at Berlin Heights settled into a *modus vivendi* with the town's conventional residents during the 1860s. While publishing a series of short-lived periodicals and discussing the latest ideas in their meetings, the radicals did business honestly and worked hard. By the late 1860s, a group of Berlin free lovers led by James Towner converted to perfectionism and settled at Oneida.[25]

Oneida was also changing. The second generation there, children who had been born in the community and grown up in communism and accustomed to complex marriage, lacked their parents' religious zeal. John Humphrey Noyes countenanced both revivalism and even spiritualism during the 1870s in an effort to turn the children of the perfectionists away from materialism and toward their Christian heritage. While the *American Socialist* (successor to the *Oneida Circular*) became a highly respected journal among American radicals, Oneidan communism entered a period of crisis that culminated in the end of complex marriage in 1879 and ultimately in the dissolution of the community.[26]

In spite of changes within the free love network, the movement's first generation actively aided the work of the newer marriage abolitionists. Much of Victoria Woodhull's work, for instance, carried the stamp of Stephen Pearl Andrews's influence. Other radicals aired their views and encouragement within the new periodicals. Warren Chase wrote to the Claflin paper that he was convinced all marriage laws should be abolished, thus making relations between men and women subject to the general law of contracts. Marx Edgeworth Lazarus continued to write for various anarchist periodicals. He praised Heywood's monthly, *The Word:* "it inculcates the essential goodness of amative pleasure, the integrity of love, in opposition to platonic hypocrisies." His experience at Ceresco and Berlin Heights had convinced J. H. Cook that dual marriage was incompatible with a higher life. As the race moves toward its millennial destiny, Cook assured postwar readers, there could be no permanent resting place between legal marriage and free love. Theron Leland also continued to condemn the "Devil Fish of ecclesiasticism" that defined sex as obscenity. He believed that it was "dawning on advanced thinkers, students of science, and on the minds of sensible men and women generally, that sex is not total depravity, nor a disastrous mistake on the part of the Creator."[27]

By the 1870s a second generation of marriage radicals had appeared who would face challenges unanticipated by their older associates. Probably the leading free lover during the 1870s and 1880s was Ezra Heywood. Beginning in 1872, Heywood, with his wife Angela Tilton, published the *Word* from their home in Princeton, Massachusetts. One historian of American anarchism, James J. Martin, has called this monthly "the first sustained voice of anarchist doctrine in America." Heywood's activism had come from the antislavery movement and such leaders as Garrison and Wendell Philips, but his anarchism he learned from Josiah Warren, "the Thomas Paine of coming Socialism." Heywood, like Warren, worked to improve the conditions of laborers. In 1872 he joined such older labor activists as Albert Brisbane, John Orvis, and William Denton to form the New England Labor Reform League.[28]

In spite of Josiah Warren's cautious public attitude toward the question of marriage, sovereignty of the individual implied the repudiation of marriage. Heywood recognized this connection, making marriage and its prospective abolition prominent features of his writings. He discussed sexual relationships in the same tone that Warren used for economic issues: "If [lovers are] free to go wrong, disciplined by ideas, they will work out their own salvation in the school of experience." The first issue of the *Word* carried an article on "Love and Marriage." "Wishing to hasten the progress of civilization towards the bed chamber and the nursery, we shall do what we can to stimulate investigation into the gravest subject of human inquiry, the true relations of the sexes." During 1873 he organized the New England Free Love League in Princeton. The League's first convention took place in Boston, in 1876, to publicly demonstrate freedom of discussion. Later issues of the *Word* would be dated YL, or Year of Love, from the 1873 founding of the Free Love League.[29]

Cupid's Yokes, first published in 1873, reiterated many of the arguments that earlier free lovers had advanced. Heywood claimed that "the secret history of the human heart proves that it is capable of loving any number of times and persons, and the more it loves the more it can love." But rather than encouraging love, civil marriage turned women over to the lusts of their husbands, while the demands of premarital chastity and lifelong monogamy forced many to live either above or below marriage. It was marriage, not free love, that opened the floodgates of sensuality and created prostitution by forbidding natural intercourse. "A system so prolific of hypocrites and martyrs," Heywood believed, "is compulsive in the most mischievous sense of that word, and will be abolished when free and virtuous people resolutely confront it." With marriage abolished and sexual relations a matter of simple contracts, individuals would become more experienced and so better able to form good unions. When men finally learned to love intelligently, they would become less lustful and more friendly and helpful to their mates. Heywood continued his attack upon marriage in the eighty thousand copies of *Uncivil Liberty* (1877).[30]

Among reformers supporting Heywood, Francis Barry was particularly enthusiastic. Barry wrote from Ravenna praising the *Word* for presenting free love so clearly. "Let the World understand," wrote Barry, "that Free Love is not a seeking, on the part of its advocates, of personal enjoyment, but a grand *work* for human redemption—a hand to hand and life and death struggle with hoary-headed and bloody-handed wrong." In another letter Barry identified the complete emancipation of women with the abolition of marriage; once woman was liberated, marriage would disappear. Even when human relations became truly free, however, contracting cohabitation for an indefinite period of time would be "prima facie evidence of an intention to commit prostitution." The only disagreement between Barry and Heywood came from the misuse of a single word. When Barry read an article referring to Angela Heywood as Ezra's wife, he protested. Barry knew Heywood was a good man and gave him the benefit of his confidence: "I do not by any means suppose that you really practice marriage." But, though men with wives could be sincere reformers, they still engaged in a form of slavery. "Why did you not speak of the lady in question as your *prostitute* or as your mistress?"[31]

Two of the important free lovers in the postwar period were westerners. Moses Hull (born 1836) grew up in rural Indiana where he joined first the United Brethren, then the Adventists, and finally the Seventh Day Adventists. He was both a minister and lecturer for the disciples of Ellen White until 1865, when his own doubts and those of his wife forced him to abandon Christian millennialism for spiritualism. His pilgrimage from the pulpit to the seance allowed Hull to doubt other Christian institutions. In 1872 he wrote that marriage, though appointed by heaven as a blessing to humanity, was as often a bane. "The radical evil, I apprehend, is in the relation of the sexes— the ownership of wife by husband, and husband by wife." He expected that a great revolution would be necessary to prepare the world for "the soul-union, the true marriage that shall follow."[32]

Hull's own experience made marriage a pressing issue. During his months-long lecture trips as a missionary of spiritualism, he struggled to maintain fidelity to his wife. In line with the claims of other spiritualists, Hull concluded by about 1867 that "man made law, God made love: one or the other has made a mistake." Writing of this realization several years later, he mentioned both divine and physiological imperatives. "The confinement of one man and one woman together sexually," he wrote in *Woodhull and Claflin's* in 1873, "may do for those who do not attempt to do much besides following along as the lamb is led to the slaughter: but to the man or woman of mind, of brain, of intellectual labor, it is a different question." Far different. Hull abandoned exclusiveness, and eventually "I told my wife all; the scene which immediately followed I will not relate." In time, however, Elvira Hull became accustomed to the idea and finally found the practice acceptable for both of them. Elvira Hull confirmed this. Rather than periods of sexual starvation while Hull was away and abuse when he returned home, they had developed a healthier life together. "Moses

Moses Hull (1836–1906).
Hull left the Seventh Day Adventist Church in 1865 and soon became a lecturer for spiritualism. It was during his months-long lecture tours that he began to enter free relationships with women other than his wife.

COURTESY OF THE LABADIE COLLECTION, DEPARTMENT OF RARE BOOKS AND SPE-
CIAL COLLECTIONS, UNIVERSITY OF MICHIGAN LIBRARY.

is a better husband—a better man for it." In 1873 the two parted by mutual agreement, and Hull entered a free union with another lecturer, Mattie Sawyer.[33]

Hull's confession seems to have caused quite a stir. Colonel Blood later claimed that his letter caused five thousand subscribers to the *Weekly* to cancel the paper.[34] Hull opened volume three of *Hull's Crucible* with a long defense of his actions and of his revelation. With the noteworthy exception of James Clay's *A Voice from Prison*, writings on free love had always tended to damn marriage and propose its destruction, leaving the details of free love practice open for speculation. Hull's dramatic departure from this upset many who were willing to imagine free love as a form of purified marriage. This was the kind of person whom Francis Barry found always "talking about 'what marriage ought to be,' 'true marriage,' etc., and going to work to patch up the system instead of abolishing it." Rather than idealize his marriage, Hull had rejected its limitations; only true free lovers could support such consistency. Austin Kent encouraged Hull, telling him that although Hull had lost popularity among spiritualists for his confession, he was a better man for telling it. "In our State," Kent wrote, "if a couple desire to part, one must commit adultery to give the other a chance to get a bill of divorce. That offers a premium on what the law calls a crime."[35] Kent, like Barry and other first generation free lovers, continued to support the movement they had begun.

Another Westerner became a leader in postwar free love. Moses Harman had grown up on a farm in Missouri and attended Arcadia College. By age twenty, in 1850, he was licensed to preach by the southern Methodist Church, but arguments with Universalists soon turned his thoughts in the direction of infidelity. After traveling and teaching in Indiana during the 1850s, Harman returned to Missouri in 1860 and quickly gained notoriety for his antislavery views. Though suffering during the Civil War, Harman remained in Missouri and married the daughter of a slain Union sympathizer. In 1877 Susan Harman died, leaving Moses with two children, Lillian and George. The Harmans moved in 1879 to Valley Falls, Kansas, where Moses worked as a teacher and was soon helping to edit the *Valley Falls Liberal*. By 1883 Harman was again notorious, this time as a free thinker. In that year he changed his paper's name from the *Kansas*

Liberal to *Lucifer, the Light Bearer* and featured articles on free thought, free love, and labor reform. *Lucifer* and its publisher inspired many of the controversies of the next two decades, surviving until after the turn of the century as the last voice of free love's second generation.[36]

Lucifer, like the *Word* and *Hull's Crucible*, would be eagerly read and supported by radicals from the 1850s. In spite of their continuing enthusiasm, however, the first generation of marriage radicals could serve as only partial guides to postwar free lovers. Josiah Warren, the first American anarchist and mentor to virtually all of the individual sovereigns, died in 1874. Austin Kent, who had been losing his struggle against paralysis for decades and living partially on charity, probably survived Warren by only a few years. In 1873 he was in his early sixties but wrote that his mental powers had deteriorated to that of a man in his eighties. Stephen Pearl Andrews died in 1886, Warren Chase in 1891, Marx Lazarus in 1895. While human mortality and changes within the free love network gave free love a new shape, changes in American society made the relation of bourgeois radicalism to the middle class more problematic and more volatile.[37]

There were several aspects of postwar free love that set it apart from the prewar movement. To begin with, middle-class radicalism was further from the middle class than it had ever been before. Prewar radicals formed their views from the materials at hand—European socialisms, revival-inspired heresies, and the assumptions of class identity. For the postwar generation, an American radical tradition and network already existed. Josiah Warren was the philosopher of this tradition, Modern Times and Berlin Heights the communal expressions, and the abolition of marriage the expected outcome. It was a tradition that originally had some relation to the middle class at every point. Ante-bellum intellectuals, for instance, shared the individualism and perfectionism typical of radicals and so could easily find connections between their principles and those of more extreme thinkers. The consolidation of American culture during the 1850s followed by the national crusade to save the Union made pragmatism and faith in institutions more typical of middle-class intellectuals; thus, individual sovereignty became more specifically the program of those who were at odds with American society.

Individuals had farther to travel to radicalism after the Civil War,

Moses Harman (1830–1910).
Harman changed the name of his paper from the *Kansas Liberal* to *Lucifer, the Light Bearer* in 1883. From that time until his death, Harman stood for free language, free thought, and free love.

COURTESY OF THE LABADIE COLLECTION, DEPARTMENT OF RARE BOOKS AND SPE-CIAL COLLECTIONS, UNIVERSITY OF MICHIGAN LIBRARY.

not only because free love was farther from the American mainstream but because postwar free lovers grew up in a middle-class environment that was more pervasive. Although a time of religious awakening, the 1830s and 1840s were also the decades when Owenism and Fourierism swept through the country. The generation of postwar radicals were children in these decades and had less experience of socialism. Their parents had largely accepted that evangelicalism and proper behavior formed the basis of their social status. The first names of Heywood, Hull, and Harman testify to the piety of their parents. Both Harman and Hull had been preachers, and Heywood had trained for the ministry. Heywood later commented that his free love ideas dated from his studies of the New Testament. Harman also made a long journey through religious doubt to radical certainty.[38]

Moses Hull provides the best example of the fusion of revivalist fervor and radical principles. Even though he had abandoned his belief in the divine inspiration of scripture, his writings contained frequent scriptural references. In his "Personal Experience" letter he asked, "Methodists, Baptists and Presbyterians prove their religion by their personal experiences. Cannot we do the same?" His letter certainly had the flavor of an evangelical conversion. Recognizing that sexual variety was God's command,

I humbly, and prayerfully yielded to the diviner impulses of my soul, and found that peace, happiness and intellectual growth for which I craved. I felt that I had been baptized with a diviner baptism, and reached a higher and purer life, had entered the "Holy of Holies," and found a divine benediction that never was reached by one who had not traversed the same road.[39]

While the religious pilgrimage of postwar free lovers tended to set them apart from prewar radicals, their tactics gave free love a new militancy. Prewar free lovers had largely guarded their language even when they advocated free love. Marriage was wrong, for spiritual or religious or legal reasons. It had to go, to be replaced by more virtuous and spiritual unions that were in many ways identical to ideal bourgeois marriages. Even James Clay's love match with Maria Cole was chaste. When Anne Denton Cridge in 1857 cited cases of women whose sexual demands outpaced their husbands', free lovers reacted with outrage. Obviously, it was a new world in which Victoria Woodhull ridiculed Joseph Treat for having intercourse with only one woman in his life.[40] Moses Hull's "Personal Experience" began open discussion of sexual desire and the replacement for marriage.

Although the comparative openness about sexuality may have been the logical conclusion of prewar radical ideals, it also reflected a fragmentation of ideology. The ante-bellum radicals mentioned few details of their purified sexual relations because they could all assume, from their understanding of the writings of health reformers, that sex without marriage would be more a matter of discipline than of sensuality. Even Moses Hull, who admitted to changing partners, said that he still had sex only once a month. Free lovers after the war were caught both by changes within what the middle class considered appropriate and by their own confusion over whether to stand by their old beliefs or claim new, more radical ideas.

More important than the changes within the free love movement were changes within American society. Writing to Ezra Heywood, Francis Barry commented, "The amount of persecution Free Lovers have had to meet in the past, at least this generation of them, has been insignificant. I am inclined to think it will not be very much more serious in the future."[41] Barry was half right. Although free lovers never received any encouragement for their activities, the actual physical restraint exercised against them was minimal. During the 1850s the most severe punishment meted out to anyone espousing or practicing free love was the six months that James Clay spent in an Augusta jail. Several of the Berlin free lovers were arrested on adultery charges, and the sentences against them sought to exile them from Berlin Heights. As we have seen, this was a signal failure of policy. Finally, although the police raid on the Free Love Club in New York City appears to have ended that organization, the several individuals arrested spent only one night in jail and meetings were soon taking place again on other premises.

More than a year before Barry's optimistic prediction, Austin Kent foresaw that the coming struggle to destroy marriage would be a bitter one. By the mid-1870s American attitudes had hardened. In the 1830s and 1840s, sexual purity had been a relatively novel idea, spread by preachers and physicians who often earned middle-class suspicion and hostility for discussing sexual behavior. The postwar purity crusaders, in their efforts to promote feminism and protect children, attacked pornography as a root cause of sexual immorality. In 1873, with the newly revised obscenity law shepherded through Congress by Anthony Comstock, purity became a matter of public policy. Comstock believed free love posed a threat to the very basis of American society. "With them," he wrote,

marriage is bondage; love is lust; celibacy is suicide. . . . All restraints which keep boys and girls, young men and maidens pure and chaste, which prevent our homes from being turned into voluntary brothels, are not to be tolerated by them.

Although Victoria Woodhull escaped Comstock's attentions relatively unscathed, other free lovers would find him a dangerous foe.[42]

Comstock struck at Ezra Heywood first. He sent decoy letters to Heywood in 1877 requesting copies of *Cupid's Yokes*. With a warrant based on this evidence in hand, Comstock appeared at a Boston meeting of the New England Free Love league, purchased a ticket, and took a seat among approximately 250 men and boys. "The address," he reported later, "was made up of abuse of myself and disgusting arguments for their cause." When Angela Heywood took the podium to deliver "the foulest address I ever heard," Ezra Heywood momentarily walked outside. Comstock followed him and exercised the warrant for his arrest. According to Comstock's account, he had to manhandle Ezra Heywood to get him away from the hall just as Angela Heywood raised the alarm. With much manly courage the special federal deputy escorted his prisoner to Charles Street Jail. That same year Comstock arrested another editor, De Robigne Bennett, also for selling *Cupid's Yokes*.[43]

In June 1878 Heywood was sentenced to two years in prison and a $100 fine. Benjamin Tucker, an anarchist editor in New Bedford, took over as editor of the *Word* during Heywood's trial and following the sentence organized the National Defense Association (NDA) to take up Heywood's cause. On August 1, 1878, the NDA held a rally at Fanueil Hall in Boston with forty-five hundred in attendance. The crowd included former abolitionists, free thinkers, and others devoted to civil liberties. Enough pressure was put on President Hayes that he pardoned Heywood. Bennett's case turned out differently. Although his fine was paid for him, and Bennett returned to his work, he was soon arrested again and sentenced to a $300 fine and thirteen months in prison. After the outcry over Heywood's pardon, Hayes was unwilling to help Bennett and rejected the petition containing two hundred thousand signatures requesting a pardon for Bennett.[44]

Out of prison, Heywood continued his campaign for free love. In 1880 he and his wife decided upon the use of free language as a means of advancing more openness in the discussion of sex. Angela Heywood found the word fuck a particularly graceful term for describing the experience of sex. Ezra facetiously called marriage the penis trust; in its place, he wrote, there should be established a fucking trust to bring the moral, social, and physical uses of sex into the domain of reason and moral obligation. This was hardly the kind of policy to calm the nation's vice hounds. Between 1882 and 1887 Comstock arrested Heywood four more times. Each time Heywood went free, either because the juries found him innocent or because officials would not prosecute. Comstock persisted. In 1889 he arrested Heywood again, this time for reprinting some material Angela had written and also for texts that had appeared in *Lucifer*. Ezra Heywood was convicted and sentenced to two years at hard labor in Charlestown Prison. He lived only one year after his release in 1892.[45]

As suggested by the reference to *Lucifer*, the Harman circle also ran afoul of the postwar guardians of morality. Moses Harman's daughter Lillian and Edwin Walker published the ceremony of their free marriage in *Lucifer*'s columns in 1886 and were promptly arrested. Both were convicted — Edwin Walker was sentenced to seventy-five days in prison, Lillian Harman to forty-five. In 1887 Moses Harman and his son George were arrested for violating obscenity laws for publishing various letters, including one on marital rape. This was part of Harman's free language policy; like Heywood, he viewed the medium of the radical journal as a means of opening discussion. In 1890 he brought another charge upon himself by publishing a letter from Richard V. O'Neill, a physician who had written about cases of heterosexual and homosexual oral sex. Sentenced to five years for the first offense, Harman gained his release after four months on a technicality. For the O'Neill letter he was again convicted; again he served only part of the sentence. He was then resentenced for the original letter, and this time served one year of hard labor. This was in 1895 and 1896, when Harman was in his mid-sixties.[46]

Other advocates of changes in sex and marriage found the Gilded Age an unfriendly time. Lois Waisbrooker, who edited *Lucifer* in the 1890s while Harman was in prison, was arrested in 1894 for publishing the journal *Foundation Principles* and was arrested in 1902 for publishing *Clothed with the Sun*. Emil Ruedebusch was fined $1,200 in 1898. Alice B. Stockham, for distributing obstetrical advice to women, was fined $250. The most tragic case of legal harassment was that of Ida C. Craddock who was released after a short time in prison in 1902 but was soon rearrested by Anthony Comstock. Rather than face more time in prison, she committed suicide. Finally, Moses Harman, in his seventies, was arrested again in 1905.[47]

Imprisonment and legal harassment could never have prevailed against the righteous determination of free love's second generation. By the time of Moses Harman's 1905 arrest, however, the movement had become largely irrelevant. Comstock and the federal laws represented only one form of defense of middle-class marriage and represented only part of the middle class. The official morality promoted by Comstock and his sponsors had little connection to the actual concerns of married couples and families. Many Americans had come to regard divorce as a safety valve for marriage, allowing the demise of clearly substandard unions. From 1860 through the early 1900s, the divorce rate nearly doubled every twenty years. As the kind of informal divorce that free love had sanctioned became unnecessary, the movement retained its radical ideology and rhetoric but lost any practical program for individuals. By persisting in perfectionism—seeking the full equality of all within a regenerated sexual union—free love distanced itself from the day-to-day concerns of America's middle class. Barry's abhorrence of those who sought to patch up marriage was, given his beliefs, well placed, since their efforts were largely successful.[48]

Married sex gained a second safety valve by the late nineteenth century as Americans became more inclined to endorse sexual pleasure. In matters as different as bathing and recreational clubs and lodges, the Gilded Age bourgeoisie began to find personal enjoyment acceptable. Sexual intercourse began to seem, if only in marriage, a proper

form of fun. Both a contributing cause and an effect of this affirma-
tion of sexual pleasure was the spread of birth-control knowledge
and technology. At the same time, the separation of sex from pro-
creation gave more protection to the health of married women, thereby
undermining another of free love's traditional attacks on marriage.[49]

It was not only American society that marginalized middle-class
radicalism; by the end of the century the radical milieu was far different. Free love as a slogan would be carried from the early twentieth
century by radicals whose connections with the movement's bourgeois
and religious roots were tenuous or nonexistent. During the late nineteenth century, avant-garde intellectuals were reading free love works
and circulating the writings of English radicals. After 1900, bohemians
in New York's Greenwich Village embraced free love as an intellectual
style and as a way of life. At the same time, with the growth of labor
agitation and the importation of European anarchists, radicalism moved
in new directions. Warrenite individual sovereignty was too friendly
to private property for European radicals like Johann Most. Emma
Goldman, probably the outstanding advocate of free love during the
early 1900s, recalled no religious struggles in the years before she
began to take on a series of lovers, including Most. Goldman also gave
little evidence of influence from native American radicalism until the
late 1890s, when she was already one of the nation's leading anarchists.[50]

Ante-bellum free love could survive only as long as radicalism had
deep roots in evangelical religion and middle-class ideology. The
movement that had grown up in the wake of utopian socialism and was
founded on the moral imperatives of revival, reform, and hygiene
could hardly continue to offer viable alternatives when the issues of
community, physiological salvation, and genuine experience no longer
moved the majority of Americans. Free lovers in the Gilded Age faced
a middle class that was committed to large-scale organization, nationalism, and sexual respectability and was indifferent to fears of artificial
relationships. Free love passed into this new age as one concomitant of
the coming freedom or as a protest against a loveless world. As in the
past, free love was part of a program for wide-ranging social change,
but it was a program that free love's first advocates would have found
confusing and surprising.

$\mathcal{N}$otes

1. Marriage and the Formation of the Middle Class

1. John Higham, *From Boundlessness to Consolidation: The Transformation of American Culture, 1848–1860* (Ann Arbor, Mich.: Clements Library, 1969), 6; Alice Felt Tyler, *Freedom's Ferment: Phases of American Social History to 1860* (Minneapolis: University of Minnesota Press, 1944), 1; Gilbert Barnes, *The Antislavery Impulse, 1830–1844* (New York: D. Appleton, 1933), 16.

2. Carroll Smith-Rosenberg, *Disorderly Conduct: Visions of Gender in Victorian America* (New York: Oxford University Press, 1985), 81–82; Louis Dumont, *Homo Hierarchicus: The Caste System and its Implications*, trans. Mark Salisbury, Louis Dumont, and Basia Gulati, (Chicago: University of Chicago Press, 1980), especially 4–20; and Robert Brain, *Friends and Lovers* (New York: Basic Books, 1976), 247. See also Sean Wilentz, *Chants Democratic: New York City and the Rise of the American Working Class, 1788–1850* (New York: Oxford University Press, 1984).

3. Stuart M. Blumin, "The Hypothesis of Middle-class Formation in Nineteenth-Century America: A Critique and Some Proposals," *American Historical Review* 90 (April 1985):299–338.

4. On the Puritan ideal of marriage and its transformation, see Christopher Hill, *The World Turned Upside Down: Radical Ideas During the English Revolution* (London: Temple Smith, 1972), 247; and John R. Gillis, *For Better, For Worse: British Marriages, 1600 to the Present* (New York: Oxford University Press, 1985), 14. On the changes in the vision of society from Puritan times, see Michael Paul Rogin, *Fathers and Children: Andrew Jackson and the Subjugation of the American Indian* (New York: Knopf, 1975), 31, 251, 252, 254. The functions of the middle-class family are carefully examined in Steven Mintz, *A Prison of Expectations: The Family in Victorian Culture* (New York: New York University Press, 1983) and in Mary P. Ryan, *Cradle of the Middle Class: The Family in Oneida County, New York, 1790–1865* (Cambridge: Cambridge University Press, 1981). See also Burton

J. Bledstein, *The Culture of Professionalism: The Middle Class and the Development of Higher Education in America* (New York: W. W. Norton, 1976), especially the introductory essay and Blumin.

5. Daniel Scott Smith and Michael Hindus, "Premarital Pregnancy in America, 1640–1971: An Overview and Interpretation," *The Journal of Interdisciplinary History* 5 (Spring 1975):551; Perry Miller, *The Life of the Mind in America from the Revolution to the Civil War* (New York: Harcourt, Brace and World, 1965), 7, 32ff; Donald G. Mathews, "The Second Great Awakening as an Organizing Process, 1780–1830: An Hypothesis," *American Quarterly* 21 (Spring 1969):36–37; Winthrop S. Hudson, "A Time of Religious Ferment," in Edwin S. Gaustad, ed., *The Rise of Adventism: Religion and Society in Mid-Nineteenth-Century America* (New York: Harper and Row, 1974), 3.

6. Barnes, *Antislavery Impulse*, 25; Carroll Smith-Rosenberg, "Sex as Symbol in Victorian Purity: An Ethnohistorical Analysis of Jacksonian America," *American Journal of Sociology* 84 (supplement):217–20, 227, 237, 243. The uses of revivalism in establishing personal identity are treated in Ryan, *Cradle of the Middle Class*, 102, 121, 154 and in Gerald Moran, "The Puritan Saint: Religious Experience, Church Membership, and Piety in Connecticut, 1636–1776," (Ph.D. dissertation, Rutgers University, 1973), 405–10, 421–26. See also Stephen Nissenbaum, *Sex, Diet, and Debility in Jacksonian America: Sylvester Graham and Health Reform* (Westport, Conn.: Greenwood Press, 1980), 4–5, 127–29, 143–45. On the new standards for moral behavior, see Thomas L. Haskell, "Capitalism and the Origins of the Humanitarian Sensibility," *American Historical Review* 90 (April/June 1985):339–61, 547–66; Norbert Elias, *The Civilizing Process: The History of Manners*, vol. 1, trans. Edmund Jephcott (New York: Urizen Books, 1978), 225; E. Anthony Rotundo, "Body and Soul: Changing Ideals of American Middle-class Manhood, 1770–1920," *Journal of American History* 15 (Fall 1982):23–38; Warren Susman, " 'Personality' and the Making of Twentieth-century Culture," in *Culture as History: The Transformation of American Society in the Twentieth Century* (New York: Pantheon), 271–85.

7. Ryan, *Cradle of the Middle Class*, 12, 80–83, 93–98, 102–3, 116, 120–23, 141, 146–47, 154–79. Paul E. Johnson, *A Shopkeeper's Millennium: Society and Revivals in Rochester, New York, 1815–1837* (New York: Hill and Wang, 1978) provides a different interpretation of evangelicalism. According to Johnson, revival was a tool of the middle class to bring order to the community. It provided self-control for the middle class and social controls for the lower classes.

8. John S. Gilkeson, *Middle-Class Providence, 1820–1940* (Princeton, N.J.: Princeton University Press, 1986), 23–54.

9. Peter Gardella, *Innocent Ecstasy: How Christianity Gave America an Ethic of Sexual Pleasure* (New York: Oxford University Press, 1985), 40–67; Eric Trudgill, *Madonnas and Magdalens: The Origins and Development of Victorian Sexual Attitudes* (New York: Holmes and Meier, 1976), 13–14; Miller, *Life of the Mind in America*, 32ff.

10. Self-control as the core of civilization is treated in Ronald G. Walters, "The Erotic South: Civilization and Sexuality in American Abolitionism," *American Quarterly* 25 (May 1973):187–88; Peter Gay *The Bourgeois Experience: Victoria to Freud*, vol. 1, *Education of the Senses* (New York: Oxford University Press, 1984), 429; Elias, *Civilizing Process*, vol. 1, 49, 183, 185–86.

11. Sylvester Graham, *A Lecture to Young Men* [1834] (New York: Arno, 1974), 16–21, 29–30. For the background to Graham's physiological theory of debility, see Nissenbaum, *Sex, Diet, and Debility*, 53–64, 105–19. See also James C. Whorton, *Crusaders for*

Fitness: The History of American Health Reformers (Princeton, N.J.: Princeton University Press, 1982), 43–44; John Ware, *Hints to Young Men, on the True Relation of the Sexes* (Boston: Tappan, Whittemore, and Mason, 1850), 5, 50–52.

12. L. D. Fleming, *Self-pollution, the Cause of Youthful Decay: Showing the Dangers and Remedy of Veneral Disease* (New York: Wellman, 1846), 38; Graham, *Lecture to Young Men*, 26, 62; R. T. Trall, *Home-Treatment for Sexual Abuses* (New York: Fowler and Wells, 1853), xii, 81.

13. Ellen K. Rothman, "Sex and Self-Control: Middle-Class Courtship in America, 1770–1870," *Journal of Social History* 15 (Spring 1982):409–25; Graham, *Lecture to Young Men*, 37; Smith and Hindus, "Premarital Pregnancy," 537–39, 550–51. For a discussion of the implications of self-control in middle-class society, see James Reed, *The Birth Control Movement and American Society: From Private Vice to Public Virtue* (Princeton, N.J.: Princeton University Press, 1983), chap. 1. Recently Michel Foucault has offered an interesting new perspective on the "Repressive Hypothesis" in *The History of Sexuality*, vol. 1, *An Introduction*, trans. Robert Hurley (New York: Vintage, 1980), 17–35. Foucault places sexual discourse into a wider social imperative to discuss, administer, and intervene in sex. Discussion of sex became far more common—indeed, pervasive—as is shown from the numerous tracts by Alcott, Graham, and others.

14. Nancy F. Cott, "Passionlessness: An Interpretation of Victorian Sexual Ideology, 1790–1850," *Signs* 4 (Winter 1978):219–36 and quote from 227. While the major portion of this argument was drawn from the Cott article, other influential works that follow the same general line of reasoning are Ann Douglas, *The Feminization of American Culture* (New York: Knopf, 1978); Daniel Scott Smith, "Family Limitation, Sexual Control, and Domestic Feminism in Victorian America," *Feminist Studies* (Winter–Spring 1973):40–57; Nancy F. Cott, *The Bonds of Womanhood: "Woman's Sphere" in New England, 1780–1835* (New Haven, Conn.: Yale University Press, 1977), 9, 200.

15. Dumont, *Homo Hierarchicus*, 20; Edward Strutt Abdy, *Journal of a Residence and Tour in the United States in 1833–34* (London: N.p., 1835), 74; Alexis de Tocqueville, *Democracy in America*, vol. 2, (New York: Knopf, 1945), 217; Louis Kern, *An Ordered Love: Sex Roles and Sexuality in Victorian Utopias—the Shakers, the Mormons, and the Oneida Community* (Chapel Hill: The University of North Carolina Press, 1981), 19–20, 23; Karen Halttunen, *Confidence Men and Painted Women: A Study of Middle-Class Culture in America, 1830–1870* (New Haven, Conn.: Yale University Press 1982), xv, 1.

16. "The Man that was Used Up," in *The Complete Tales and Poems of Edgar Allen Poe*, ed. Hervey Allen (New York: Modern Library, 1938), 405–12; Nathaniel Hawthorne, *The Blithedale Romance*, (New York: W. W. Norton, 1958), 115.

17. James Fenimore Cooper, *Notions of the Americans: Picked Up by a Travelling Bachelor*, vol. 1 [1825] (New York: Frederick Ungar, 1963), 153, 155, 177; Halttunen, *Confidence Men and Painted Women*, quote on 93 and xiv, xv, 13, 20–21, 34, 50–51, 71, 75, 79–80, 98.

18. Halttunen, *Confidence Men and Painted Women*, xv xvi; Alexander Walker, *Woman Physiologically Considered. . . .* (Hartford, Conn.: Silas Andrus and Son, 1839), 179; Nelson Sizer, *Thoughts on Domestic Life; or, Marriage Vindicated and Free Love Exposed* (New York: Fowler and Wells, 1858), 21.

19. John Mather Austin, *A Voice to the Married. . . .* (New York: Kiggins and Kellogg, 1841), 277; A. J. H. Duganne, "Unhappy Marriages," *Harbinger* 6 (December 4, 1847):33–34.

20. Sizer, *Thoughts on Domestic Life*, 21; Orson Fowler, *The Family*, vol. 1, *Matrimony, as Taught by Phrenology and Physiology* (New York: O. S. Fowler, 1859) [hereafter *Matri-*

mony], 242; Lorenzo Fowler, *Marriage: Its History and Ceremonies; with a Phrenological Exposition of the Functions and Qualifications for Happy Marriages* (New York: Fowler and Wells, 1847), 145.

21. Robert A. Abzug, *Passionate Liberator: Theodore Dwight Weld and the Dilemma of Reform* (New York: Oxford University Press, 1980), 23, 47–50, 76–94, 123–52; Gerda Lerner, *The Grimké Sisters from South Carolina: Rebels Against Slavery* (Boston: Houghton Mifflin, 1967), 24, 66–76, 86, 101, 123–25, 135–48.

22. Gilbert H. Barnes and Dwight L. Drumond, eds., *Letters of Theodore Dwight Weld Angelina Grimké Weld and Sarah Grimké, 1822–1844*, vol. 2 (New York: D. Appleton-Century, 1934), 533, 537, 635–36.

23. Ibid., 557, 576–80, 560.

24. "Influence of Females," *Liberator* 2 (March 3, 1833):36; "Marriage," *Liberator* 2 (July 21, 1832):116; "Model of a Wife," *Liberator* 4 (May 24, 1834):84; George Henry, *The Marriage of the Lamb, or Wedlock and Padlock, Temporal and Spiritual* (Oneida: the author, 1856), 416; Walker, *Woman*, xv.

25. William Alcott, *The Young Husband, or Duties of Man in the Marriage Relation* [1838] (New York: Arno, 1972), 42, 108, 110, 115, 116; Abzug, *Passionate Liberator*, 206; Nissenbaum, *Sex, Diet, and Debility*, 136–37.

26. Ronald G. Walters, *The Antislavery Appeal: American Abolitionism After 1830* (Baltimore: Johns Hopkins University Press, 1976), 93–94; Trudgill, *Madonnas and Magdalens*, 45; Ware, *Hints to Young Men*, 29–30; Alcott, *Young Husband*, 18–21, 38–39, 105–06.

27. Frederick Marryat, *A Diary in America with Remarks on Its Institutions* (New York: Knopf, 1962), 422, 425; Frances Trollope, *Domestic Manners of the Americans* (New York: Knopf, 1949), 75. Among the travel accounts, see Frances Wright, *Views of Society and Manners in America* (Cambridge, Mass.: Belknap Press of Harvard University, 1963), 218–19; Isabella Lucy Bird, *The Englishwoman in America* (Madison: University of Wisconsin Press, 1966), 94; Harriet Martineau, *Society in America* (Gloucester, Mass.: Peter Smith Publisher, 1962) 291, 294; and Frances Trollope, *Domestic Manners of the Americans*, ed. Donald Smalley (New York: Knopf, 1949), 75. For scholarly views of the question of separate spheres, see Carl N. Degler, *At Odds: Women and the Family in America from the Revolution to the Present* (New York: Oxford University Press, 1980); Cott, *Bonds of Womanhood*, 201–03; Cott, "Passionlessness"; and Suzanne Lebsock, *The Free Women of Petersburg: Status and Culture in a Southern Town, 1784–1860* (New York: W. W. Norton, 1984), 232–36.

28. Peter Cominos, "Late Victorian Sexual Respectability and the Social System," *International Review of Social History* 8 (1963):21, 37, 217, 244–47; Bryan Strong, "Toward a History of the Experiential Family: Sex and Incest in the Nineteenth-Century Family," *Journal of Marriage and the Family* 35 (August 1973):457–66; G. J. Barker-Benfield, *The Horrors of the Half-Known Life: Male Attitudes Toward Women and Sexuality in Nineteenth-Century America* (New York: Harper and Row, 1976), 8, 9, 17, 20, 22, 30, 48–49; Brain, *Friends and Lovers*, 43, 46, 120–22.

29. Ware, *Hints to Young Men*, 29; R. J. Culverwell, *Guide to Health and Long Life . . .* (London: the author, 1845), 40; "The Wife," *Liberator* 3 (April 16, 1833):32; Alcott, *Young Husband*, 224–26, 237.

30. John R. Gillis, "From Ritual to Romance: Toward a New History of Love" (unpublished ms.); Lantz et al., "Pre-Industrial Patterns in the Colonial Family in America: A Content Analysis of Colonial Magazines," *American Sociological Review* 33

(June 1968):413–26; Barnes and Drumond, *Letters of Theodore Dwight Weld*, 635–36, 538, 587.

31. Cooper, *Notions of the Americans*, 196; Fowler, *Matrimony*, 336; Barnes and Drumond, *Letters of Theodore Dwight Weld*, 538, 588; Abzug, *Passionate Liberator*, 199–200.

32. Lewis Perry, *Childhood, Marriage, and Reform: Henry Clarke Wright 1797–1870* (Chicago: University of Chicago Press, 1980), 3–53, 55, 172, 228, 231–39.

33. *Marriage and Parentage; or, The Reproductive Element in Man, as a Means to his Elevation and Happiness*, 2d ed. [1855] (New York: Arno, 1974), 19, 140, 165–68, 177–79, 184–85, 189, 193–95.

34. Ibid., 203; "Marriage," *Liberator* 5 (July 4, 1835):108; Barnes and Drumond, *Letters of Theodore Dwight Weld*, 587, 637.

35. Based upon an analysis of Nissenbaum, *Sex, Diet, and Debility*, 175–89. See also Ware, *Hints to Young Men*, iii–iv and William Alcott, *The Physiology of Marriage* (Boston: J. P. Jewett, 1856), v, 14.

2. Marriage and Utopia, 1825 to 1850

1. Marianne (Dwight) Orvis, *Letters From Brook Farm, 1844–1847*, ed. Amy L. Reed [1928] (Philadelphia: Porcupine Press, 1972), 94–95.

2. William Owen, "Diary of William Owen, From November 10, 1824, to April 20, 1825," ed. Joel W. Hiatt, in *Indiana Historical Society Publications*, vol. 4 (Indianapolis: Bobbs-Merrill, 1906), 14, 15.

3. Ibid., 9–11, 14.

4. John Humphrey Noyes, *History of American Socialisms* [1870] (New York: Hillary House, 1961), 30; Arthur Bestor, *Backwoods Utopias: The Sectarian Origins and Owenite Phase of Communitarian Socialism in America: 1663–1829* (Philadelphia: University of Pennsylvania Press, 1950, 2d ed., 1970), 60, 92–93; Arthur Bestor, "Patent-Office Models of the Good Society: Some Relationships Between Social Reform and Westward Expansion," in Bestor, *Backwoods Utopias*, 230–31.

5. Robert Dale Owen, *A New View of Society or Essays on the Formation of the Human Character Preparatory to the Development of a Plan for Gradually Ameliorating the Condition of Mankind* [1816] (London: MacMillan, 1972), 75–76. See also John F. C. Harrison, *Quest for the New Moral World: Robert Owen and the Owenites in Britain and America* (New York: Scribner's 1969), 5–7.

6. Owen, *New View of Society*, 59, 85, 90; Bestor, *Backwoods Utopias*, 62–66; Harrison, *Quest for the New Moral World*, 5–7, 87.

7. Bestor, *Backwoods Utopias*, 68–74; Richard William Leopold, *Robert Dale Owen: A Biography* [1940] (New York: Octagon Books, 1969), 18–21.

8. William Owen, "Journal," 17, 41–44, 53; Bestor, *Backwoods Utopias*, 94–95, 100–01, 122–23.

9. *Robert Owen in the United States*, ed. Oakley C. Johnson (New York: Humanities Press, 1970), 23, 24, 28–29, 32–33.

10. Robert Dale Owen, *To Holland and to New Harmony: Robert Dale Owen's Travel Journal, 1825–1826*, ed. Josephine M. Elliott (Indianapolis: Indiana Historical Society, 1969), 237; Bestor, *Backwoods Utopias*, 160–61.

11. Noyes, *History of American Socialisms*, 56; Bestor, *Backwoods Utopias*, 162–66; Leopold, *Robert Dale Owen*, 31.

12. Noyes, *History of American Socialisms*, 41, 43.

13. William Bailie, *Josiah Warren: The First American Anarchist* [1906] (New York: Arno, 1972), 1–4; Noyes, *History of American Socialisms*, 49–50; Robert Dale Owen, *Threading my way: Twenty-seven Years of Autobiography* (New York: G. W. Carleton, 1874), 276; Paul Brown, *Twelve Months in New Harmony; Presenting a Faithful Account of the Principal Occurrences Which Have Taken Place There Within that Period; Interspersed with Remarks* [1827] (Philadelphia: Porcupine Press, 1972), 13–17, 25, 33.

14. *New Harmony as Seen by Participants and Travellers* [N.p.] (Philadelphia: Porcupine Press, 1975).

15. *A Vindication of the Rights of Woman with Strictures on Political and Moral Subjects*, ed. Charles W. Hagelman, Jr. (New York: W. W. Norton, 1967), 35, 82, 122, 182.

16. *Enquiry Concerning Political Justice and Its Influence on Modern Morals and Happiness*, ed. Isaac Krammick (Middlesex, England: Penguin Books, 1976), 703, 761–63.

17. *Alcuin: A Dialogue*, ed. Lee R. Edwards (New York: Grossman Publishers, 1971), 24, 75, 85, 87, 88.

18. Robert Dale Owen, *Journal*, 235; "A Sketch," *New Harmony Gazette* 1 (October 29, 1825):33, 41–42; "Gray Light IV," *New Harmony Gazette* 1 (January 11, 1826):124.

19. *Robert Owen in the United States*, 69–73.

20. Bestor, *Backwoods Utopias*, 125–26; *Indiana Journal* (November 14, 1826):3, quoted in *Backwoods Utopias*, 223 n.; *Education and Reform at New Harmony: Correspondence of William Maclure and Marie Duclos Fretageot, 1820–1833* [hereafter cited as Maclure Letters], ed. Arthur E. Bestor, Jr. (Indianapolis: Indiana Historical Society, 1948), 346–47.

21. Maclure Letters, 351; "Sunday Conversations," *New Harmony Gazette* 1 (August 9, 1826):364–65.

22. Maclure Letters, 349, 355; Bestor, *Backwoods Utopias*, 223.

23. *New Harmony as Seen by Participants and Travellers*; Maclure Letters, 349, 355.

24. "Divorce," *New Harmony Gazette* 2 (September 10, 1828):366–67; Owen, *Threading My Way*, 281; Brown, *Twelve Months in New Harmony*, 86–87.

25. "Married," *New Harmony Gazette* 1 (April 5, 1826):222; Auguste Carlier, *Marriage in the United States*, trans. B. Joy Jeffries [1867] (New York: Arno, 1972), 35–36, 113–14.

26. Bestor, *Backwoods Utopias*, 202, 227; Whitney Cross, *The Burned-over District: The Social and Intellectual History of Enthusiastic Religion in Western New York, 1800–1850* (Ithaca, N.Y.: Cornell University Press, 1950), 152.

27. Bailie, *Josiah Warren*, 9–18; *Free Enquirer* 3 (February 26, 1831):137–38.

28. James M'Knight, *Discourse Exposing Robert Owen's System as Practiced by the Franklin Community, at Haverstraw* (New York: John Gray, 1826), 3–6, 8–13, passim; Bestor, *Backwoods Utopias*, 203–04.

29. Noyes, *History of American Socialisms*, 161–67, Bestor, *Backwoods Utopias*, 204–13.

30. E., "Mr. Owen," *Correspondent* 1 (April 7, 1827):172; Sean Wilentz, *Chants Democratic: New York City and the Rise of the American Working Class, 1788–1850* (New York: Oxford University Press, 1984), 153–55.

31. *The Radical: and Advocate of Equality* [1834] (Westport, Conn.: Hyperion Press, 1976), 10, 13, 35, 38–39.

32. A. J. G. Perkins and Theresa Wolfson, *Frances Wright: Free Enquirer. The Study of a Temperament* [1939] (Philadelphia: Porcupine Press, 1972), 53, 141–57, 166–71, 215–96, 310, 312; "Nashoba," *New Harmony Gazette* 3 (February 6, 1828):132; Wilentz, *Chants Democratic*, 190–211.

33. "Constancy," *New Harmony Gazette* 3 (June 11, 1828):262–63; *Moral Physiology; or, A Brief and Plain Treatise on the Population Question* [1859] (New York: Arno, 1972); *Divorce: Being a Correspondence Between Horace Greeley and Robert Dale Owen* [1860] (New York: Source Book, 1972); Leopold, *Robert Dale Owen*, 49–103, 142ff, 272–75.

34. John Austin, *A Voice to the Married* (New York: Kiggins and Kellogg, 1841), x, 276.

35. Noyes, *History of American Socialisms*, 104–05; Paul F. Boller, Jr., *American Transcendentalism, 1830–1860: An Intellectual Inquiry* (New York: G. P. Putnam's Sons, 1974), ix–xiv; Arthur W. Brown, *Margaret Fuller* (New York: Twayne Publishers, 1964), 27–36; Octavius Brooks Frothingham, *Transcendentalism in New England: A History* (New York: G. P. Putnam's Sons, 1876), 51–52, 76ff.

36. Boller, *American Transcendentalism*, 22; Frothingham, *Transcendentalism in New England*, 12–13, 103; Frederick C. Dahlstrand, *Amos Bronson Alcott: An Intellectual Biography* (Rutherford, N.J.: Fairleigh Dickinson University Press, 1982), 12.

37. Yehousha Arieli, *Individualism and Nationalism in American Ideology* (Cambridge, Mass.: Harvard University Press, 1964), 281; Ralph Waldo Emerson, *Representative Men: Seven Lectures* (Boston: Phillips, Sampson, and Co, 1849), 174; Amos Bronson Alcott, "Observations on the Principles and Methods of Infant Instruction" (1830), in Alcott, *Essays on Education (1830–1862)*, (Gainesville, Fl.: Scholar's Facsimile and Reprint, 1960), 19; Alcott, "Doctrine and Discipline of Human Culture" (1836), in Alcott, *Essays on Education*, 51.

38. Alcott, "Doctrine and Discipline," 40, 48; Dahlstrand, *Amos Bronson Alcott*, 20–21, 30–32; Frothingham, *Transcendentalism in New England*, 147.

39. Dahlstrand, *Amos Bronson Alcott*, 53; Anne C. Rose, *Transcendentalism as a Social Movement, 1830–1850* (New Haven, Conn.: Yale University Press, 1981), 18–24, 28–38; Boller, *American Transcendentalism*, xx, 3–21.

40. Frothingham, *Transcendentalism in New England*, 137, 140; Emerson's "Human Life" essay is quoted in Boller, *American Transcendentalism*, xvi. See also John L. Thomas, "Romantic Reform in America, 1815–1865," *American Quarterly* 17 (Winter 1965):656–81.

41. "Woman," *Dial* 1 (January 1841):362–66. The inappropriateness for women of the male model of individuality and autonomy has been explored by Carol Gilligan, *In a Different Voice: Psychological Theory and Women's Development* (Cambridge, Mass.: Harvard University Press, 1982).

42. Brown, *Margaret Fuller*, passim. See also Margaret Vanderhaar Allen, *The Achievement of Margaret Fuller* (University Park, Penn.: The Pennsylvania State University Press, 1979); Boller, *American Transcendentalism*, 24; and Poe, "The Literati of New York City. Some Honest Opinions at Random Respecting Their Autorial Merits, with Occasional Words of Personality," *Godey's Lady's Book* (August 1846):72.

43. *Woman in the Nineteenth Century*, in Bell Gale Chevigny, *The Woman and the Myth: Margaret Fuller's Life and Writings* (Old Westbury, N.Y.: Feminist Press, 1976), 240, 245, 248, 263, 252–56, 268–69, 271, 278.

44. Emerson quote in Rose, *Transcendentalism as a Social Movement*, 162; Emerson, *Representative Men*, 157; "Free Love," *Dial* 3 (October 1842):199.

45. Dahlstrand, *Amos Bronson Alcott*, 17–20, 28–36, 53, 70, 104, 113, 122–27, 139–47.

46. Clara Endicott Sears, *Bronson Alcott's Fruitlands* [1915] (Philadelphia: Porcupine

Press, 1975), 2–4, 8–9; Richard Francis, "Circumstances and Salvation: The Ideology of the Fruitlands Utopia," *American Quarterly* 25 (May 1973):206, 210–12, 215, 218; Dahlstrand, *Amos Bronson Alcott*, 188–96.

47. Sears, *Bronson Alcott's Fruitlands*, 14, 21, 47, 71, 112, 121, 126, 134; Rose, *Transcendentalism as a Social Movement*, 122, 124; Dahlstrand, *Amos Bronson Alcott*, 193–202.

48. Rose, *Transcendentalism as a Social Movement*, 129–30; Francis, "Circumstances and Salvation," 218, 219.

49. Charles Lane quoted in Noyes, *History of American Socialisms*, 144, 519. See also Francis, "Circumstances and Salvation," 221–22.

50. Francis, "Circumstances and Salvation," 215; Lindsay Swift, *Brook Farm: Its Members, Scholars, and Visitors* [1900] (New York: Corinth Books, 1961), 15–17, 20; Rose, *Transcendentalism as a Social Movement*, 132–35; Boller, *American Transcendentalism*, 2–3, 28.

51. Swift, *Brook Farm*, 27, 30–34, 40–44, 48–49, 50, 69–76; Rose, *Transcendentalism as a Social Movement*, 131.

52. Noyes, *History of American Socialisms*, 143; Nathaniel Hawthorne, *The Blithedale Romance* (New York: W. W. Norton, 1958), 42–45, 94.

53. Swift, *Brook Farm*, 53–57, 113, 117.

54. Swift, *Brook Farm*, 175–76; Orvis, *Letters From Brook Farm*, 26, 33.

55. Orvis, *Letters From Brook Farm*, 12–13, 57, 69.

56. Frances Wright, *Views of Society and Manners in America* ed. Paul R. Baker (Cambridge, Mass.: Harvard University Press, 1963), 23; and Isabella Lucy Bird, *The Englishwoman in America* (Madison: University of Wisconsin Press, 1966), 364.

57. Orvis, *Letters From Brook Farm*, 41; Swift, *Brook Farm*, 22–26, 275–77. Both Frothingham and Boller believe that Fourierism spoiled the community before finances actually ruined it.

58. Rose, *Transcendentalism as a Social Movement*, 209–25; Boller, *American Transcendentalism*, xix, 133–38; Dahlstrand, *Amos Bronson Alcott*, 209, 235–36, 255–66.

59. Arthur E. Bestor, Jr., "Albert Brisbane—Propagandist for Socialism in the 1840s," *New York History* 28 (April 1947):131–49; "American Phalanxes: A Study of Fourierist Socialism in the United States (with Special Reference to the Movement in Western New York)" 2 vols. (Ph.D. dissertation, Yale University, 1938), chap. 1; Carl J. Guarneri, "Utopian Socialism and American Ideas: The Origins and Doctrine of American Fourierism" (Ph.D. dissertation, The Johns Hopkins University, 1979), chap. 1.

60. Whitney R. Cross, *The Burned-over District: The Social and Intellectual History of Enthusiastic Religion in Western New York, 1800–1850* (Ithaca, N.Y.: Cornell University Press, 1950), 328–29; Bestor, "American Phalanxes," 4, 25–27, 30.

61. Octavius Brooks Frothingham, *Transcendentalism in New England: A History* (New York: G. P. Putnam's Sons, 1876), 155; "Fourierism and the Socialists," *Dial* 3 (July 1842):86–88.

62. Michael Barkun, "Communal Societies as Cyclical Phenomena," *Communal Societies* 4 (1984):35–48; Lindsay Swift, *Brook Farm* [1900] (New York: Corinth Books, 1961), 178–80; Bestor, "American Phalanxes," 51–59; Wilentz, *Chants Democratic*, 356–57.

63. Cross, *The Burned-over District*, 322–26; Swift, *Brook Farm*, 181–82.

64. Guarneri, "Utopian Socialism," ii–iii, 8–9, 98–100; Bestor, "American Phalanxes," 9–13.

65. Frank Manuel, *The Prophets of Paris* (Cambridge, Mass.: Harvard University Press,

1962), 215; New York *Tribune*, 30 August 1842, 7 April 1842, 3 March 1842 (all p. 1); Albert Brisbane, *Social Destiny of Man or Association and Reorganization of Industry* [1840] (New York: Augustus M. Kelley, 1969), 251.

66. Manuel, *The Prophets of Paris*, 215–29; Roland Barthes, "Fourier," from *A Barthes Reader*, ed. Susan Sontag (New York: Hill and Wang, 1982), 334–67; Bestor, "Albert Brisbane," 146; Guarneri, "Utopian Socialism," 41–46, 127–28, 131–33, 200–01; Yehousha Arieli, *Individualism and Nationalism in American Ideology* (Cambridge, Mass.: Harvard University Press, 1964), 236.

67. *A Popular View of the Doctrines of Charles Fourier* [1844] (Philadelphia: Porcupine Press, 1972), 39–40; Brisbane, *Social Destiny*, vi–x, 2–3, 8–9, 18–19, 49, 105, 113, 164, 248–49.

68. New York *Tribune*, 2 March 1842, 15 March 1842, 16 March 1842, 26 March 1842, 2 May 1843 (all p. 1).

69. Bestor, "American Phalanxes," 63, 84, 150–240; Carl Guarneri, "The Fourierist Movement in America," *Communities* (Winter 1985):50–54.

70. Guarneri, "Fourierist Movement," 50–54.

71. Douglass C. North, *The Economic Growth of the United States, 1790–1860* (New York: W. W. Norton, 1966), 204; Karen Halttunen, *Confidence Men and Painted Women: A Study of Middle-Class Culture in America, 1830–1870* (New Haven, Conn.: Yale University Press, 1982), 153, 186; Wilentz, *Chants Democratic*, 15, 357, 387–88.

72. Donald M'Laren, *Boa Constrictor, or Fourier Association Self-exposed as to its Principles and Aims* (Rochester, N.Y.: Canfield and Warren, 1844), 18 (M'Laren was quoting James 1:14); Bestor, "American Phalanxes," 262–69, 273–75, 282–83.

73. Barthes, "Fourier," 343 n.; Charles Fourier, *The Utopian Vision of Charles Fourier: Selected Texts on Work, Love, and Passionate Attraction*, trans. Jonathan Beecher and Richard Bienvenu (Boston: Beacon Press, 1971), 172–73, 175–77.

74. John Humphrey Noyes, *History of American Socialisms* [1870] (New York: Hillary House, 1961), 143; Guarneri, "Utopian Socialism," 135, 144.

75. New York *Tribune*, 7 April 1842, p. 1; Brisbane, *Social Destiny*, 5, 6, 133; "The Isolated Household," *Harbinger* 1 (June 21, 1845):22.

76. New York *Tribune*, 16 April 1842, 23 May 1842, 3 August 1842, 4 November 1842, 13 July 1842 (all p. 1).

77. "The Condition of Women in Harmony," *Phalanx* 1 (August 10, 1844):234–36; New York *Tribune*, 7 June 1843, p. 1. See also anon., "Domestic Relations in a Utopian Community," *Phalanx* 1 (February 8, 1844):317–19.

78. Godwin, *Doctrines of Fourier*, 86–88; "The Isolated Family," *Harbinger* 1 (September 27, 1845):251–53.

79. M'Laren, *Boa Constrictor*, 23; *Harbinger* 2 (April 18, 1846):302; [Greeley?], "Association and Marriage," *Harbinger* 2 (May 25, 1846):312.

80. "Society," *Harbinger* 6 (December 12, 1846):8. Lazarus mentioned "Society" in a letter, from Brook Farm to his uncle, George Mordecai. Lazarus probably did not live there permanently, but he doesn't seem to have lived anywhere permanently during the later 1840s. Marx Lazarus to George Mordecai, November 1846, George Mordecai Papers, Southern Historical Collection, University of North Carolina, Chapel Hill. Lazarus also made out a will at Brook Farm, leaving his estate to the cause of association. George Ripley witnessed the document. Will of Marx Lazarus, George Mordecai Papers, Southern Historical Collection, University of North Carolina, Chapel Hill.

81. George Ripley, "Review of Love in the Phalanstery," *Harbinger* 7 (September 23,

1848):167; Victor Hennequin, *Love in the Phalanstery* (New York: DeWitt and Davenport, 1849), 1–2, 4, 26.

82. Jean Strouse, *Alice James: A Biography* (Boston: Houghton Mifflin, 1980), 3–17.

83. "The Observer and Hennequin," *Harbinger* 7 (October 21, 1848):197; "Love and Marriage," *Harbinger* 7 (October 28, 1848):203.

84. "Love in the Phalanstery" and "Reply," *Harbinger* 8 (November 11, 1848):12–13; "Letter from AEF," *Harbinger* 8 (December 2, 1848):36.

85. *Harbinger* 8 (December 2, 1848):36–37, (December 9, 1848):44–45, (December 16, 1848):53–54, (December 30, 1848):60–61.

86. *Harbinger* 8 (December 30, 1848):68–69; "The Love Question," *Harbinger* 8 (January 6, 1849):77–78.

3. Spiritual Wives and Elective Affinity

1. Whitney Cross, *The Burned-over District: The Social and Intellectual History of Enthusiastic Religion in Western New York, 1800–1850* (Ithaca, N.Y.: Cornell University Press, 1950), 31–32.

2. "Cases of Monomania," *Liberator* 5 (April 25, 1835):68.

3. Benjamin Warfield, *Perfectionism*, vol. 2 (New York: Oxford University Press, 1931), 239; William Hepworth Dixon, *Spiritual Wives*, vol. 2 (London: Hurst and Bleckett, 1868), 24–25; vol. 1, 85–86; "The Autobiography of Stephen Pearl Andrews," Stephen Pearl Andrews Papers, State Historical Society of Wisconsin, 175.

4. Robert C. Fuller, *Mesmerism and the American Cure of Souls* (Philadelphia: University of Pennsylvania Press, 1982), 23; Arthur M. Schelsinger, Jr., *The Age of Jackson* (Boston: Little, Brown, 1945), 186.

5. William L. Stone, *Matthias and His Impostures: or, The Progress of Fanaticism* (New York: Harper and Brothers, 1835), 296–98; Michael Hull Barton, "A Letter on Free-Loveism," *Practical Christian* 15 (November 18, 1854):59.

6. Stone, *Matthias and His Impostures*, 171, 172.

7. Dixon, *Spiritual Wives*, vol. 2, 12–17, 30; Warfield, *Perfectionism*, 244.

8. Stephen Nissenbaum, *Sex, Diet, and Debility in Jacksonian America: Sylvester Graham and Health Reform* (Westport, Conn.: Greenwood Press, 1980), 25, 143–45.

9. Ellen K. Rothman, "Sex and Self-Control: Middle-Class Courtship in America, 1770–1870," *Journal of Social History* 15 (Spring 1982):409–25; Henry Reed Stiles, *Bundling: Its Origin, Progress and Decline in America* (privately issued by the author, 1871), 113, 131.

10. Constance Noyes Robertson, ed., *Oneida Community: An Autobiography, 1851–1870* (Syracuse, N.Y.: Syracuse University Press, 1970), 2–6.

11. Ernest R. Sandeen, "John Humphrey Noyes as the New Adam," *Church History* 40 (March 1971):83; Dixon, *Spiritual Wives*, vol. 2, 30, 55, 177.

12. Dixon, *Spiritual Wives*, vol. 2, 177; Robert David Thomas, *The Man Who Would Be Perfect: John Humphrey Noyes and the Utopian Impulse* (Philadelphia: University of Pennsylvania Press, 1977), 106; *First Annual Report of the Oneida Association: Exhibiting its History, Principles, and Transactions to Jan. 1, 1849* (Oneida Reserve: The Association, 1849), 2; Robertson, *Oneida Community*, 8–10.

13. Robertson, *Oneida Community*, 11–12; *First Annual Report*, 14.

14. *First Annual Report*, 21–26; "The Oneida Association," *Oneida Circular* 1 (December 28, 1851):31.

15. *First Annual Report*, 17; "Fourierism," *Oneida Circular* 2 (December 22, 1852):41.

16. Carroll Smith-Rosenberg, *Disorderly Conduct: Visions of Gender in Victorian America* (New York: Knopf, 1985), 133; Cross, *The Burned-over District*, 341–45; quoted in Leon Festinger, Henry W. Riecken, and Stanley Schachter, *When Prophecy Fails* (New York: Harper and Row, 1956), 22; Robert H. Abzug, *Passionate Liberator: Theodore Dwight Weld and the Dilemma of Reform* (New York: Oxford University Press, 1980), 247–49.

17. Smith-Rosenberg, *Disorderly Conduct*, 131–35.

18. Moritz Busch, *Travels Between the Hudson and the Mississippi, 1851–1852* trans. Norman H. Binger (Lexington: University of Kentucky, 1971), 16, 34; Fuller, *Mesmerism*, 17–18, 23, 30; Warren Chase, *Life-line of the Lone One; or, Autobiography of the World's Child*, 5th ed. (Boston: William White, 1868), 112–13; Marianne (Dwight) Orvis, *Letters from Brook Farm, 1844–1847*, ed. Amy L. Reed [1928] (Philadelphia: Porcupine Press, 1972), 13, 24; Emma Hardinge, *Modern American Spiritualism: A Twenty Years' Record of the Communion between the Earth and the World of Spirits* [1870] (New Hyde Park, N.Y.: University Books, 1970), 22.

19. Fuller, *Mesmerism*, 3–4, 46, 71–72. The vulnerability of the United States to contagious disease is graphically described in Charles Rosenberg, *The Cholera Years: The United States in 1832, 1849, and 1866* (Chicago: University of Chicago Press, 1962), 1–7, passim. New York *Tribune*, 8 March 1943, p. 1, reported 9,176 deaths in 1842 and broke down the deaths by category: epidemic, endemic, and contagious disease accounted for 2,320 of the deaths.

20. Ralph Waldo Emerson, *Representative Men: Seven Lectures* (Boston: Phillips, Sampson, and Co., 1849), 100; Signe Toksvig, *Emanuel Swedenborg, Scientist and Mystic* (New Haven, Conn.: Yale University Press, 1948) 154, passim; John Humphrey Noyes, *History of American Socialisms* (New York: Lippincott, 1870), 538–39; Cross, *The Burned-over District*, 342; Emanuel Swedenborg, *The Delights of Wisdom Pertaining to Conjugial Love* (New York: American Swedenborg Printing and Publishing Society, 1905), 45.

21. *Henry James, Senior. A Selection of His Writings*, ed. Giles Gunn (Chicago: American Library Association, 1974), 41–45, 49, 55–58.

22. "The Doctrine of Love and Charity," *Age* 1 (September 25, 1852):26; George Bush, *Mesmer and Swedenborg; or, the Relation of the Developments of Mesmerism to the Doctrines and Disclosures of Swedenborg* (New York: John Allen, 1847), iii, 16–21, 51, 57–65, 70–71, 137. During 1844 Bush published a journal concerned with biblical prophecy entitled the *Hierophant*.

23. Andrew Jackson Davis, *The Magic Staff; an Autobiography of Andrew Jackson Davis* (New York: J. S. Brown & Co., 1857), 26, 68, 161, 182–83, 188, 192–93, 199–200, 202–04, 316, 333; Andrew Jackson Davis, *The Principles of Nature, Her Divine Revelations, and a Voice to Mankind* (New York: S. S. Lyon & Wm. Fishbough, 1847), xi, xivff.

24. Davis, *Principles of Nature*, 1–25, 689, 706, 729, 733, 735.

25. Andrew Jackson Davis, *Beyond the Valley* (Boston: Colby & Rich, 1885), 30–33.

26. "The Brotherhood at Cincinnati," *Univercoelum* 1 (April 29, 1848):345–46; John O. Wattles, "The Crisis—Universal Unity," *Herald of Truth* (January 1847):41–49; J. P. Cornell, "The New Philosophy," *Herald of Truth* 1 (February 1847):150–54; John O. Wattles, "Harmonising," *Herald of Truth* 1 (March 1847):179, 183; Kenneth William McKinley, "A Guide to the Communistic Communities of Ohio," *The Ohio State Archae-*

ological and Historical Quarterly 46(1937):1–15; Noyes, *History of American Socialisms*, 316ff.

27. Swedenborg, *Conjugial Love*, 34, 40, 49–50, 53, 130–35, 228, 354–61; Toksvig, *Emanuel Swedenborg*, 51–52.

28. "Our Plans for Social Reform," *Univercoelum* 1 (March 11, 1848):233–34; FMW, "Love," *Univercoelum* 3 (April 21, 1848):331.

29. Davis, *Magic Staff*, 394–416, 494–547; *Sandusky Daily Commercial Register*, 7 June 1857.

30. Andrew Jackson Davis, *The Great Harmonia; Concerning Physiological Vices and Virtues, and the Seven Phases of Marriage* (Boston: Sanborn, Carter, & Bazin, 1855), 71–72, 104, 226, 275–76, 293–300, 408–12, 418–23; Andrew Jackson Davis, *Memoranda of Persons, Places, and Events* . . . (Boston: William White, 1868), 248. Mr. and Mrs. Davis supported divorce in their journal, *Herald of Progress*, published in New York during 1860–64. Davis's commitment to the one true marriage seemingly took him to the bizarre expedient of divorcing his second wife, Mary Fenn Davis, after twenty-nine years of marriage, in 1885. Davis, *Beyond the Valley*, 94–114, 291–92.

31. Cross, *The Burned-over District*, 345–49; John B. Ellis, *Free Love and Its Votaries* [1870] (New York: AMS, 1971), 405; John Weiss, ed., *Life and Correspondence of Theodore Parker*, vol. 1 [1863] (New York: Da Capo Press, 1970), 428; R. Laurence Moore, "Spiritualism and Science: Reflections on the First Decade of the Spirit Rappings," *American Quarterly* 24 (October 1972):481–84, and "Spiritualism," in E. S. Gaustad, ed., *The Rise of Adventism: Religion and Society in Mid-Nineteenth-Century America* (New York: Harper and Row, 1974), 85; Frank Podmore, *Mediums of the 19th Century*, vol. 1 [1902] (New York: University Books, 1963), 208.

32. Robert W. Delp, "Andrew Jackson Davis: Prophet of American Spiritualism," *Journal of American History* 54 (June 1967):46–49; Ann Braude, "Spirits Defend the Rights of Women: Spiritualism and Changing Sex Roles in Nineteenth-Century America," in Yvonne Yazbeck Haddad and Ellison Banks Findly, eds., *Women, Religion, and Social Change* (New York: State University of New York Press, 1985), 419–31; Hardinge, *Modern American Spiritualism*, 60.

33. Hardinge, *Modern American Spiritualism*, 22; "Spiritual Communications," *Age* 1 (January 1, 1853):248; "The Mode of Acquiring Knowledge from the Spiritual World," *Age* 1 (April 16, 1853):488.

34. Moore, "Spiritualism and Science," 477.

35. Andrew Jackson Davis, *The Philosophy of Special Providence: A Vision* (Boston: Bela Marsh, 1850), 45, and Davis, *Magic Staff*, 470.

36. Dixon, *Spiritual Wives*, vol. 1, 99; Moore, "Spiritualism and Science," 91; Charlotte Fowler Wells Manuscript, Spiritualism Collection, Division of Rare Books and Manuscripts, Cornell University, 18 [number written 17]; C. Hammond, *Light from the Spirit World* (Rochester, N.Y.: W. Heughes, 1852), 187ff; "The Doctrine of Affinity," *Spiritual Telegraph* 1 (June 12, 1852).

37. Dixon, *Spiritual Wives*, vol. 2., 252; F. C. Ewer, *Two Eventful Nights, or, the Fallibility of "Spiritualism"* (New York: H. Dayton, 1856), 12; "Free Love," *Age of Progress* 2 (July 12, 1856):620; Charles Partridge, "The 'Times' on 'Free-Love'," *Spiritual Telegraph* (September 29, 1855):86.

38. Smith-Rosenberg, *Disorderly Conduct*, 134–35. Vieda Skultans, *Intimacy and Ritual: A Study of Spiritualism, Mediums and Groups* (London: Routledge, Kegan Paul, 1974), 4, 45. In her study of modern spiritualistic circles in Wales, Skultans has shown that

spiritualism can provide both a network of sympathetic individuals and healing for women in conflict with their husbands or other men.

39. Noyes, *History of American Socialisms*, 541, 543, 547; Charles Wilkins Webber, *Spiritual Vampirism: The History of Etherial Softdown, and her friends of the "New Light"* (Philadelphia: Lippincott, 1853), 18–19.

40. Chase, *Life-line of the Lone One*, 10–33, 41–104, 112–26; Noyes, *History of American Socialisms*, 411–12.

41. Noyes, *History of American Socialisms*, 418, 423; Chase, *Life-line*, 126–27.

42. Chase, *Life-line*, 95–97, 127–130, 147–61, 167–74; Dixon, *Spiritual Wives*, vol. 1, 99.

43. "Autobiography of Stephen Pearl Andrews," 174–75, 227, 259.

44. "A Private Chapter of the Origin of the War. by Stephen Pearl Andrews. Third Paper," "Fourth Paper," and "Fifth Paper," Stephen Pearl Andrews Papers, State Historical Society of Wisconsin; Madeline B. Stern, *The Pantarch: A Biography of Stephen Pearl Andrews* (Austin: University of Texas Press, 1968), 3, 15–18, 20–31, 33–46, 55.

45. Stern, *The Pantarch*, 46–71, 74–77; Theron Leland, "Letter from One of the 'Old Guard'," *American Socialist* 1 (April 13, 1876):18.

46. Lori D. Ginzburg, " 'Moral Suasion is Moral Balderdash': Women, Politics, and Social Activism in the 1850s," *Journal of American History* 73 (December 1986):601–22; Louis Filler, *The Crusade Against Slavery, 1830–1860* (New York: Harper and Row, 1960), 192–217.

4. Modern Times and the Emergence of Free Love

1. Charlotte Fowler Wells Manuscript, Spiritualism Collection, Division of Rare Books and Manuscripts, Cornell University Library, 1, 13.

2. Josiah Warren, "A Scrap of history" and "Lecture notes," in the Josiah Warren Papers, Labadie Collection, Department of Rare Books and Special Collections, University of Michigan Library; Josiah Warren, *Equitable Commerce* (New Harmony, Ind.: Warren, 1846), i, 4.

3. "Our state of difficulties," *Peaceful Revolutionist* (February 5, 1833):6; Manuscript Journal of Josiah Warren, Josiah Warren Papers, Workingmen's Institute Library, New Harmony, Indiana.

4. Warren, *Equitable Commerce*, 13, 19; Josiah Warren, *True Civilization: An Immediate Necessity and the Last Ground of Hope for Mankind* [1863] (New York: Burt Franklin, 1967), 83.

5. William Bailie, *Josiah Warren: The First American Anarchist* [1906] (New York: Arno, 1972), 9–18, 42–45; Warren, *Equitable Commerce*, 13, 19; Warren, *True Civilization*, 87; "Social Experiment," *Free Enquirer* 3 (February 26, 1831):137–38; Journal of Josiah Warren.

6. James J. Martin, *Men Against the State: The Expositors of Individualist Anarchism in America, 1827–1908* (New York: Libertarian Book Club, 1953), 39–40, 50–55, 64–68; Warren, "Practical Applications of the Elementary Principles of 'True Civilization.' . . .", proof sheets of part three of the "True Civilization" series in the Warren Papers, Labadie Collection, Division of Rare Books and Special Collections, University of Michigan Library, 8–10 [hereafter cited as "Elementary Principles"]; Kenneth William McKinley, "A Guide to the Communistic Communities of Ohio," *Ohio Archaeological and Historical Quarterly* 46 (1937):12.

7. Madeline B. Stern, *The Pantarch: A Biography of Stephen Pearl Andrews* (Austin: University of Texas Press, 1968), 71; Warren, "Lecture notes," Warren Papers, Labadie Collection, Division of Rare Books and Special Collections, University of Michigan Library.

8. Theron Leland, "Letters from one of the 'Old Guard,' " *American Socialist* 1 (April 13, 1876):18; "Correspondence," *American Socialist* 2 (July 12, 1877):221; "Individual Sovereignty. What Killed the Phalansters?" *American Socialist* 1 (June 1, 1876):73.

9. Charlotte Fowler Wells Manuscript, 13–19.

10. Martin, *Men Against the State*, 70–72; Bailie, *Josiah Warren*, 59–60.

11. Resident of Utopia quoted in John Humphrey Noyes, *History of American Socialisms* [1870] (New York: Hilary House, 1961), 98. For Warren's accomplishments as an inventor, see Bailie, *Josiah Warren*, 2, 35, 39, 40–41, 47–49.

12. Martin, *Men Against the State*, 70–73; Charles Codman, "A Brief History of 'The City of Modern Times' Long Island N.Y. and a glorification of some of its Saints," typescript of original manuscript, Brentwood Public Library, 5, 20; *Periodical Letter* (August 1854):32, (September 1854):34, 43–45, (December 1854):69.

13. Moncure Conway, "Modern Times," *The Fortnightly Review* 6 (July 1, 1865):425–26; "Elementary Principles," from 17 to end, past where pagination stops; *Periodical Letter* (August 1854):19; Charles Shively, "Samuel Bowers' Doctrine of Nudity at Fruitlands and Modern Times," paper given at the National Historic Communal Societies Association Conference, October 1986. The nudist was Samuel Bowers, a former resident of Fruitlands.

14. Henry Edger, *Modern Times, The Labor Question, and the Family: A Brief Statement of Facts and Principles* (New York: Calvin Blanchard, [1855]), 3; Alfred Owen Aldridge, "Mysticism in Modern Times, L.I.," *Americana* 36 (October 1942):555–70; Codman, "A Brief History," 11; E. Newbery, *Manual of the Science of the Nature and Perfectibility of Mankind* (New York: George Evans, 1847), passim.

15. Josiah Warren quoted in Noyes, *History of American Socialisms*, 99.

16. Stephen Pearl Andrews, *The Science of Society* (London: C. W. Daniel, 1913), 15, 33, 62.

17. "Dr. Marx Edgeworth Lazarus," *Nichols Journal* 1 (November 1, 1853):63; [Mary Gove Nichols], *Mary Lyndon; or, Revelations of a Life. An Autobiography* (New York: Stringer and Townsend, 1855), 285, 291, 295; Ellen Mordecai to George Mordecai, April 10, 1848, George Mordecai Papers, Southern Historical Collection, University of North Carolina, Chapel Hill.

18. Noyes, *History of American Socialisms*, 212; Marx Edgeworth Lazarus, *The Trinity in its Theological, Scientific, and Practical Aspects, Analyzed and Illustrated* (New York: for the author by Fowlers and Wells, 1851). "Society" appeared in vols. 3 and 4 of the *Harbinger*, from October 24, 1846 to January 25, 1847; "Cannibalism" appeared in vols. 4 and 5.

19. Marx Edgeworth Lazarus, *Love vs. Marriage*, part 1 (New York: Fowler and Wells, 1852), 62, 69.

20. Ibid., 103–05, 107, 164, 167.

21. Ibid., 49, 60, 210–211.

22. Ibid., 40, 54, 55, 92.

23. Ibid., 45; Marx Edgeworth Lazarus, *Passional Hygiene and Natural Medicine; Embracing the Harmonies of Man with his Planet* (New York: Fowler and Wells, 1852), 429–31.

24. Andrews published the *Tribune* letters and his own final replies, made after Greeley closed the columns of the paper to him, in *Love, Marriage, and Divorce and the Sovereignty of the Individual* [1853] (New York: Source Book, 1972), 24–25, 38–40.

25. Ibid., 11, 22, 27, 31, 46–50, 69.

26. Ibid., 21, 22, 69.

27. WSH, "Modern Times," *Practical Christian* 13 (Oct. 9, 1852):47.

28. *History of the Hopedale Community.* . . . , ed. William S. Heywood [1897] (Philadelphia: Porcupine Press, 1972), 247; Roger Wunderlich, "Low Living and High Thinking at Modern Times, New York (1852–1864)" (Ph.D. dissertation, State University of New York at Stony Brook, 1986), 268–69; Conway, "Modern Times," 427; George MacDonald, *Fifty Years of Free Thought* (New York: The Truth Seeker, 1929), 450–51.

29. Leland, "Individual Sovereignty," 73 and "Old Guard," 18; William Hayward to Josiah Warren, December 8, 1852, Josiah Warren Papers, Labadie Collection, Division of Rare Books and Special Collections, University of Michigan Library; MacDonald, *Fifty Years of Free Thought*, 450–51.

30. Leland, "Old Guard," 18; J. H. Cook, "Way Marks," *American Socialist* 3 (August 1, 1878):24; "Letter to SPA," *Woodhull and Claflin's Weekly* 3 (October 28, 1871), and "Cerebral Development and Freedom," *Woodhull and Claflin's Weekly* 3 (October 28, 1871):13.

31. Bertha-Monica Stearns, "Two Forgotten New England Reformers," *New England Quarterly* 6 (March 1933):59–84; John B. Blake, "Mary Gove Nichols, Prophetess of Health," *Proceedings of the American Philosophical Society* 106 (June 29, 1962):219–34; Janet Hubly Noever, "Passionate Rebel: The Life of Mary Gove Nichols, 1810–1884" (Ph.D. dissertation, University of Oklahoma, 1983); Thomas Nichols, *Woman in All Ages and Nations* . . . (New York: Fowler and Wells, 1849), 71, 207–15, 229.

32. *Esoteric Anthropology (The Mysteries of Man)* (London: Nichols, n.d.), 96, 100. The London edition was issued, and apparently toned down, a decade or more after the American edition appeared. Stephen Nissenbaum has especially stressed the Grahamite connection of the Nicholses' free love theories. See Stephen Nissenbaum, *Sex, Diet, and Debility in Jacksonian America: Sylvester Graham and Health Reform* (Westport, Conn.: Greenwood Press, 1980), 167–69.

33. Stearns, "Two Forgotten New England Reformers," 72; New York *Tribune*, 21 July 1853, p. 5; 22 July 1853, p. 7.

34. Taylor Stoehr, *Free Love in America* (New York: AMS, 1979), 12; Stern, *The Pantarch*, 82–85; Wunderlich, "Low Living and High Thinking," 221–22 n.

35. "Institute of Desarollo: A School of Life," *Nichols Journal* 1 (October 1853):49; "Our School of Life," *Nichols Journal* 1 (November 1, 1853):58–59.

36. "The Question of Marriage," *Nichols Journal* [3] (September 2, 1854):27; Thomas Nichols and Mary Gove Nichols, *Marriage: Its History, Character, and Results; Its Sanctities, and Its Profanities; Its Science and Its Facts* (Cincinnati: Valentine Nicholson, 1854), 13, 27, 81–82.

37. "Elementary Principles," 17.

38. Both Warren's broadside and Mary Nichols's reply are included in "Individuality —Protest of Mr. Warren—Relations of the Sexes," *Nichols Journal* 1 (October 1853):52.

39. Nichols, *Marriage*, 201–02.

40. "Question of Marriage," 27–28; Nichols, *Marriage*, 100, 102–05, 289, 298.

41. Nichols, *Marriage*, 96, 299, 300, 362.

42. Periodical Letter (August 1854):19–20; (July 1854):13.

43. Codman, "A Brief History," 16.

44. Warren, "Our State of Difficulties," 6 and "Social experiment," 137–38; Caroline Cutter Warren to Josiah Warren, October 21, 1855, and May 27, 1855, Josiah Warren Papers, Labadie Collection, Division of Rare Books and Special Collections, University of Michigan Library.

45. "Conversational Development" is in the Journal of Josiah Warren but is separated from the first part (written in 1840) by a number of blank pages. Two of Warren's last public statements on the marriage question were in a postwar free love journal, *Word* (January 1872):3, and in an issue a few months later (June 1872):3. He was answered sharply by Olivia Shepard in the same journal, (May 1873):4; Josiah Warren, *Practical Applications of the Elementary Principles of True Civilization. . . .* (Princeton, Mass.: the author, 1873); Wunderlich, "Low Living and High Thinking," 250.

46. Lazarus, *Love vs. Marriage*, 55; John B. Ellis, *Free Love and Its Votaries, or American Socialism Unmasked* [1870] (New York: AMS, 1971), 400; Conway, "Modern Times," 428.

47. Quoted without reference in Ellis, *Free Love*, 388, 396; Edger, *Modern Times*, 12–13; Conway, "Modern Times," 421, 425. See also Noyes, *History of American Socialisms*, 101.

48. Ellis, *Free Love*, 388, 391–92; Ellis's work can be used only with great caution. I believe the "Miss Smith" story is false. Ellis's quotations from a long-time resident seem to me more likely to be genuine, but I have used material from this source only when it was consistent with material from other eyewitness accounts. These same cautions apply to my use of Ellis in the following chapter. See also Edger, *Modern Times*, 12.

49. Edger, *Modern Times*, 12–15; Codman, "A Brief History," 17.

50. Codman, "A Brief History," 17; Ellis, *Free Love*, 396; Conway, "Modern Times," 425.

51. Martin, *Men Against the State*, 80–82.

52. Edger, *Modern Times*, 2.

5. The Free Love Counterculture, 1853 to 1860

Much of the material in this chapter appeared in John C. Spurlock, "The Free Love Network in America, 1850–1860," *Journal of Social History* 21 (June 1988).

1. *Liberator* 26 (July 25, 1856):120; *Liberator* 26 (August 22, 1856):140; *Liberator* 26 (September 5, 1856):148; *Liberator* 26 (September 26, 1856):150. This exchange is discussed in Lewis Perry, *Childhood, Marriage, and Reform: Henry Clarke Wright, 1797–1870* (Chicago: University of Chicago Press, 1980), 253–54. Perry has an extended discussion of the relationship between antislavery and marriage radicalism in *Radical Abolitionism: Anarchy and the Government of God in Antislavery Thought* (Ithaca, N.Y.: Cornell University Press, 1973), 188–230.

2. A. D. Mayo, "The Real Controversy Between Man and Woman," *Una* 1 (February 1, 1853):3; E. H. W., "Woman and Marriage," *Una* 1 (November 1853):170–71.

3. Mari Jo and Paul Buhle, eds., *The Concise History of Woman Suffrage* (Urbana: University of Illinois Press, 1987), 171, 185; Paulina Wright Davis, *A History of the National Woman's Rights Movement for Twenty Years. . . .* [1871] (New York: Source Book Press, 1970), 10–11.

4. [Francis Barry], "From the Lecturing Field," *Social Revolutionist* 3 (April 1857):127;

Hannah F. M. Brown, *The False and True Marriage; the Reason and Results* (Cleveland: E. Cowles, 1859), 6, 9–11, 15, 16.

5. Mrs. H. F. M. Brown, "Reply to 'B'," *Agitator* 1 (September 15, 1858):6; "L. A. Hine and the Marriage Question," *Agitator* 2 (November 15, 1858):28; Warren Chase, "Seduction," *Agitator* 2 (December 1, 1858):34; Stephen Pearl Andrews, "Free Love," *Agitator* 2 (December 15, 1858):43; George Roberts, "Freedom," *Agitator* 3 (March 15, 1860):91.

6. Andrew Jackson Davis, *The Magic Staff* (New York: J. S. Brown, 1857), 470, 492; Warren Chase, *The Life-line of the Lone One*, 5th ed. (Boston: William White, 1868), 156–59.

7. William Denton, "Notes from the Lecturing Field," *Social Revolutionist* 1 (April 1856):121; Anne Denton Cridge, "My Soul's Thralldom and Its Deliverance: An Autobiography," *Social Revolutionist* (December 1856):169–72 and *Social Revolutionist* 3 (January 1857):18; J. H. Powell, *William Denton, the Geologist and Radical: A Biographical Sketch* (Boston: J. H. Powell, 1870), 5–28.

8. Denton, "Notes," 121; William Denton, "Spiritualism, Socialism, and Free Love," *Social Revolutionist* 1 (April 1856):124–25; William Denton, "Reform Schools," *Vanguard* 1 (March 14, 1857):7.

9. Alfred Cridge, "Congenial Relations," *Vanguard* 1 (March 21, 1857):21. Patterson's letters and the Cridges' replies continued to appear in the *Vanguard* for several months. Exchanges referred to here are in vol. 1 (July 11, 1857):148; (July 25, 1857):164–65; (August 5, 1857):186–87; (September 26, 1857):238.

10. *Proceedings of the Free Convention, Held at Rutland, Vt., July 25th, 26th, and 27th, 1858* (Boston: J. B. Yerrinton and Son, 1858), 11–13, 24–31, 43–49, 53–55, 71.

11. Ibid., 56–62.

12. "Organs of Modern Socialism," *New York Herald*, 14 July 1858, p. 4.

13. *Social Revolutionist* 1 (May 1856):145–46; James H. Cook, "Questions and Answers," *Social Revolutionist* 1 (February 1856):94; Francis Barry, *Social Revolutionist* 1 (May 1856):147.

14. *Social Revolutionist* 1 (May 1856):145–46; "From Francis Barry," *Oneida Circular* 7 (March 4, 1858):24.

15. Thomas and Mary Nichols, "The Reason Why," *Nichols Journal* 1 (April 1853):5; "Organs of Modern Socialism," 4; John Patterson, "A Dream," *Herald of Truth* 1 (January 1847):50–54; William F. Vartorella, "The Other 'Peculiar Institution': The Free Thought and Free Love Reform Press in Ohio During Rebellion and Reconstruction, 1861–1877" (Ph.D. dissertation, Ohio University, 1977), xxviii–xxx.

16. Stephen Pearl Andrews, Horace Greeley, and Henry James, Sr., *Love, Marriage, and Divorce* . . . [1853] (New York: Source Book, 1972), 53; New York *Tribune*, 22 July 1853, p. 7. Thomas Nichols probably did some mental calculations to convince himself that twenty thousand people saw his periodical. It is unlikely that twenty thousand copies were printed or that twenty thousand people had even heard of Thomas Nichols. *Social Revolutionist*, extra (following December number, 1856).

17. William Hepworth Dixon, *New America* (Philadelphia: J. B. Lippincott, 1867), 421 (Dixon is quoting a document prepared by Noyes); "Marriage Discussion," *Oneida Circular* 3 (October 28, 1854):562.

18. "S. P. Andrews and the Tribune," *Oneida Circular* 2 (January 29, 1853):86; "Sovereignty of the Individual," *Oneida Circular* 2 (May 14, 1853):206; TLP, "A Definition of Free Love," *Oneida Circular* 11 (April 10, 1862):36; AWC, "New Institutions for

New Society," *Oneida Circular* 6 (August 26, 1857):126; *Oneida Circular* n.s. 7 (June 27, 1870):116; Dixon, *New America*, 420.

19. "What is it to be a Free Lover?" *Social Revolutionist* 3 (March 1857):77; Thomas Nichols, *"Free Love a Doctrine of Spiritualism;"* A Discourse delivered in Foster Hall, Cincinnati, December 22, 1855 (Cincinnati: F. Bly, 1856), 20.

20. Thomas Nichols and Mary Nichols, *Marriage* (Cincinnati: Valentine Nicholson, 1854), 317 and discussion of spiritualism following 407; "Letter from Dr. and Mrs. Nichols: Giving an account of their conversion," *Vanguard* 1 (May 2, 1857):66–67; Mary Gove Nichols, "A Letter from Mrs. Gove Nichols to her Friends," *Nichols Monthly* (November 1854):67; Thomas Nichols, "The Progressive Union: A Society for Mutual Protection in Right," *Nichols Monthly* (June 1855):53–59; "The Progressive Union. Third Report," *Nichols Monthly* (August/September 1855):195–96.

21. "To Dr. T. L. and Mrs. M. S. G. Nichols. Sectism and Sexuality," *Social Revolutionist* 2 (July 1856):26–30; L. A. Hine, "Free Love," *Social Revolutionist* 2 (August 1856):47–48 followed by the editors' "Remarks," 48–49; *Social Revolutionist* 4 (July 1857):6–7; Barry letter, *Social Revolutionist* 3 (March 1857):80.

22. Philip Gleason, "From Free Love to Catholicism: Dr. and Mrs. Thomas L. Nichols at Yellow Springs," *Ohio Historical Quarterly* 70 (October 1961):283–307; "Conversions to Catholicism," *Spiritual Telegraph* (April 18, 1857):404–05; "Letter from Dr. and Mrs. Nichols: Giving an account of their conversion," *Vanguard* 1 (May 2, 1857):66–67 and (May 16, 1857):81–83; Alfred Cridge, "The 'Law of Progression in Harmony;' Its Logical Sequence," *Social Revolutionist* 4 (July 1857):6–7.

23. The scripture reference is to James 2:20; "The Free Lovers: Practical Operation of the Free-Love League in the City of New-York," *New York Daily Times*, 10 October 1855, pp. 1–2; "A Rich Development," *New York Daily Times*, 19 October 1855, p. 4; George MacDonald, *Fifty Years of Free Thought*, (New York: The Truth Seeker, 1929), 207–08.

24. *Social Revolutionist* 3 (April 1857):127–28.

25. Thomas Nichols, "The Progressive Union," *Nichols Monthly* (June 1855):53–59; "The Progressive Union. Third Report of the Central Bureau," *Nichols Monthly* (August/September 1855):194–96.

26. "The Progressive Union," *Nichols Monthly* (June 1855):59; *Nichols Monthly* (August/September 1855):145, 187; "The Progressive Union. Fourth Report of the Central Bureau," *Nichols Monthly* (October/November 1855):303–06. According to J. H. Noyes, the Oneida archives contained four of the Progressive Union lists. These contained 324, 527, 506, and 155 names respectively, with some duplication of names from list to list. See, *Oneida Circular* n.s. 7 (June 27, 1870):116.

27. Gleason, "From Free Love to Catholicism," 289–90; *Nichols Monthly* (June 1856):6 and (August 1856):77.

28. *Nichols Monthly* (August 1856):77, 123. See also Gleason, "From Free Love to Catholicism"; and Bertha-Monica Stearns, "Memnonia: The Launching of Utopia," *New England Quarterly* 15 (June 1942):280–95.

29. M. E. Morse, "The Ceresco Union," *Social Revolutionist* 1 (February 1856):103–04; Letter from Thomas P. Wright, *Social Revolutionist* 1 (January 1856):29–30; J. H. Cook, "Way-Marks," *American Socialist* 3 (August 1, 1878):246.

30. "Rising Star Community," *Social Revolutionist* 1 (January 1856):6–7; John Patterson, "We so Love to Talk our Religion," *Vanguard* 1 (April 11, 1857):41–42.

31. "Dr. T. L. Nichols Letter," *Spiritual Telegraph* (September 1, 1855):70; John B.

Ellis, *Free Love and Its Votaries, or American Socialism Unmasked* [1870] (New York: AMS, 1971), 353, 356, 358, 359. As in the last chapter, I use evidence from Ellis with great caution. I assume that Ellis interviewed the eyewitness many years after the events recounted. That would explain why the resident forgot some crucial events (for instance, he told Ellis that all of the free lovers were acquitted). In general, however, the story conforms to other evidence. A much different perspective than Ellis's, and in many respects a better account, is Alvin Warren, "Reminiscences of Berlin Heights," *Our New Humanity* 1 (June 1896):27–42.

32. Francis Barry, "Individual Freedom," *Social Revolutionist* 1 (February 1856):48; J. K. Moore, "Government and Reform, or Theism and Atheism," *Social Revolutionist* 3 (June 1857):181.

33. Joseph Treat, "Berlin Movement," *Social Revolutionist* 3 (January 1857):15–16; "Berlin Heights," *Social Revolutionist* 4 (August 1857):63; Francis Barry, "Practical Socialism," *Social Revolutionist* 2 (September 1856):73–74; Francis Barry, "Practical Socialism," *Social Revolutionist* 3 (March 1857):81–82; Cook, "Way-Marks," 246; Warren, "Reminiscences of Berlin Heights," 30–32.

34. Warren, "Reminiscences of Berlin Heights," 37–38.

35. *Sandusky Daily Commercial Register* [the paper was unpaginated], 25 August 1857 and 8 September 1857; Ellis, *Free Love and Its Votaries*, 362–64; 366–67; Warren, "Reminiscences of Berlin Heights," 32.

36. *Sandusky Daily Commercial Register*, 21 November 1857; "Legal Annoyances," *Social Revolutionist* 4 (December 1857):189.

37. "November No. of the Social Revolutionist Burned by a Mob!" *Social Revolutionist* 4 (December 1857):189–90; "The Free Lovers Again," *Sandusky Daily Commercial Register*, 4 December 1857.

38. "The Free Love Settlement at Berlin Heights, Ohio," *New York Times*, 21 July 1858, p. 3; "The 'Free Love' Iniquity: A Movement to Suppress the Nuisance at Berlin Heights. . . ." *New York Times*, 27 July 1858, p. 2; "Pugnacious Reformers," *New York Times*, 3 August 1858, p. 3. Overton quoted in William F. Vartorella, "The Other Peculiar Institution" (Ph.D. dissertation, Ohio University, 1977), 70. Warren, "Reminiscences of Berlin Heights," 39.

39. Ellis, *Free Love and Its Votaries*, 372–76; "The Berlin Free Lovers Redividius," *New York Times*, 25 June 1858, p. 2; "Organs of Modern Socialism," 4.

40. The *Free Press* accounts were reprinted in the New York *Tribune* and the *New York Times*. "Rescue of a Young Wife from Free Love at Berlin," New York *Tribune*, 30 June 1858, p. 6, and "The Berlin Free Lovers-Letter from a Deserted Wife," *New York Times*, 14 July 1858, p. 2.

41. William F. Vartorella, "Free Love and Sexual Anarchism: A Brief History of the 'Berlin Movement,' and the role of the Towner Clan" (unpublished paper, n.d., Center for Communal Studies, University of Southern Indiana), 8; Warren, "Reminiscences of Berlin Heights," 31–32.

42. Job Fish, "The Free Love Community," *Firelands Pioneer* 23 (1925):322–23.

43. Warren, "Reminiscences of Berlin Heights," 33–34.

6. Free Love Portraits

1. "The Free Lovers: Practical Operation of the Free-Love-League in the City of New York," *New York Daily Times*, 10 October 1855, p. 2.

2. "The Progressive Union," *Nichols Monthly* (August/September 1855):59.

3. Madeline B. Stern, *The Pantarch: A Biography of Stephen Pearl Andrews* (Austin: University of Texas Press, 1968), 3–18, 33–46; "The Autobiography of Stephen Pearl Andrews," Stephen Pearl Andrews Papers, State Historical Society of Wisconsin; "Short autobiography of Marx Edgeworth Lazarus," Labadie Collection, Division of Rare Books and Special Collections, University of Michigan Library; Marx Edgeworth Lazarus to George Mordecai, November 1846 and December 30, 1846, and Will of Marx Edgeworth Lazarus, March 30, 1847, in George Mordecai Papers, Southern Historical Collection, University of North Carolina, Chapel Hill; Edgar MacDonald, ed., *The Education of the Heart: The Correspondence of Rachel Mordecai Lazarus and Maria Edgeworth* (Chapel Hill: The University of North Carolina Press, 1977), 328.

4. William F. Vartorella, "The Other 'Peculiar Institution': The Free Thought and Free Love Press in Ohio during Rebellion and Reconstruction" (Ph.D. dissertation, Ohio University, 1977), 199; "Letter from Austin Kent," *Practical Christian* 14 (September 10, 1853):38–39; "From Austin Kent on Free-Loveism," *Practical Christian* 15 (September 23, 1854):42; "Free Love: Number One," *Practical Christian* 15 (October 7, 1854):46; "Free Love: Number Four," *Practical Christian* 15 (November 18, 1854):58; "Letter," *Social Revolutionist* (March 1857):87–88; *Mrs. Woodhull and her "Social Freedom"* (Clinton, Mass.: Independent Radical Tract Society, 1873), 6, 10; Austin Kent, *Free Love; or, A Philosophical Demonstration of the Non-exclusive Nature of Connubial Love* (Hopkinton, N.Y.: the author, 1857).

5. James Clay, *A Voice From Prison; or, Truths for the Multitude, and Pearls for the Truthful* (Boston: Bela Marsh, 1856), iii–vi, 24, 27, 84, 228–29, 345, 354–58.

6. Ibid., 28–30, 71–72; William O. Reichert, *Partisans of Freedom: A Study in American Anarchism* (Bowling Green, Ohio: Bowling Green State University Popular Press, 1976), 285; Roger Wunderlich, "Low Living and High Thinking in Modern Times, New York (1852–1864)" (Ph.D. dissertation, State University of New York at Stony Brook, 1986), 272–73.

7. Kent, *Social Freedom*, 2; Clay, *Voice From Prison*, 27, 38, 56.

8. "Autobiography of Stephen Pearl Andrews," 50, 175, 258–59.

9. Stephen Pearl Andrews, *The Science of Society* (London: C. W. Daniel, Ltd., 1913), 15; "Autobiography of Stephen Pearl Andrews," 60, 62–63.

10. Marx Edgeworth Lazarus, "Short Autobiography;" *The Trinity in its Theological, Scientific, and Practical Aspects, Analyzed and Illustrated* (New York: for the author by Fowlers and Wells, 1851). Pagination was separate. *Incarnation*, 4, 44, 48.

11. Lazarus, "Short Autobiography;" *Trinity*, 5, 6.

12. Marx Edgeworth Lazarus, *Love vs. Marriage* (New York: Fowler and Wells, 1852), 41 and "Short Autobiography"; Kent, *Social Freedom*, 10; Lazarus wrote for anarchist journals like the *Sentinel* while Kent received space in *Hull's Crucible*.

13. James Turner, *Without God, Without Creed: The Origins of Unbelief in America* (Baltimore: Johns Hopkins University Press, 1985); Joseph Treat, "Theology," *Vanguard* (March 14, 1857):2–3; Letter from Joseph Treat, *Practical Christian* 12 (July 19, 1851):24. [It is possible that this was a different Joseph Treat.] Charles Latchar, who committed suicide at Berlin Heights, was also a professed atheist; Vartorella, "The Other 'Peculiar Institution'," 56.

14. C. M. Overton, "What Is It to Be a Free Lover?" *Social Revolutionist* 3 (March 1857):77–78 and "The Philosophy of Reform," *Vanguard* 1 (March 21, 1857):181–89; Alvin Warren, "Reminiscences of Berlin Heights," *Our New Humanity* (June 1896):40.

15. Warren, "Reminiscences of Berlin Heights," 41.

16. Mary Orme [pseud.], "The Artist," *Godey's Lady's Book* 33 (April 1845):154; Karen Halttunen, *Confidence Men and Painted Women: A Study of Middle-Class Culture in America, 1830–1870* (New Haven, Conn.: Yale University Press, 1982), xiv–xv, 1–35, and passim. Also see Louis J. Kern, *An Ordered Love* (Chapel Hill: The University of North Carolina Press, 1981).

17. Andrews, *The Science of Society*, 58 and *Love, Marriage, and Divorce and the Sovereignty of the Individual* [1853] (New York: Source Book, 1972), 90; Clay, *Voice From Prison*, 26.

18. Lazarus, *Trinity*, 10; Lazarus, *Love vs. Marriage*, 35; Marx Edgeworth Lazarus, *Comparative Psychology and Universal Analogy* (New York: Fowlers and Wells, 1852), viii.

19. Andrews, *Love, Marriage, and Divorce*, 12–13; Kent, *Social Freedom*, 4.

20. Clay, *Voice From Prison*, 45; Marx Edgeworth Lazarus, *Passional Hygiene and Natural Medicine; Embracing the Harmonies of Man with his Planet* (New York: Fowler and Wells, 1852), iv.

21. Alfred Cridge, "Minor Morals, So-called," *Vanguard* 1 (September 6, 1857):212; Jacqueline S. Wilkie, "Submerged Sensuality: Technology and Perceptions of Bathing," *Journal of Social History* 19 (Summer 1986):649–64.

22. Clay, *Voice From Prison*, 27; Stephen Pearl Andrews, "Free Love," *Agitator* 2 (December 15, 1858):43; John 3:5.

23. "Autobiography of Stephen Pearl Andrews," 51–52; Lazarus, "Short Autobiography."

24. "The Marriage Question: Courtship Before and After Marriage," *Social Revolutionist* 1 (May 1856):134–35; "Marriage Question," *Social Revolutionist* 1 (April 1856):111–13; "Autobiography of Stephen Pearl Andrews," 54; John Humphrey Noyes, "Free Love II," *Oneida Circular* n.s. 1 (February 13, 1865):377; Clay, *Voice From Prison*, 68.

25. "Autobiography of Stephen Pearl Andrews," 283.

26. Alfred Cridge, "Congenial Relations," *Vanguard* 1 (March 21, 1857):21; John Patterson, "Marriage and Individual Sovereignty Again," *Vanguard* 1 (August 5, 1857):186–87; Warren, "Reminiscences of Berlin Heights," 31–32, 34–35; Stern, *The Pantarch*, 87–98.

27. "Glimpses of Life," *Social Revolutionist* 3 (January 1857):29–31; Warren, "Reminiscences of Berlin Heights," 30–32.

28. Francis Barry in "The Lecturing Field," *Social Revolutionist* 3 (April 1857):127. According to William F. Vartorella in "The Other 'Peculiar Institution'," 36, Cora Barry was at least nominally the head editor of *Age of Freedom*, which succeeded the *Social Revolutionist* at Berlin Heights.

29. Minerva Putnam, "Glimpses of Life," 30, and "A Woman's Experience in Freedom," *Social Revolutionist* 3 (March 1857):71–72.

30. The *Sandusky Daily Commercial Register* ["The Free Lovers Again," 4 December 1857] not only reported that the women burned the papers, but that they then turned on Francis Barry and would have shaved his head if they had caught him. The story may not be true. True or not, the story was inspired by Barry's long hair (he also went barefoot, it seems). It also represents a symbolic castration of the man whose sexual aggressions seemingly threatened the safety of the women's families. "The Lady's Letter," *Practical Christian* 15 (December 30, 1854):69. On women's attitudes toward marriage, see Nancy F. Cott, *The Bonds of Womanhood: "Woman's Sphere" in New England, 1780–1835* (New Haven, Conn.: Yale University Press, 1977), 193.

31. On Clay, see Warren, "Reminiscences of Berlin Heights," 32 and throughout. Lazarus wrote encouraging words to the *Word* 17 (September 1889):[3–4]. See also Kent, *Social Freedom*. Andrews is also discussed in the next chapter. As will be shown, other people who embraced free love continued in the cause after the war, including Francis Barry, J. H. Cook ["one of the few survivors of the Berlin movement, who adhered to the principles of that movement, to the bitter end." Quoted from Warren, "Reminiscences of Berlin Heights," 35], Theron Leland, and Stephen Pearl Andrews. Aside from Thomas Nichols, the only prewar free lover specifically referred to as having abandoned free love was the *Social Revolutionist* editor John Patterson [Warren, "Reminiscences of Berlin Heights," 35].

32. "A Bad Book Gibbetted," *New York Daily Times*, 17 August 1855, p. 2.

33. "The Free Love System: Origin, Progress—and Position of the anti-Marriage Movement" *New York Daily Times*, 8 September 1855, p. 2.

34. Ibid.; Elizabeth Cady Stanton, Susan B. Anthony, Matilda Joslyn Gage, eds., *The History of Woman Suffrage*, vol. 1, 1848–1861 [1881] (New York: Arno and New York Times, 1969), 37; Charles Wilkins Webber, *Spiritual Vampirism: The History of Etherial Softdown, and her Friends of the "New Light"* (Philadelphia: Lippincott, Grambo, 1853), passim; [Mary Gove Nichols], *Mary Lyndon or, Revelations of a Life. An Autobiography* (New York: Stringer and Townsend, 1855), passim. In fact, Mary Gove had become enamored of Brisbane's philosophy during a visit to New York City or Philadelphia in 1841, long before she moved to the city in 1845. See *Mary Lyndon*, 324, and Irving T. Richards, "Mary Gove Nichols and John Neal," *New England Quarterly* 7 (June 1934):346.

35. *Mary Lyndon*, 5–22, 66–69.

36. Ibid., 74–76.

37. Mary S. Gove, *Lectures to Ladies on Anatomy and Physiology* (Boston: Saxton and Peirce, 1842), vi; Janet Noever, "Passionate Rebel: The Life of Mary Gove Nichols, 1810–1884" (Ph.D. dissertation, University of Oklahoma, 1983), 21, 28, 39–48; Bertha-Monica Stearns, "Two Forgotten New England Reformers," *New England Quarterly* 6 (March 1933):60–62; Richards, "Mary Gove Nichols and John Neal," 344, 352–53; John B. Blake, "Mary Gove Nichols, Prophetess of Health," *Proceedings of the American Philosophical Society* 106 (June 29, 1962): 219–234.

38. Gove, *Lectures to Ladies*, 10, 11, 18, 82, 178.

39. Stephen Nissenbaum, *Sex, Diet, and Debility in Jacksonian America: Sylvester Graham and Health Reform* (Westport, Conn.: Greenwood Press, 1980), 128–29, 136, 140–42; Carroll Smith-Rosenberg, "Sex as Symbol in Victorian Purity: An Ethnohistorical Analysis of Jacksonian America," *American Journal of Sociology* 85 (supplement):332–56.

40. Gove, *Lectures to Ladies*, 217–18, 225.

41. Nancy F. Cott, "Passionlessness: An Interpretation of Victorian Sexual Ideology, 1790–1850," *Signs* 4 (Winter 1978):219–36; Nissenbaum, *Sex, Diet, and Debility*, 30; Gove, *Lectures to Ladies*, 219. Bonnie G. Smith, in *Ladies of the Leisure Class: The Bourgeoises of Northern France in the Nineteenth Century* (Princeton, N.J.: Princeton University Press, 1981), 82, indicates that pervasive ignorance of sexuality could indeed be enforced. "Northern bourgeois women," Smith writes, "went to the marriage bed ignorant of the sexual act."

42. Mary Gove Nichols, *Experience in Water-cure: A Familiar Exposition of the Principles and Results of Water Treatment, in the Cure of Acute and Chronic Diseases* (New York: Fowler and Wells, 1849), 74; Thomas Nichols, *Esoteric Anthropology* (London: Nichols and Co., n.d.), 100; Nissenbaum, *Sex, Diet and Debility*, 167.

43. *Mary Lyndon*, 156, 249–63, 273; Noever, "Passionate Rebel," 71, 91–97, and ff.

44. Gove, *Lectures to Ladies*, 219, 273; *Mary Lyndon*, 309–10.

45. "The Artist," *Godey's Lady's Book* 33 (April 1845):155–56.

46. Mary Gove, *Agnes Morris; or, the Heroine of Domestic Life. . . .* (New York: Harper and Brothers, 1849), 96.

47. "Marrying a Genius," *Godey's Lady's Book* 32 (September 1844):104–07; "The Evil and the Good," *Godey's Lady's Book* 33 (July 1845):36–38.

48. For the phrenological version of love, see Lorenzo Niles Fowler, *Marriage* (New York: Fowler and Wells, 1847) or Orson Fowler, *The Family*, 3 vols. (New York: O. S. Fowler, 1859); Henry C. Wright, *Marriage and Parentage* [1855] (New York: Arno, 1974), 168; Johann Wolfgang von Goethe, *Elective Affinities*, trans. R. J. Hollingdale (Middlesex, England: Penguin Books, 1971).

49. *Mary Lyndon*, 338–39, 358, 365, 366, 369.

50. Ibid., 374, 379, 380, 385.

51. "Individuality—Protest of Mr. Warren—Relations of the Sexes," *Nichols Journal* 1 (October 1853):52.

52. Ibid.; Thomas and Mary Nichols, *Marriage* (Cincinnati: Valentine Nicholson, 1854), 202, 369.

53. "The Evil and the Good," 36; *Mary Lyndon*, 360.

54. *Mary Lyndon*, 153, 385.

55. Noever, "Passionate Rebel," 297; Webber, *Spiritual Vampirism*, 6–18.

56. Richards, *Mary Gove Nichols*, 341; *Mary Lyndon*, 360; Nichols, *Experience in Water-cure*, 29.

57. Philip Gleason, "From Free Love to Catholicism: Dr. and Mrs. Thomas L. Nichols at Yellow Springs," *Ohio Historical Quarterly* 70 (October 1961):283–307; Bertha-Monica Stearns, "Memnonia: The Launching of a Utopia," *New England Quarterly* 15 (June 1942):280–95.

58. Emile Durkheim, *Suicide: A Study in Sociology*, trans. John A. Spauldin and George Simpson, ed. George Simpson (New York: Free Press, 1951), 257.

59. "Letter from Dr. and Mrs. Nichols: Giving an account of their conversion," *Vanguard* 1 (May 2, 1857):66–67 and (May 16, 1857):81–83; Gleason, "From Free Love to Catholicism," 283–307.

60. I am grateful for the many comments I received on this paper from participants in Carol Gilligan's seminar, "On the Psychology of Love," at Douglass College, Spring 1985. The connection between Mary's conversion and the value of Catholicism in preventing suicide was suggested to me by Kathleen Wallace.

61. "The Artist," 156; Noever, "Passionate Rebel," 253–54; "Letter from Dr. and Mrs. Nichols," *Vanguard* 1 (May 16, 1857):81–83.

62. Mary Gove Nichols to Paulina Wright Davis, n.d., Paulina Wright Davis Papers, Vassar College Library.

7. Free Love Versus the Middle Class, 1865 to 1900

1. George Fredrickson, *The Inner Civil War: Northern Intellectuals and the Crisis of the Union* (New York: Harper and Row, 1965), 2, 36–39, 56–63, 122; "The social significance of our institutions . . ." [Boston, 1861], in *Henry James, Senior: A Selection of his Writings*, ed. Giles Gunn (Chicago: American Library Association, 1974), 105–20, and quotes on 115–17.

2. James J. Martin, *Men Against the State: The Expositors of Individualist Anarchism in America, 1827–1908*, third printing (Colorado Springs, Colo.: Ralph Myles, 1970), 84, 95; Josiah Warren, *True Civilization: An Immediate Necessity and the Last Ground of Hope for Mankind* [1863] (New York: Burt Franklin & Co., 1967), 16–17, 51–55.

3. "The Autobiography of Stephen Pearl Andrews," Stephen Pearl Andrews Papers, State Historical Society of Wisconsin, 108, 170–71; Warren Chase, *American Crisis; or, Trial and Triumph of Democracy* (Boston: Bela Marsh, 1862); Alvin Warren, "Reminiscences of Berlin Heights," *Our New Humanity* 1 (June 1896):35; William F. Vartorella, "Free love and sexual anarchism: A brief history of the 'Berlin Movement' and the role of the Towner clan," (unpublished paper, n.d., Center for Communal Studies, University of Southern Indiana), 10; Prospectus of *The New Republic*, in *Herald of Progress* 3 (June 28, 1862):7.

4. "Austin Kent on Non-resistance," *Practical Christian* 13 (September 25, 1852):42; Austin Kent, *Mrs. Woodhull and her "Social Freedom"* (Clinton, Mass.: Independent Radical Tract Society, 1873), 10.

5. Thomas Low Nichols, *Forty Years of American Life: 1821–1861* [1864] (New York: Stackpole Sons, 1937), 5, 150–51; Edgar E. MacDonald, ed., *The Education of the Heart* (Chapel Hill: The University of North Carolina Press, 1977), 328; Marx Edgeworth Lazarus, "Short Autobiography," Labadie Papers, Division of Rare Books and Special Collections, University of Michigan Library.

6. Hal D. Sears, *The Sex Radicals: Free Love in High Victorian America* (Lawrence: Regents Press of Kansas, 1977), 153–56; *Herald of Progress* 1 (August 4, 1860):5.

7. G., "Social Petroleum," *Oneida Circular* N.S. 1 (March 13, 1865):409; Chase, *American Crisis*, 79.

8. Fredrickson, *The Inner Civil War*, 184–88.

9. Ibid., chaps. 5 and 7; David J. Pivar, *Purity Crusade: Sexual Morality and Social Control, 1868–1900* (Westport, Conn.: Greenwood Press, 1973), 24–43, 50–62, 78–79.

10. Anthony Comstock, *Frauds Exposed; or, How the people are deceived and robbed, and youth corrupted* [1880] (Montclair, N.J.: Patterson Smith, 1969), 388, 389; Heywood Broun and Margaret Leech, *Anthony Comstock: Roundsman of the Lord* (New York: Literary Guild of America, 1927), 60–78, 80, 83–88, 91–93, 141–42, 152–55, 185.

11. William L. O'Neill, *Everyone was Brave: The Rise and Fall of Feminism in America* (Chicago: Quadrangle, 1969), 18–19; letter from Mary Gove Nichols to Paulina Wright Davis, n.d., in the Paulina Wright Davis Papers, Vassar College Library.

12. Francis Barry, "Men," *Revolution* (May 7, 1868):279; Elizabeth Cady Stanton, "Marriages and Mistresses," *Revolution* (October 15, 1868):233–34 and "Does the Revolution Believe in Marriage?" *Revolution* (April 8, 1869):212; Paulina Wright Davis, *A History of the National Woman's Rights Movement for Twenty Years. . . .* [1871] (New York: Source Book Press, 1970), 64, 69–70, 83; O'Neill, *Everyone was Brave*, 21.

13. Johanna Johnston, *Mrs. Satan: The Incredible Saga of Victoria C. Woodhull* (New York: G. P. Putnam's Sons, 1967), 35–69; Alpha, "Victoria Woodhull: The Coming Woman," *Revolution* (February 11, 1869):86.

14. Davis, *History of the National Woman's Rights Movement*, 95–111; "The New Rebellion. The Great Secession Speech of Victoria C. Woodhull. . . . ," in Davis, *History of the National Woman's Rights Movement*, 112–19; Johnston, *Mrs. Satan*, 103.

15. "A speech on the principles of social freedom. . . ." [1871], in *The Victoria Woodhull Reader*, ed. Madeline B. Stern (Weston, Mass.: M&S Press, 1974), 15–16, 19–

20, 23 (note that all of the speeches and articles in the *Woodhull Reader* have separate pagination). Johnston, *Mrs. Satan*, 128–34.

16. Madeline B. Stern, *The Pantarch: A Biography of Stephen Pearl Andrews* (Austin: University of Texas Press, 1968), 112–28; Johnston, *Mrs. Satan*, 135–37; "A speech on the impending revolution . . ." [1872], in *Woodhull Reader*, 16, 28.

17. Johnston, *Mrs. Satan*, 142–47; Kent, *Mrs. Woodhull's "Social Freedom"*, 2.

18. "Victoria C. Woodhull's Complete and Detailed Version of the Beecher-Tilton Affair" [1872], in *Woodhull Reader*, 16; Johnston, *Mrs. Satan*, 159–96; Broun and Leech, *Anthony Comstock*, 102–22.

19. "Beecher-Tilton Affair," 13.

20. Vartorella, "Free Love and sexual anarchism," 11; "A Card," *Woodhull and Claflin's Weekly* 5 (April 19, 1873):6; Joseph Treat, *Beecher, Tilton, Woodhull, the Creation of Society. All four of them exposed, and if possible reformed, and forgiven, in Dr. Treat's celebrated letter to Victoria C. Woodhull* (New York: the author, 1874), passim. My speculation about Treat being in love with one of the Claflins is based entirely on language in his pamphlet. If he was, in fact, infatuated with a Claflin, it was probably Utica.

21. Treat, *Beecher, Tilton, Woodhull*, 3, 4, 7–12. Woodhull probably penned few, if any, of the articles or speeches attributed to her. Benjamin Tucker, one of her lovers and traveling companions and a committed free lover, believed that the Claflin sisters had vague ideas of the writings that appeared under their names but that neither was capable of writing any of it. See Johnston, *Mrs. Satan*, 207–08, 214–15. Colonel Blood wrote that Stephen Pearl Andrews was given the information for the Beecher-Tilton exposé and then rewrote the material, adding the elements that caused the most uproar. See Colonel Blood, "What Broke Down the Woodhull Paper?" *American Socialist* 3 (April 18, 1878):123.

22. Austin Kent, "Emancipation of Woman," *Hull's Crucible* 3 (January 8, 1874):2. For the Treat letters, see *Word* (May 1874):2; (June 1874):3; and July and August 1874.

23. Blood, "What Broke Down the Woodhull Paper?", 123. Leland's letters appeared July 12, 1877, 221, and April 25, 1878, 133. Johnston, *Mrs. Satan*, 237–302.

24. O'Neill, *Everyone was Brave*, 29; Aileen S. Kraditor, in *The Ideas of the Woman Suffrage Movement, 1890–1920* (New York: W. W. Norton, 1965, 1981), 114.

25. *Woodhull and Claflin's Weekly* 5 (July 5, 1873):3–5; *Word* 3 (August 1874):4; Vartorella, "Free Love and sexual anarchism," 11–14; Spence C. Olin, Jr., "Bible communism and the Origins of Orange County," *California History* 58 (Fall 1979):220–33; Robert S. Fogarty, "Nineteenth Century Utopian," *Pacific Historian* 10 (Fall 1972):70–76.

26. Constance Noyes Robertson, *Oneida Community: The Breakup, 1876–1881* (Syracuse, N.Y.: Syracuse University Press, 1972), 15–21.

27. Warren Chase, "Marriage Laws," *Word* 2 (February 1874):4; Lazarus letter in *Word* 17 (September 1889):3–4; J. H. Cook, "Millennial Fraternity," *Oneida Circular* n.s. 2 (October 9, 1865):236 and in *Woodhull and Claflin's Weekly* 3 (October 28, 1871):13; Leland's letter appeared in *Proceedings of the Indignation Meeting held in Fanueil Hall, Thursday evening, August 1, 1878. . . .* (Boston: Benjamin Tucker, 1878), 63.

28. Martin, *Men Against the State*, 105–06, 125; *Word* 1 (July 1872):1.

29. For a good example of Warren's caution, see "Criticism," *Word* 1 (June 1872):2. For an example of the controversy Warren attracted by his caution, see Olivia F. Shepard, "Libertinism," *Word* 2 (May 1873):4; Ezra Heywood, *Cupid's Yokes: or, The Binding Forces of Conjugal Life* [1874] (New York: Arno, 1974), 5; *Word* 1 (May 1872):4; "Free Love League," *Word* 5 (May 1876):1–2.

30. Heywood, *Cupid's Yokes*, 5, 7–9, 14, 19–20; Sears, *The Sex Radicals*, 157.

31. Francis Barry, "Correspondence," *Word* 2 (July 1873):3; "Anti-Marriage," *Word* 3 (October 1874):3; "Wife Holding," *Word* 5 (April 1877):3.

32. Daniel Hull, *Moses Hull* (Wellesley, Mass.: Maugus, 1907), 13–32; Moses Hull, *That Terrible Question*, 3d ed. (New York: D. M. Bennett, [1872]), 5, 8, 10.

33. Moses Hull, *Terrible Question*, 17 and "A Personal Experience," *Woodhull and Claflin's Weekly* 6 (August 23, 1873):3–4; Elvira Hull, "Facts are stubborn things," *Woodhull and Claflin's Weekly* 6 (September 6, 1873):5; Sears, *The Sex Radicals*, 16.

34. Remarkable if true, but probably not true. Blood, 'What Broke Down the Woodhull Paper," 123.

35. Moses Hull, "The General Judgment," *Hull's Crucible* 3 (January 8, 1874):1–2; Francis Barry, "Letter to A. Briggs Davis," *Word* 4 (September 1875):3; "Letter from Austin Kent," *Hull's Crucible* 3 (January 1, 1874):7.

36. Sears, *The Sex Radicals*, 28–33, 55.

37. Martin, *Men Against the State*, 102; Austin Kent, *Mrs. Woodhull's "Social Freedom"*, passim, and "My Confession," *Hull's Crucible* 3 (January 8, 1874):3; Stern, *The Pantarch*, 149; Robert S. Fogarty, ed., *Dictionary of American Communal and Utopian History* (Westport, Conn.: Greenwood Press, 1980), "Warren Chase"; MacDonald, *Education of the Heart*, 328.

38. Ezra Heywood, "Wife Holding," *Word* 5 (April 1877):3; Sears, *The Sex Radicals*, 30.

39. Hull, "Personal Experience," 3–4.

40. Anne Denton Cridge, "The Other Side," *Social Revolutionist* 4 (October 1857):122. For a response, see *Social Revolutionist* 4 (December 1857): 192ff; Treat, *Beecher, Tilton, Woodhull*, 12.

41. Francis Barry, *Word* 5 (May 1875):3.

42. Austin Kent, "The Emancipation of Woman," *Hull's Crucible* 3 (January 8, 1874):2; O'Neill, *Everyone was Brave*, 25; Pivar, *Purity Crusade*, 78–79; John C. Burnham, "The Progressive Era Revolution in American Attitudes toward Sex," *Journal of American History* (March 1973):885–908; Anthony Comstock, *Traps for the Young*, ed. Robert Bremner [1883] (Cambridge, Mass.: Belknap Press of Harvard University Press, 1967), 159.

43. Comstock, *Traps*, 163–66; Broun and Leech, *Anthony Comstock*, 170–75; Sears, *The Sex Radicals*, 165–68.

44. Sears, *The Sex Radicals*, 166–71; *Proceedings of the Indignation Meeting*, 3.

45. Sears, *The Sex Radicals*, 172–82.

46. Ibid., 83–86, 89–92, 107–12; Hugh O. Pentecost, "A Good Man Sent to Prison," *Twentieth Century Library* 1 (May 31, 1890):1–10.

47. Sears, *The Sex Radicals*, 229–34, 262–63.

48. William L. O'Neill, *Divorce in the Progressive Era* (New Haven, Conn.: Yale University Press, 1967), viii, 6–7, 12, 20. See also Hal Sears, "Sex Radicals in High Victorian America," *Virginia Quarterly Review* 48 (Summer 1972):377–92.

49. Jacqueline S. Wilkie, "Submerged Sensuality: Technology and Perceptions of Bathing," *Journal of Social History* 19 (Summer 1986):649–64; John S. Gilkeson, Jr., *Middle-Class Providence, 1820–1940* (Princeton, N.J.: Princeton University Press, 1986), 215–46; James Reed, *The Birth Control Movement and American Society: From Private Vice to Public Virtue* (Princeton, N.J.: Princeton University Press, 1983), chaps. 2 and 5. See

also Peter Gay, *The Bourgeois Experience: Victoria to Freud*, vol. 1, *Education of the Senses*, and vol. 2, *The Tender Passion* (New York: Oxford University Press, 1984 and 1986).

50. O'Neill, *Divorce*, 104–11, 164–65; Emma Goldman, *Living My Life*, vol. 1 [1931] (New York: Dover, 1970), 17–25, 36, 145, 216, 219–20; Alice Wexler, *Emma Goldman: An Intimate Life* (New York: Pantheon Books, 1984), 48–51; Martin, *Men Against the State*, 219–33; Christopher Lasch, *The New Radicalism, 1889–1963: The Intellectual as a Social Type* (New York: Knopf, 1965).

Bibliographical Essay

Background and Middle-Class Formation

John Humphrey Noyes's *History of American Socialisms* (1870) is the key source for the historian of the ante-bellum free love movement. Noyes comprehended the importance of sex and religion and the challenge of the home to community better than any author of his time. My second chapter takes its form from Noyes's scheme of nationwide socialist movements—Owenism followed by Fourierism with the Brook Farm experiment as the mediating experience. More than the record of experiences recounted by Noyes, however, the insights of the Yankee saint have frequently informed my interpretation of sources and the people behind the sources.

There have been extremely useful historical works since 1870 dealing with issues of religion and sexuality, though in general they tend to stress one or the other. Whitney Cross, in *The Burned-over District* (1950), traced the course of revival religion throughout the early nineteenth century, showing the impress of enthusiasm upon reform and other social phenomenon. We can gauge Cross's accomplishment only by realizing that his work has never been duplicated. Such recent works as Paul E. Johnson's *Shopkeeper's Millennium* (1978) and Mary P. Ryan's *Cradle of the Middle Class* (1981) assume that they can rely upon Cross as background for their studies.

Johnson and Ryan bring us to issues of class formation. Cross probably took the middle class for granted and never thought to mention that revival not only explained unusual behaviors among his yeoman but also offered them a self-understanding that determined, in time, what behavior would be usual. While Johnson is much more concerned with the uses of revival by the middle class, his work—especially his introduction—draws attention to the place of evangelical religion in the growth of middle-class consciousness. Ryan's work influenced my interpretation through her assumption that the connection between the middle class and religious experience needed to be carefully examined. The historical issues involved in the study of the middle class are clearly stated by Stuart M. Blumin in "The Hypothesis of Middle-class Formation in Nineteenth-Century America: A Critique and Some Proposals," *American Historical Review* 90 (April 1985).

Ryan also spends a large part of her work dealing with issues relating to the middle-class family. This has been vital to my understanding of the basis for the bourgeois family, since the concepts valued by the middle class persisted in the alternative middle class. Middle-class courtship has been clearly and creatively treated in Ellen K. Rothman's "Sex and Self-Control: Middle-class Courtship in America, 1770–1870," *Journal of Social History* 15 (Spring 1982) and in Karen Halttunen's *Confidence Men and Painted Women* (1982). Rothman recaptures the understanding that early nineteenth-century youth had of courtship, and Halttunen studies the cultural constraints they applied to courtship during the century in an effort to exorcise the demon of artificiality. My understanding of romantic love during the early nineteenth century has been largely shaped by John Gillis's forthcoming essay, "From Ritual to Romance: Toward a New History of Love."

Youth has been the subject of Stephen Nissenbaum's *Sex, Diet, and Debility in Jacksonian America* (1980) and of Carroll Smith-Rosenberg's essay on "Sex as Symbol in Victorian Purity," in *American Journal of Sociology* 84 Supplement (1978). Both historians point to the need of ante-bellum youth to establish personal discipline that would, in turn, order the chaotic worlds of urban living, commerce, and economic competition they were entering. The form that this personal discipline took was probably best described by Peter Cominos in "Late Victorian

Sexual Respectability and the Social System," *International Review of Social History* 8 (1963).

Sexual purity became a primary value for the youth who matured and entered the middle class during the 1830s and 1840s. An understanding of the value placed upon a kind of compulsive purity, and of the forms of courtship and marriage implied by the search for genuineness, may begin with historical works but should be extended to include writings by the purity crusaders. Sylvester Graham's *Lecture to Young Men* (1834) and William Alcott's *Physiology of Marriage* (1856) and *Moral Philosophy of Courtship and Marriage* (1857) are some of the best examples of the genre. The most interesting book on the subject of purity that came to my attention was one concerning women: Robert T. Wakely's *Woman and Her Secret Passions* (1846). Henry C. Wright was a major figure in the marriage debates of the period and his work *Marriage and Parentage* (1855) conveys both the importance placed upon marriage and the ambiguity of marriage and love. Wright's work is more useful to the historian thanks to an excellent biography by Lewis Perry, *Childhood, Marriage, and Reform* (1980).

Utopian Socialism

Arthur Bestor has written the basic works on both Owenism and Fourierism in America: "American Phalanxes" (Ph.D. dissertation, Yale University, 1938) and *Backwoods Utopias* (1950). Owenism has received a great deal of attention, including J. F. C. Harrison's *Quest for the New Moral World* (1969) and Barbara Taylor's *Eve and the New Jerusalem* (1983). Both of these books stress Owen's connection with Enlightenment philosophy, and Professor Taylor's work is especially useful in showing the growth of feminism within Owenism. For some reason Fourierism in America lacks a major, published, analytical treatment (other than Noyes). The best recent work is Carl Guarneri's "Utopian Socialism and American Ideas" (Ph.D. dissertation, The Johns Hopkins University, 1979).

Since my interest was in the development of ideas concerning marriage within socialist movements, the most useful sources were the periodical literature, especially *New Harmony Gazette* and *Free Enquirer* for Owenism and Brisbane's *Tribune* articles and the *Phalanx* and the *Harbinger* for Fourierism.

Transcendentalism had its own periodical literature. During the early 1840s, the *Dial* expressed many of the movement's most important ideas. My understanding of the New View, however, is especially indebted to Anne C. Rose's *Transcendentalism as a Social Movement, 1830–1850* (1981). The basic resources on Brook Farm are still Lindsay Swift's *Brook Farm* (1900) supplemented by Marianne Dwight Orvis's *Letters From Brook Farm, 1844–1847* (1928). Fruitlands has also had little scholarly treatment. Clara Endicott Sears's *Bronson Alcott's Fruitlands* (1915) has fortunately been supplemented by Richard Francis's "Circumstances and Salvation: The Ideology of the Fruitlands Utopia," *American Quarterly* 25 (May 1973).

Religious Radicalism

My discussion of perfectionism relied heavily upon the two volumes of William Hepworth Dixon's *Spiritual Wives* (1868). The Onedia *First Annual Report* (1849) and the *Oneida Circular* (from 1851) were basic sources for Oneidan perfectionism. Constance Noyes Robertson's *Oneida Community* (1970) includes an introduction that gives an excellent summary of the community's history. Lawrence Foster's *Religion and Sexuality* (1981) and Louis J. Kern's *An Ordered Love* (1981) both contain long, analytical discussion of the Oneida community. Robert David Thomas's *The Man Who Would Be Perfect* (1977) deals with John Humphrey Noyes's early development.

Spiritualism has also received serious scholarly attention recently. R. Laurence Moore's articles (referred to in the discussion of spiritualism) are contained in *In Search of White Crows* (1977). The connections between spiritualism and the experience of women has been investigated by Carroll Smith-Rosenberg in *Disorderly Conduct* (1985). Ann Braude's "Spirits Defend the Rights of Women: Spiritualism and Changing Sex Roles in Nineteenth-century America," in Yvonne Yazbeck Haddad and Ellison Banks Findly, eds., *Women, Religion, and Social Change* (1985), has given a careful and very useful consideration of the woman as medium, tying her role as true woman to her role as the conduit of spiritual communication.

Mesmerism, one of the background ideologies to spiritualism, has also been studied recently by Robert C. Fuller, in *Mesmerism and the American Cure of Souls* (1982).

On Swedenborg, Signe Toksvig's *Emanuel Swedenborg, Scientist and Mystic* (1948) proved very helpful. George Bush, one of Swedenborg's American disciples, attempted to connect mesmerism and Swedenborg's thought in *Mesmer and Swedenborg* (1847) and so helped elucidate the philosophy of both.

Andrew Jackson Davis was the subject of an article by Robert W. Delp, "Andrew Jackson Davis: Prophet of American Spiritualism," *Journal of American History* 54 (June 1967). I found Davis's own autobiography, *The Magic Staff* (1857), far more interesting. I cannot claim the same fascination with other works by Davis. His *Principles of Nature* (1847) is massive and should be read by committed spiritualists only. Even his work on marriage and sexual relations, *The Great Harmonia*, volume 4 (1855), largely reiterates the work of others. S. B. Brittan's journal the *Univercoelum* (1848–1849) tried to present Davis's philosophy to a wider public. It also heralded the findings of many related investigators.

The *Herald of Truth* was the organ of the Cincinnati Brotherhood and, along with an article in the *Univercoelum*, contains about all we know of this protospiritualist group in Ohio.

Warren Chase was an important figure in prewar radicalism, but he has attracted little historical attention. His autobiography, *Life-line of the Lone One*, 5th edition (1868), is interesting as an account of his simultaneous agnosticism and of his growing interest in spiritual matters.

Modern Times

Although the basic work on Josiah Warren is still William Bailie's *Josiah Warren* (1906), the best treatment of Josiah Warren's life, thought, and various communal experiments is in James J. Martin's *Men Against the State* (1953). Roger Wunderlich has provided probably the most extensive investigation of Modern Times in his dissertation, " 'Low Living and High Thinking' at Modern Times, New York (1851–1864)" (State University of New York at Stony Brook, 1986).

Warren's ideas were not complex and did not substantially change after he presented them in *Equitable Commerce* (1846). Caroline Cutter Warren wrote a series of letters to her husband from New Harmony, showing the affection that still existed between the two even after their long separation, and also expressing her desire that the separation be continued. These letters are in the Josiah Warren Papers, Labadie Collection, Division of Rare Books and Special Collections, University of Michigan, Ann Arbor. The Labadie Collection also contains Warren's "Lecture Notes," various letters to and from Warren, a memoir of his experience at New Harmony, and other materials that proved useful to me in recapturing the individual sovereign's attitudes. The Division of Rare Books and Special Collections also contains photocopies of Warren's *Peaceful Revolutionist*.

The development of Warren's ideas and his solution to the marriage problem appear in his "Journal" and "Conversational Development," both part of the same manuscript at the Workingmen's Institute Library, in New Harmony, Indiana.

Other useful accounts are in Henry Edger's *Modern Times, The Labor Question, and the Family* (1855), in Moncure Conway's "Modern Times," *Fortnightly Review* 6 (July 1, 1865), and in John Ellis's *Free Love and Its Votaries* (1870).

The Free Love Counterculture

Information about the counterculture came largely from various radical journals, especially the *Una*, the *Agitator*, the *Oneida Circular*, and the *Social Revolutionist*. The *Social Revolutionist* was by far the most useful of these publications. Taylor Stoehr, who edited *Free Love in America* (1979), introduced his work with a long and useful essay on free love.

Berlin Heights has received some historical treatment, especially by William Vartorella. His dissertation, "The Other Peculiar Institution" (Ohio University, 1977), proved useful. Berlin Heights was news, from time to time, in the *Sandusky Daily Commercial Register* (especially in the fall of 1857), in the Detroit *Free Press*, and in other nearby newspapers. Reprints of these articles are available in the New York *Tribune* and in the *New York Daily Times*. The *Times* also provided me with virtually all of my information about the Free Love Club. Alvin

Warren's memoir "Reminiscences of Berlin Heights," *Our New Humanity* 1 (June 1896), gave an insider's view of Berlin Heights.

Free Love Ideology

The *Social Revolutionist* provided some of the most succinct (and extreme) statements on free love and related movements. The *Oneida Circular* took a hand in trying to define free love, though it was clearly fighting a rearguard action. The books that I believe best express free love ideas are: Marx Edgeworth Lazarus, *Love vs. Marriage* (1852); Stephen Pearl Andrews, *Love, Marriage, and Divorce and the Sovereignty of the Individual* (1853); Thomas and Mary Nichols, *Marriage* (1854); James A. Clay, *A Voice from Prison* (1856); and Austin Kent, *Free Love or, A Philosophical Demonstration of the Non-Exclusive Nature of Connubial Love* (1857).

Responses to Free Love

Andrews's pamphlet *Love, Marriage, and Divorce, and the Sovereignty of the Individual* was partly a compilation of letters to the *Tribune* by Andrews and Henry James and answers to them by Horace Greeley. This rather neatly establishes the reformist and conservative positions as opposed to Andrews's view of free love. In general, most answers to free love lacked Greeley's moderation and James's intelligence. Perhaps the best examples of free love baiting is from the *New York Daily Times* in 1855: "A Bad Book Gibbetted" (August 17) and "The Free Love System: Origin, Progress—and Position of the anti-Marriage Movement" (September 8). The latter article, though intensely hostile, is also the first attempt at a history of the movement and does a good job of establishing the general context for free love (Owenism to Fourierism to free love).

An interesting series of articles and responses appeared in the *Practical Christian* from September 1854 through early 1855. The author of the free love articles was Austin Kent, and Adin Ballou, the periodical's editor, responded to Kent's arguments. On December 30, 1854, Ballou devoted the front page of the journal to "True Love vs. Free Love," highlighting the "Testimony of a True Hearted Woman." Only part of the page was "The Lady's Letter" (though by far the most interesting part). A woman who had been reading Kent's arguments in favor of free love had written to Henry C. Wright giving her viewpoint of the dangers of free love for the married woman. Ballou included some comments of his own and Wright's anti–free love letter in his front page spread.

John B. Ellis's *Free Love and Its Votaries* (1870) is the most unusual anti–free love polemic. Half or more of the book deals with the Oneida community. Separate chapters detail the atrocities of Modern Times, Berlin Heights, and spiritualism. Ellis included long quotations from informants and material taken verbatim from other books (often without references and sometimes without quotation marks). Much of the material on Oneida, for instance, came straight out of Dixon. One of the crimes that the Berlin free lovers were accused of was of writing to periodicals throughout the country condemning free love but wording the letters in such a way that they really were spreading propaganda in favor of free love. It is sometimes hard not to suspect Ellis of this. His treatment of Berlin Heights is hilarious, as he recounts how the opponents of free love were defeated again and again by the intelligence, patience, and determination of the free lovers. Part of the story tells how one of the champions of virtue stumbled upon the free lovers bathing naked and stayed for an hour watching them.

Free Love Portraits

Stephen Pearl Andrews. Although Andrews wrote a great deal, his autobiography remained unpublished. The manuscript is in the Stephen Pearl Andrews Papers, State Historical Society of Wisconsin, along with other documents relating to Andrews's life and thought. The short biography of Andrews by Madeline Stern, *The Pantarch* (1968), does a good job of narrating Andrews's life but gives little attention to the development of his thought.

Marx Edgeworth Lazarus. Edgar MacDonald, ed., *The Education of the Heart* (1977), and Ruth K. Nueremberger, "Some Notes on the Mordecai Family,' *Virginia Magazine of History and Biography* 49 (October 1941), contain some biographical information on Lazarus. His letters to his uncle, George Mordecai, in the George Mordecai Papers, Southern Historical Collection, University of North Carolina, Chapel Hill, also contain information about Lazarus's life and give some insights into his thinking during the 1840s and 1850s. The Mordecai family was quite close-knit, so other members—particularly Marx's aunt—made some comments about Lazarus in letters sprinkled through this collection. Lazarus wrote a short autobiography for Joseph Labadie, now in the Labadie Collection, Division of Rare Books and Special Collections, University of Michigan, Ann Arbor. Lazarus also wrote a series of letters to Labadie during the 1870s.

Austin Kent. In addition to *Free Love* (1857) and Kent's letters to the *Practical Christian* beginning in 1852, there are few sources about Kent. I learned of his paralysis in *Mrs. Woodhull and her "Social Freedom"* (1873) and a few other details from his correspondence to postwar free love journals, such as *Hull's Crucible.*

James Clay. The best source is *A Voice from Prison* (1856).

Mary Gove Nichols. In contrast to the meager information about some free lovers, Mary Nicholas has attracted a good deal of scholarly interest, including a recent Ph.D. dissertation: Janet Noever, "Passionate Rebel" (University of Oklahoma, 1983). Noever has strangely little to say about Nichols's free love and on several points seems more interested with merely describing the life of her subject than in explaining her thinking or the reasons for her actions. Biographical information about Mary Nichols is available in Bertha-Monica Stearns's "Two Forgotten New England Reformers," *New England Quarterly* 6 (March 1933), and "Memnonia: The Launching of a Utopia," *New England Quarterly* 15 (June 1942). Philip Gleason's "From Free Love to Catholicism," *Ohio Historical Quarterly* 70 (October 1961), does a good job of describing Memnonia and the Nicholses' conversion. John B. Blake's "Mary Gove Nichols, Prophetess of Health," *Proceedings of the American Philosophical Society* 106 (June 29, 1962), concentrates on Mary Nichols's career as a physiological lecturer and unlicensed physician.

There are also many primary sources on Mary Nichols. Irving T. Richards published her letters to John Neal in "Mary Gove Nichols and John Neal," *New England Quarterly* 7 (June 1934). Her *Lectures to Ladies on Anatomy and Physiology* (1842) and *Experience in Water-cure* (1849) contain valuable insights into Mary Nichols's life and thought. The most interesting sources for a study of Mary Nichols, however, are the fictionalized attack on her by Charles Wilkins Webber, *Spiritual Vampirism* (1853), and her autobiographical answer, *Mary Lyndon* (1855). Depending on whether one gives more credence to Webber (as Stoehr does) or Nichols (as Noever does), the interpretation of her life changes dramatically.

Postwar Free Love

George Fredrickson's *Inner Civil War* (1965) formed the basis for my discussion of the effects of the Civil War on intellectuals. I relied heavily upon William L. O'Neill's *Divorce in the Progressive Era* (1967) and *Everyone was Brave* (1969) for my picture of postwar feminism and attitudes toward marriage. James Reed's *Birth Control Movement and American Society* (1983) shaped my general understanding of late nineteenth-century sexuality. David Pivar's *Purity Crusade* (1973) and Heywood Broun and Margaret Leech's *Anthony Comstock* (1927) delineated the postwar establishment of sexual standards.

Sources for postwar free love are very good. Hal Sears's *The Sex Radicals* (1977) provides a good overview of the movement, concentrating especially on the Harman circle in Kansas. Additional information on Moses Hull came from Martin's *Men Against the State* (1953) and Daniel Hull's biography of his brother, *Moses Hull* (1907). Both *Woodhull and Claflin's Weekly* and the *Word* provided valuable news about the continuing activities of first-generation free lovers and about the network that came into existence following the war.

Index